P9-ASB-259

Social Network Analysis

For Sophie and Lukas

Social Network Analysis

history, theory & methodology

Christina Prell

Los Angeles | London | New Delhi
Singapore | Washington DC

© Christina Prell 2012

First published 2012
Reprinted 2013

Apart from any fair dealing for the purposes of research or private study, or criticism or review, as permitted under the Copyright, Designs and Patents Act, 1988, this publication may be reproduced, stored or transmitted in any form, or by any means, only with the prior permission in writing of the publishers, or in the case of reprographic reproduction, in accordance with the terms of licences issued by the Copyright Licensing Agency. Enquiries concerning reproduction outside those terms should be sent to the publishers.

SAGE Publications Ltd
1 Oliver's Yard
55 City Road
London EC1Y 1SP

SAGE Publications Inc.
2455 Teller Road
Thousand Oaks, California 91320

SAGE Publications India Pvt Ltd
B 1/I 1 Mohan Cooperative Industrial Area
Mathura Road, Post Bag 7
New Delhi 110 044

SAGE Publications Asia-Pacific Pte Ltd
3 Church Street,
10-104 Samsung Hub
Singapore 049483

Library of Congress Control Number: 2011920330

British Library Cataloguing in Publication data

A catalogue record for this book is available from the British Library

ISBN 978-1-4129-4714-5
ISBN 978-1-4129-4715-2 (pbk)

Typeset by C&M Digitals (P) Ltd., Chennai, India
Printed and bound by CPI Group (UK) Ltd., Croydon, CR0 4YY
Printed on paper from sustainable resources

CONTENTS

ABOUT THE AUTHOR

Christina Prell is an Assistant Professor in Sociology at the University of Maryland, College Park. She uses mixed methods to explore the role that social networks play in different research contexts. Such contexts include natural resource governance and management; social capital and communities; and network evolution and agent-based modelling. She was been involved in a number of successful funded projects involving social network analysis, and she has taught social network analysis for a number of years at the Masters level. This book comes from her experience as both a researcher and teacher of social networks and the network analytic approach.

INTRODUCTION: WHAT ARE SOCIAL NETWORKS?

We are increasingly aware of the interdependencies of social life: the twenty-first century is characterized by communication and transportation technologies that shrink the world, make it smaller, and thus help bring individuals geographically far from one another into close social contact. We live in a world that is paradoxically small and wide: each of us is embedded in local communities, yet at the same time more and more of us hold contacts that span the globe, and further, each of us is arguably only a few 'links' away from anyone else in the world (Milgram, 1967; Watts, 1999).

These interdependencies have both positive and negative consequences. Our knowledge that the world is both large and small makes us more sensitive to the idea that our actions affect those around the world, and whom we know in our local social circles could very well connect us with someone in a distant land. However, these same interdependencies have shown us some dark sides: asocial and terrorist groups can be both local and global, using their local links to spread global messages of hate and intolerance.

Thus, the social relations that knit together our modern world can have multiple effects, and a local occurrence in one area of the world can affect the rest. Yet there is a big gap between this intuitive understanding of how our social world works and a more precise understanding of how these interactions and relationships form. Filling this gap is important if we want to understand what kind of interventions (if any) we can make to improve a variety of social conditions, and in addition, understanding of these kinds of interactions and relationships can also help our understanding of the world.

This book attempts to fill this gap by providing an overview of an increasingly popular approach for studying social relations and their structuring: social network analysis (SNA). This approach involves theoretical concepts, methods and analytical techniques to uncover the social relations that the individuals and groups together, the structure of those relations, and how relations and their structures influence (or are influenced by) social behaviour, attitudes, beliefs and knowledge.

The growing popularity of this approach coincides with the growing awareness in our society of the interdependencies and complexities of social systems in particular, but also ecological ones as well; social policy makers, for example, are increasingly turning their attention to the role of networks for understanding a range of problems on the local, regional, societal and even global level. With regards to the environment, a number of scholars and policy makers are also starting to see the importance of understanding social networks for providing insights into the ways humans understand, value and manage the natural world.

The literature on social networks is vast: there are three journals that focus entirely on social networks – *Connections, Journal of Social Structure* and *Social Networks* – and there are a number of books that focus on the techniques, concepts, theories and mathematics that form the field.

This book differs from others in its emphasis and scope. Whereas many introductory books on SNA are more suitable for learners with a background in statistics or sociology, or both, this book is aimed primarily for an audience of newcomers to the field, who might not have much confidence in their knowledge of sociology, statistics or mathematics. A second audience is for those already familiar with SNA, but have yet to tackle some of the newer trends in methods and techniques, such as Exponential Random Graph Models (ERGMs) or actor-based models, such as those found in the software application SIENA. Finally, a third audience consists of those looking to teach SNA, and are in need of some examples of how to get students started with software applications, and friendly introductions to some of the mathematics involved. This book is designed to serve all of these three audiences. It is a book for the social network novice on learning how to study, think about and analyse social networks; the intermediate user, who has not yet come across some of the newer developments or trends in the field; and the teacher, who is looking for a range of exercises, as well as an up-to-date historical account of the field.

The book aims to offer a full overview of this field – historical origins; common theoretical perspectives and frameworks used in the field; traditional and more recent analytical procedures; and fundamental mathematical equations necessary for gaining a foothold in the field. After reading this book and following the exercises within, you should have a good basic understanding of social networks and social network analysis, literally from metaphor to models.

A word on organization: I have chosen to organize the book in three Parts. Part I offers a lot of background and fundamental concepts for later parts of the book. Thus, Part I includes a chapter on basic terminology (Chapter 1); an up-to-date historical account of social network analysis (Chapter 2); and a chapter on how to think about and design a research study involving social network data gathering and analysis (Chapter 3). This last chapter also includes within it a summary of the most common theoretical frameworks used in social network analysis, these being (i) social capital, (ii) social exchange, (iii) social influence network theory, (iv) social selection network theory, and (v) biased net theory.

Part II introduces readers to most of the fundamental, analytical concepts used in social network analysis, and organizes these concepts in terms of 'levels'. By this

I mean that I break down the notion of a 'social network' as being composed of a series of levels such as actors (e.g. individuals); relations connecting actors together (e.g. friendship); dyads (i.e. pairs of actors); triads (i.e. structures composed of three actors); subgroups; and entire networks. Each level is given its own chapter, where relevant concepts, theories, analytical techniques and examples are given.

In presenting these concepts as levels, this book is keeping pace with the SNA field: increasingly, SNA researchers are conceptualizing and researching social networks from a multilevel approach (Blau, 1993; Coromina and Coenders, 2006; DiPrete and Forristal, 1994; Klein Ikkink and van Tilburg, 1999; Lubbers, 2003; Lubbers et al., in press; van Duijn et al., 1999; Van Emmerik, 2006; Van Emmerik, in press;). In doing so, this enables researchers to not only see the relative contribution of each network level to the processes or phenomena under investigation, but also to study how these levels interact with each other. Further, in adopting a levels-oriented approach, and starting with the individual actor level, this book begins at a point that most readers are familiar with, i.e. the individual as an actor within a particular environment. Studying the social world from the viewpoint of individuals is reflective of the more traditional approach to social sciences, but it is also more intuitive and familiar to the average reader. Thus, beginning the study of networks with individuals, and then building up to higher and higher levels of structure, makes sense from a pedagogical angle.

The concepts presented in Part II lay a foundation for Part III, which introduces the idea of statistical significance in relation to social network data, and some of the most common statistical models and techniques to date. The tie-based and actor-based models introduced in this chapter are considered to be among the more recent methodological developments in the SNA field, and their power lies within their ability to provide distribution models suitable for the interdependent nature of network data. As such, these models provide a good means for statistical testing, as well as explaining network structure.

Part III is followed by the Appendices, designed to offer some in-depth examples of how to use two popular software applications within SNA. The first, UCINET, is referred to throughout many chapters of the book, yet an in-depth introduction to the software is provided in Appendix 1. The second software application is Siena, which is used for the more advanced statistical models such as ERGMs and actor-based models. I chose these two applications over others (e.g. Pajek, R or Pnet) for a number of reasons. With regards to UCINET, the menu for this software is organized in a way which is more consistent with the way social scientists think about social networks, and thus, the way in which networks are presented in this book. In addition, UCINET has grown within the social networks field, versus its near rival, Pajek, which was developed by graph theorists, and was intended more for use with very large networks. With regards to my choice for using Siena, this application can handle both ERGMs and actor-based models, thus you can use it for both cross-sectional and longitudinal statistical modelling of networks. Siena has, in the time period of this book being written, also been re-designed to work within the R software environment; this is an environment especially well-suited for statisticians and analysts of large-scale networks. If readers are interested in learning RSiena, I encourage them to visit the website: http://stat.gamma.rug.nl/siena_r.htm.

Beyond these introductory remarks on social networks and the organization of this book, I would like to conclude this chapter with some acknowledgements. In the initial proposal stage of this book, I was influenced by a number of colleagues, namely, Caroline Haythornthwaite, Chris Rojek, Steve Borgatti and Fil Agneessens. These discussions greatly inspired me as I set about trying to outline this book and make decisions on what topics to include. Along the way, at various other stages, the following people have been instrumental to helping me complete this book: in alphabetical order, this list includes Fil Agneessens; Jackie Beckhelling; Professor Klaus Hubacek; Professor David Krackhardt; Dr Mark Reed; Professor Michael Savage; Professor John Scott; and Professor John Skvoretz. I would like to offer a special thanks to Professor Martin Everett, from University of Manchester and Professor Tom Snijders, from Oxford University.

And finally, I thank my family – my immediate and extended family – and especially Klaus, Sophia and Lukas.

REFERENCES

Blau, P. M. (1993) 'Multilevel structural analysis', *Social Networks,* 15: 201–15.
Coromina, L. and Coenders, G. (2006) 'Reliability and validity of egocentered network data collected via web: A meta-analysis of multilevel multitrait multimethod studies', *Social Networks,* 28: 209–31.
DiPrete, T. A. and Forristal, J. D. (1994) 'Multilevel models: Methods and substance', *Annual Review of Sociology,* 20: 331–57.
Klein Ikkink, K. and Van Tilburg, T. (1999) 'Broken ties: reciprocity and other factors affecting the termination of older adults' relationships', *Social Networks,* 21: 131–46.
Lubbers, M. J. (2003) 'Group composition and network structure in school classes: a multilevel application of the p* model', *Social Networks,* 25: 309–32.
Lubbers, M. J., Molina, J. L., Lerner, J., Brandes, U., Ávila, J. and McCarty, C. (in press) 'Longitudinal analysis of personal networks. The case of Argentinean migrants in Spain', *Social Networks.*
Milgram, S. (1967) 'The small world problem', *Psychology Today,* 1(1): 60–7.
Van Duijn, M. A. J., Van Busschbach, J. T. and Snijders, T. A. B. (1999) 'Multilevel analysis of personal networks as dependent variables', *Social Networks,* 21: 187–210.
Van Emmerik, I. J. H. (2006) 'Gender differences in the creation of different types of social capital: A multilevel study', *Social Networks,* 28: 24–37.
Van Emmerik, I. H. (in press) 'Gender differences in the creation of different types of social capital: A multilevel study', *Social Networks.*
Watts, D. J. (1999) 'Networks, dynamics and the small world phenomenon', *American Journal of Sociology,* 105: 493–527.

PART I

BACKGROUND
UNDERSTANDING

BECOMING FAMILIAR WITH SOCIAL NETWORKS

Each one of us has our own social networks, and it is easiest to start understanding social networks through thinking about our own. So what social networks do you have? These might include friendship networks, your network of colleagues at work, and the network of individuals you know from participating in various clubs and organizations. It is quite normal to be a member of many different social networks, and in fact, social network analysis encourages you to think along these lines by separating your various social networks according to different relations. Thus, a friendship network would be one relation, an advice network a different one, and a dislike network still another relation.

Breaking down social networks according to relations is aided by how a researcher phrases questions to a respondent. For example, if I start to ask you a series of specific questions regarding the different kinds of social networks you have, it becomes easier for you, the respondent, to conceptualize all the different social networks to which you belong.

Look at the questions below and make an attempt to answer these questions for yourself. In most cases, these questions will generate new lists of names, and in some instances, you will find the same individuals popping up as answers time and time again:

- who is in your immediate family?
- who do you tend to socialize with on weekends?
- whom do you turn to for advice in making important decisions about your professional career?
- whom do you turn to for emotional support when you experience personal problems?
- whom would you ask to take care of your home if you were out of town, for example watering the plants and picking up the mail?

Take a moment and answer each of the above questions, writing down the names of people who come to mind for each question. You will probably notice two things: that each question generates a slightly different list, and that certain names appear repeatedly in different lists. Each list represents a different social network for you and there is most likely overlaps in these networks. We can label these lists to give a name to the relation that the social network represents. Thus, you can have a 'family' network, a 'socializing' network, a 'career advice' network, an 'emotional support' network and 'home-care' network. In addition, you can add some more information about yourself and about each person in the lists, for example, their age and gender. Below is a fictitious example for the list entitled 'family':

In Table 1.1, I have simply listed the people in Susie's immediate family. The list is Susie's social network for the relation of 'family'. All the people listed in this social network are the *actors* in the network. As you will see, actors are also referred to in social network analysis as *nodes* and as *vertices*. In social network analysis, there are often multiple terms for the same concept, as this field has developed in many different disciplines. For example, an 'actor' is a more socio-logical term, whereas nodes and vertices are terms derived from graph theory. The network represented by the list in Table 1.1 is a specific kind of network in SNA, which is called an '*ego network*'. Ego networks are comprised of a focal actor (called ego) and the people to whom ego is directly connected. These people to whom ego is connected are referred to as '*alters*'. In this case, Susie is the ego and the alters are Janice, Emily and John. Susie holds a tie with each family member, and each family member's gender and age has also been listed. Gender and age are considered additional information on each particular actor, and we refer to these additional pieces of actor information as *actor attributes*. Actor attributes are the same sort of attributes you come across in more tradi-tional social science research. They include categories such as age, gender, socio-economic class, and so forth.

Table 1.1   Susie's immediate family

Name	Gender	Age
Susie	Female	25
Janice	Female	21
Emily	Female	47
John	Male	48

Through this simple example, you have already learned a fair amount about social network analysis. In particular, you have learnt some of the fundamental terminology on which social network analysis is based, namely actors, nodes, vertices, ego and ego network, alters, ties, relations and actor attributes. A social network consists of all these pieces of information, and more formally, a *social network* can be defined as a set of relations that apply to a set of actors, as well as any additional information on those actors and relations.

Our example above, as simple as it is, can still provide us with a means for introducing some more SNA terms. Susie's ego network of her family represents a *state relation*. State relations have a degree of permanency or durability that make it relatively easy for a researcher to detect. Examples of state relations include kinship, affective relations such as trust or friendship, and affiliations such as belonging to the same club or church. State relations stand in contrast to *event relations*, which are more temporary sorts of relations that may or may not imply a more durable relation. Examples of event relations include attending the same meeting or conference; having a cup of coffee together; sending an email; giving advice; talking with someone; and fighting with someone. Event relations may or may not indicate a more permanent state. Usually, however, we think of event relations as individual occurrences.

Actors, vertices and nodes = the social entities linked together according to some relation

ego = the focal actor of interest

alters = the actors to whom an ego is tied

tie = what connects A to B, e.g. A is *friends* with B = A is *tied* to B.

relation = a specified set of ties among a set of actors. For example, friendship, family, etc.

actor attributes = additional information on each particular actor, for example, age, gender, etc.

ego network = social network of a particular focal actor, ego, ego's alters and the ties linking ego to alters and alters to alters

social network = a set of relations that apply to a set of social entities, and any additional information on those actors and relations

---

Figure 1.1   SNA terminology

DESCRIBING SOCIAL NETWORKS THROUGH GRAPHS AND GRAPH THEORY

Let's move on from this starting point. We can make a visual representation of Susie's network by drawing a graph. A *graph or digraph* is a visual representation of a social network, where actors are represented as nodes or vertices and the ties are represented as *lines*, also called *edges* or *arcs*.

When we represent social networks as graphs and describe social networks in terms of graphs, we use terms and concepts derived from graph theory, a branch of mathematics that focuses on the quantification of networks. Although social network analysis is not the same as graph theory, many of the fundamental concepts and terms are borrowed from this field, and so it is worthwhile to spend a bit of time familiarizing oneself with some of graph theory's basics.

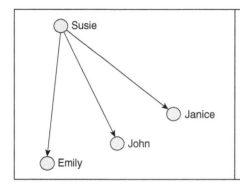

Susie	Graphs consist of a set of undirected lines among a set of nodes. They are visual depictions of social networks.
Janice	Digraphs consist of a set of directed lines among a set of nodes.
John	Graphs are composed of nodes, also called vertices, which are connected through lines.
Emily	Directed lines are referred to as arcs. Undirected lines are edges.

Figure 1.2   Digraph

In graph theory, ones says that there are *n* number of nodes and *L* number of lines. Thus, in the above graph, $n = 4$ and $L = 3$. In addition, we discuss how nodes are adjacent with each other. A node is adjacent to another node if the two share a tie between them. Thus, Susie is adjacent to each member of her family. She shares a tie with each member of her family.

To help you become better acquainted with some of the graph theory basics, I shall expand on our first example of a social network. A family network, as stated above, is one of many social networks of which an actor can be a member. Another network could be a friendship network. Friendship networks tend to span across different contexts: we have friends at our places of work, from our school, from our neighbourhood, and so forth. Sometimes these friends overlap, for example, a friend from our workplace might also live in our neighbourhood. For purposes of this present example, I would like to focus your attention on a very clearly bounded sort of friendship network, that is, the friends you have at work. For example, suppose I were to ask you the following question: 'Whom in your workplace would you consider to be your friend?' Most likely, your answer would not include every person with whom you work, but rather those people you feel closer to or more intimate with than the others. This would be considered your friendship network at work. Notice that this is quite different than if I were to ask you, 'Whom do you consider to be your friend?' without specifying whether or not I was interested in your workplace or not. In speci-fying the workplace, I have thus created a *boundary* around this particular network, i.e. I have defined what sorts of actors can be considered to be inside the network and which ones are outside my realm of interest. By specifying the boundary, I have, in essence, specified my population of interest for this particu-lar network study. Network boundaries are an important issue which will be taken up later in this book. For now, it is good enough for you to understand that the boundary of this particular network is a particular, specified workplace.

Now suppose I were to ask the exact same question to each of your colleagues. That is, each person in your workplace were asked to nominate colleagues with whom they felt they shared a friendship tie. In asking every person at your work place the same question, I have moved from studying one particular person's ego network to studying a *complete network*. A complete network is one where an entire set of actors and the ties linking these actors together are studied. Once again, I can display a complete network as a graph, as shown in Figure 1.3.

Now I can introduce additional terms from graph theory to further describe this particular social network. You will notice that the above graph contains lines with arrowheads. The lines represent ties, and the arrowheads indicate the direction of the ties. In SNA terms, we would say this graph shows a *directed relation*, and in graph theory, a graph with directed lines is referred to as a *digraph*. The directed lines making up the digraph are referred to as arcs. Arcs have *senders* and *receivers*, where senders are the ones who nominate, and receivers are the nominees. In

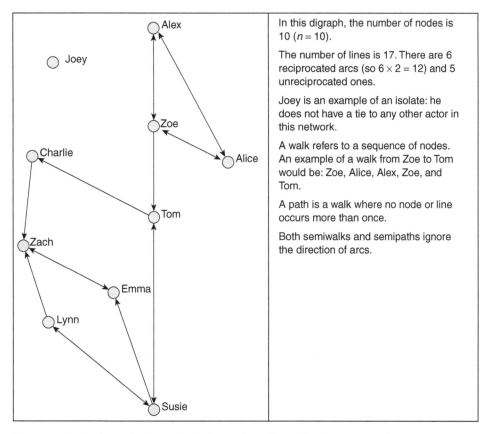

In this digraph, the number of nodes is 10 ($n = 10$).

The number of lines is 17. There are 6 reciprocated arcs (so $6 \times 2 = 12$) and 5 unreciprocated ones.

Joey is an example of an isolate: he does not have a tie to any other actor in this network.

A walk refers to a sequence of nodes. An example of a walk from Zoe to Tom would be: Zoe, Alice, Alex, Zoe, and Tom.

A path is a walk where no node or line occurs more than once.

Both semiwalks and semipaths ignore the direction of arcs.

Figure 1.3   A digraph showing 'Who is friends with whom at work'

the present example, the senders are the respondents who answered the question 'Whom in this workplace would you consider to be your friend?', and the receivers are those actors who were nominated by the respondents as friends.

If we did not want to pay attention to the direction of the lines, we could simply remove the arrowheads. In graph theory, a network that contains undirected lines is referred simply to as a graph, and the undirected lines are referred to as *edges*. Graphs, i.e. those which contains only edges, are considered the simplest to study, and thus you might choose to ignore the direction of the lines for this very reason. However, a graph might result from the nature of the relation being studied; for example, if the relation being studied is marriage, the marriage tie can be assumed to flow in both directions, so there is no need to represent that relation as a digraph.

You will also notice the Joey does not have any ties to other nodes in this graph. In this instance, Joey is an isolate, i.e. a node that does not have ties to any other actors in a network.

Displaying a social network as a graph or digraph invites a researcher to start describing certain aspects of the network. For example, we can discuss how close or far apart two nodes are from one another through the number of arcs or edges linking the two together. Considerations of distance between nodes involve the concepts of semiwalks, walks, semipaths and paths. I shall describe each of these briefly below:

In Figure 1.3, one can take a *walk* from Zoe to Tom by passing through Alex, Alice and Zoe. Notice that we are paying attention to the direction of the arcs in taking this walk, and that we passed by Zoe twice. Thus, a walk is a sequence of nodes, where all nodes are adjacent to one another, where each node follows the previous node, and where nodes and lines can occur more than once. The beginning node and the ending node in a walk can be different. Thus, the length of the walk is the number of lines that occur in a walk, and the lines that occur more than once in the walk are counted each time they occur. The walk from Zoe to Tom, as described above, is length 4. A much shorter walk from Zoe to Tom would be length 1.

A semiwalk simply ignores the direction of arcs. Thus, a semiwalk from Tom to Zoe is possible, even though the direction of the arc would suggest otherwise.

The notion of paths and semipaths builds on these ideas. A *path* is a walk in which no node and no line occurs more than once on the walk. Thus Zoe, Tom, Charlie and Zack would be an example of a path. Again, a semipath is a path that ignores the direction of arcs.

Although this seems like a lot of vocabulary, these terms and concepts are the building blocks for describing, analysing and theorizing social networks. In the remaining space of this chapter, we shall explore two other fundamentals regarding social network analysis. These are modes of networks and network matrices.

NETWORK MATRICES

The previous section focused on the display of networks as graphs and digraphs, and the terminology from graph theory used to describe these. Although visualizing networks as graphs and digraphs is useful, the reliance solely on these visual representations can become cumbersome and even chaotic as a network grows in size. For this reason (among others) network data are also organized as network matrices.

You are probably already familiar with a case-by-variable matrix: this is a matrix where rows in the matrix represent the individual cases, e.g. the respondents in your study, and columns represent certain variables related to these cases, such as age, gender, nationality and so on. Such a case-by-variable matrix is shown in Figure 1.4, with the cases represented by numbers in the rows, and the variables shown as columns. Each cell in this matrix contains a value that corresponds to the different levels of measurement (dichotomous, nominal, ordinal, interval and ratio). The values for age correspond to the level of interval, gender to dichotomous (where 1 = male and 2 = female), and nationality to nominal (where 1 = UK, 2 = USA, 3 = Canada and 4 = Australia).

A network matrix is slightly different to this case-by-variable matrix. In a network matrix, data are organized as case-by-case matrices (called adjacency matrices) or by case-by-events (called incidence matrices). The cells represent the presence or absence of ties. A cell is the intersection of a row with a column. Figure 1.5 is a very simple adjacency matrix. Here, each actor is represented twice: once in the row and once in the column. This matrix represents the graph based on friendship as we discussed above.

You will see that all the names in this social network are listed in the rows, and these names are abbreviated at the top of each column (thus, Susie becomes S and Emma becomes E, etc.). In addition, the rows and columns have been numbered. For example, Susie is referred to as row 1 and column 1.

	Age	Gender	Nationality
1	19	1	4
2	18	1	3
3	21	2	2
4...	22	2	1

Figure 1.4   Example of a case-by-variable matrix

```
                                    1   • An adjacency matrix is a case-by-case matrix.
                   1 2 3 4 5 6 7 8 9 0   • A binary matrix consists of 1s and 0s.
                   S E Z T L Z A J A C   • The rows in a matrix are represented by i and
                   - - - - - - - - - -     the columns by j.
    1   Susie      0 1 0 1 1 0 0 0 0 0   • The values of cells are referred to as a (i,j). For
    2   Emma       0 0 1 0 0 0 0 0 0 0     example, the cell representing Susie's tie with
    3   Zach       0 1 0 0 0 0 0 0 0 0     Emma is a(1,2) = 1.
    4   Tom        1 0 0 0 0 0 0 0 0 1   • Senders are found in rows; Receivers in
    5   Lynn       1 0 1 0 0 0 0 0 0 0     columns.
    6   Zoe        0 0 1 0 0 1 0 1 0     • The diagonal of the matrix represents a
    7   Alex       0 0 0 0 0 1 0 0 1 0     sender's tie with herself. The diagonal tends
    8   Joey       0 0 0 0 0 0 0 0 0 0     to be ignored
    9   Alice      0 0 0 0 0 1 1 0 0 0     in SNA.
   10   Charlie    0 0 1 0 0 0 0 0 0 0
```

Figure 1.5   Matrix of a friendship network

The adjacency matrix in the above example records who sends a tie to whom through the use of 1s and 0s. Thus, Susie, in row 1, sends a tie to Emma, in column 2, and this is recorded by inserting a 1 in the cell intersecting row 1 and column 2 (highlighted above). In social network analysis, we use notation to designate which cell we are speaking about: thus, the individual rows in a matrix are referred to as i; the columns as j; and the value in a particular cell as the letter a. Taken together, this notation allows one to specify a particular cell in matrix as $a(i,j)$. In the above matrix, we can refer to the cell representing Susie's nomination of Emma as '$a(1,2) = 1$'.

Because all the values in the cells are 1's and 0's in Figure 1.5, we call this matrix a *binary adjacency matrix*. A binary matrix contains only 1s and 0s in its cells. As a binary matrix records senders to receivers as rows to columns, the diagonal of this matrix represents the relationship of the sender to itself. In most situations, social network analysts find the diagonal in a matrix uninteresting, as in most social situations, the analyst is not interested in actors' relationships with themselves, but rather the relationships actors have with one another. Thus, the cells along the diagonal are usually recorded as 0s or they are ignored altogether.

The above matrix is also an example of what we call an *asymmetric* matrix. An asymmetric matrix is one that records the direction of ties in a social network. A *symmetric* matrix, by contrast, contains data for an undirected network. This distinction between asymmetric and symmetric matrices is made clearer in Figure 1.6. In the asymmetric matrix, the top right half of the diagonal does not match the bottom left half. In the symmetric matrix, both the upper and lower half of the matrix are the same, as these data are undirected. Another way of thinking about these undirected ties is to see these ties from senders to receivers as being *reciprocal*. For example, Susie nominates Emma as a friend and Emma nominates Susie as a friend.

Asymmetric matrix						Symmetric matrix					
		1 2 3 4 5						1 2 3 4 5			
		S E Z T L						S E Z T L			
		- - - - -						- - - - -			
1	Susie	- 1 0 1 1				1	Susie	- 1 0 1 1			
2	Emma	0 - 1 0 0				2	Emma	1 - 1 0 0			
3	Zach	0 1 - 0 0				3	Zach	0 1 - 0 1			
4	Tom	1 0 0 - 0				4	Tom	1 0 0 - 0			
5	Lynn	1 0 1 0 -				5	Lynn	1 0 1 0 -			

Figure 1.6   Asymmetric vs symmetric matrices

By contrast, in the asymmetric matrix, the ties may or may not be reciprocal. For example, Susie sends Lynn a tie and Lynn reciprocates that tie, but Susie also sends Emma a tie and Emma does not reciprocate that tie.

In addition to issues of symmetry, and how they reflect the direction of ties, a matrix can also convey the intensity of a tie by the values found within the cell. Thus, for example, a cell containing the value of 4 represents a stronger or more intense tie than a cell containing the value of 3, 2 or 1 (the strength of ties is a topic for the next chapter, and so more discussion will be given at that time). Such a matrix is referred to as a valued matrix or valued network, to convey the fact that values greater than 1s or 0s are also contained in the matrix. Figure 1.7 is an example of a valued matrix.

												1
			1	2	3	4	5	6	7	8	9	0
			S	E	Z	T	L	Z	A	J	A	C
			-	-	-	-	-	-	-	-	-	-
1	Susie		0	1	0	3	4	0	0	0	0	0
2	Emma		0	0	3	0	0	0	0	0	0	0
3	Zach		0	4	0	0	0	0	0	0	0	0
4	Tom		3	0	0	0	0	0	0	0	0	1
5	Lynn		3	0	1	0	0	0	0	0	0	0
6	Zoe		0	0	0	1	0	0	1	0	5	0
7	Alex		0	0	0	0	0	1	0	0	5	0
8	Joey		0	0	0	0	0	0	0	0	0	0
9	Alice		0	0	0	0	0	4	4	0	0	0
10	Charlie		0	0	1	0	0	0	0	0	0	0

Figure 1.7   Valued matrix

This valued matrix is based on the same friendship relation discussed earlier, but here, we have added information to the data: here some of these friendship ties are stronger than others. Thus, 1 = a friend or more likely an acquaintance, but 5 = a very close friend. Valued graphs do not necessarily reflect ideas of tie strength or intensity; the values can also represent, for example probabilities (e.g. the probability of a tie being present or absent).

Social network analysts organize social network data into matrices for a number of reasons. Top of the list is that the display of network data in graph form can easily become confusing and even chaotic the larger a network becomes. It is difficult to see how the network is structured and any interesting pattern gets lost. By structuring the data into a matrix, we can then start running a variety of quantitative analyses to start picking out the structural features and overriding patterns in the data.

ONE-MODE AND TWO-MODE NETWORKS

In the previous section we looked at matrices of complete networks. The notion of a complete network can be broken down further into the concepts of one-mode networks and two-mode networks. Our previous examples regarding friendship have been examples of one-mode networks. One-mode networks are networks where we study how all actors are tied to one another according to one relation, like friendship. One-mode networks are structured as adjacency matrices, and can be either binary or valued. With two-mode networks, we look at how actors are tied to (or affiliated with) particular events. Examples of two-mode networks include attendance at meetings and membership in an organization. Whereas one-mode networks deal with one set of data (one relation pertaining to one set of actors), two-mode networks deal with two different sets of data. A common example of a two-mode network is one where rows pertain to actors and the columns to events these actors attend. Thus, actors can be tied to one another via events, and similarily, you can conceptualize events as being linked together via actors (more on this dual-portrayal of these data can be found below). Actors and events are only one example of two-mode networks. Another example is that of affiliation networks, i.e. ones where actors are shown in the rows and their affiliations to particular third bodies, e.g. organizations, are depicted in the columns. You could imagine a range of different kinds of two-mode networks; the important distinction here from one-mode networks would be the idea that two separate kinds of entities are being reflected in the matrix, where one set of entities is found in the rows of the matrix, and another in the columns.

The matrices in which two-mode network data are organized are referred to as *incidence matrices*, and when displayed visually, they are referred to as *bipartite graphs*. An example of an affiliation network is given in Figure 1.8, displayed as both a bipartite graph and an incidence matrix.

The digraph and incidence matrix shown in Figure 1.8 show a set of actors and their attendance (or non-attendance) to four separate events. These events are two meetings and two social events. An actor's attendance to one of these events is shown in the incidence matrix through inserting a 1 in the cell below the particular event. Thus, for example, Susie has attended meetings 1 and 2 (M1 and M2) and social event 1 (S1). In the digraph, the actors' attendance is conveyed through arcs sent from the actors to the events.

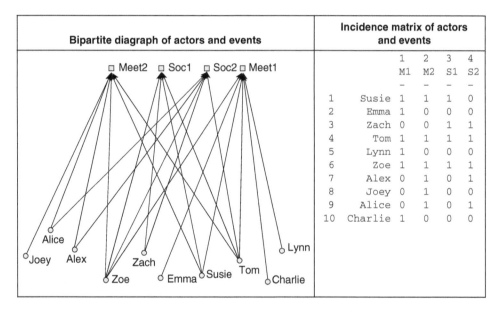

Figure 1.8   Bipartite diagraph and incidence matrix

From the incidence matrix, we can derive two new adjacency matrices: a case-by-case matrix and an event-by-event matrix. In Figure 1.9 you can see these two new matrices and their respective digraphs.

Figure 1.9 shows how a single incidence matrix can be transformed into two adjacency matrices. Although there exists some special analyses for dealing with two-mode data, in general, most social network analyses are performed on one-mode data, i.e. on adjacency matrices. Thus, it is important to understand how two-mode data can be transformed into one-mode data.

One-mode network (case-by-case)											Two-mode network (affiliation-by-affiliation)				
	1	2	3	4	5	6	7	8	9	10			1	2	3	4
	S	E	Z	T	L	Z	A	J	A	C			M1	M2	S1	S2
1 Susie	3	1	1	3	1	3	1	1	1	1	1	Meet1	6	3	3	2
2 Emma	1	1	0	1	1	1	0	0	0	1	2	Meet2	3	6	3	4
3 Zach	1	0	2	2	0	2	1	0	1	0	3	Soc1	3	3	4	3
4 Tom	3	1	2	4	1	4	2	1	2	1	4	Soc2	2	4	3	5
5 Lynn	1	1	0	1	1	1	0	0	0	1						
6 Zoe	3	1	2	4	1	4	2	1	2	1						
7 Alex	1	0	1	2	0	2	2	1	2	0						
8 Joey	1	0	0	1	0	1	1	1	1	0						
9 Alice	1	0	1	2	0	2	2	1	2	0						
10 Charlie	1	1	0	1	1	1	0	0	0	1						

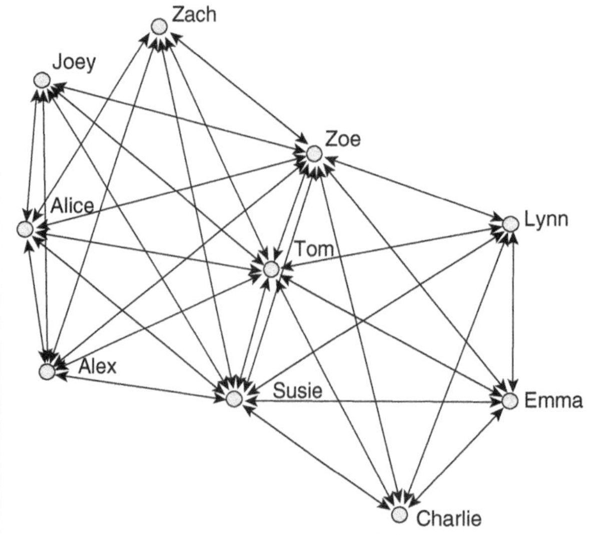

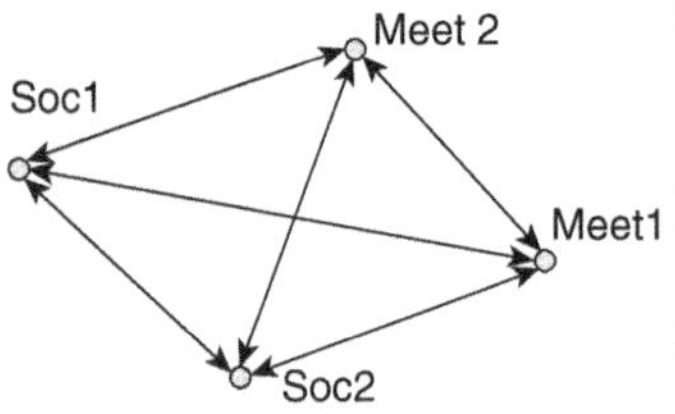

Figure 1.9   One-and two-mode networks

SUMMARY AND CONCLUSION

In this chapter we covered some fundamental concepts regarding social networks and social network analysis. In particular, you learned what comprises a network, namely actors and social ties, the graph theoretic terms for describing those networks, e.g. graphs, nodes and lines, and some basics in structuring the data as matrices and as one-mode or two-mode networks.

In Section 2, you will learn about networks from a 'levels' approach, starting with the 'actor' level and ending with the 'complete network' level. Before doing this, however, I will continue my introduction to social networks by offering you a brief history to the field. This can be found in the next chapter.

2

A BRIEF HISTORY OF SOCIAL NETWORK ANALYSIS

Social network analysis (SNA) did not evolve via a neat, linear process. It is therefore difficult to write a simple account given the multiple individuals and groups that played a role in its shaping. Social network analysis resulted from multiple interactions among academics; some of these interactions accumulated into their own unique research groups and sub-disciplines, some interactions spanned across disciplines, and some resulted in more formal, institutional frameworks that worked to promote and build the field as its own 'discipline'. Today, many see social network analysis as its own 'paradigm' (Leinhardt, 1977). This means that social network analysis is perceived as a unique approach to understanding (primarily) the social world. It is an approach that comes with it a conceptual, methodological and analytical tool-kit.

Previous historical accounts of network analysis locate the beginnings as having taken place largely in the US and Britain (Scott, 2000; Wellman, 1988) yet a more recent book by Freeman (2004) has expanded this view of SNA's origins to include a wider array of European countries, including France, Hungary, the Netherlands and Sweden. Scott's (2000) history organizes SNA's development according to specific methodological advances, for example, the development of the use of graph theory and the research on cliques. Freeman's (2004) and Wellman and Berkowitz's (1988) accounts organize the history largely in geographical terms, i.e. focusing on which countries, universities and research centres developed social network analytic concepts or tools. Wasserman and Faust (1994) opt to present each concept's and/or technique's history separately. In spite of these differences in presentation, all of these historical accounts tend to agree that SNA, as a field in its own right, emerged during the 1960s and 1970s at Harvard's sociology department, where Harrison White led a group of young scholars focusing on social network concepts and analytic techniques.

These previous accounts have informed, but not determined, the present chapter. Rather than try to give a complete overview of SNA's history, I have opted to focus on the history of those concepts and techniques emphasized in this book. Linton Freeman's (2004) book still remains the most complete, and up-to-date historical account of SNA, and the present chapter does not attempt to succeed this research. This chapter *does* attempt to frame SNA's history differently, to emphasize certain aspects of its history that have hitherto remained slightly buried. In particular, this chapter presents SNA's early history as emerging from three social science disciplines: psychology (more specifically the Gestalt psychologists and social psychologists), sociology and social anthropology. Especially in the early days, these disciplinary divides offered unique takes on how to approach the study of social networks; for example, the psychologists' research was largely experimental, and emphasized the interplay between cognitions and social relations. In contrast, social anthropologists were more interested in studying social networks in natural settings, and thus made use of social networks as an analytical concept for generating theoretical concepts regarding systemic-level conflicts. Sociologists, primarily those at Harvard University, were able to combine much of the previous work found in both social psychology and social anthropology to make use of graph theory and matrix algebra to explore important sociological concepts such as roles and positions.

Thus early SNA history can be seen as emerging from particular disciplinary trajectories, and these are presented here. Previous historical accounts of SNA do discuss the multidisciplinarity nature of SNA's beginnings, yet none have attempted to explore, explicitly, these unique disciplinary contributions. This chapter takes up that challenge. Yet before proceeding further, I wish to state openly a few limitations of framing SNA's history via this 'disciplinary' approach; first, even in the early days, there were individuals who did cross disciplinary boundaries in their explorations of social networks. Examples include Elisabeth Bott, who studied anthropology with Warner in the US before moving to England to work with psychologists at the Tavistock Institute in London. The research team composed of Elton Mayo (a psychologist) and Lloyd Warner (a social anthropologist) represent another example of early interdisciplinary SNA research. Finally, mathematicians were often involved in the early stages of SNA's history; examples are found in the work of Cartwright and Harary (1956) as well as Luce and Perry (1949). In fact, while I do not highlight mathematics as its own trajectory, one should keep in mind that mathematics, especially the sub-field of graph theory, played an enormous role in helping social scientists early on formalize concepts and measures regarding social networks.

Thus, in what follows, I offer readers a view of how certain early thinkers from psychology, sociology and social anthropology shaped particular pathways for the development of social network analysis.

(SOCIAL) PSYCHOLOGY TRAJECTORY

Although social network analysis is today seen as a multidisciplinary pursuit, historical accounts tend to agree that the field was more or less started through the efforts of Jacob Moreno, a student of psychiatry from Vienna, who immigrated to the US in 1925 and developed the field of 'sociometry', widely considered the precursor to social network analysis. As such, I shall begin this historical account with Moreno, and in so doing, briefly touch upon some of Moreno's contemporaries and other potential influences from around this time period.

Jacob Moreno

Moreno studied psychiatry, and through his studies, he became acquainted with Gestalt psychology, a sub-field in psychology that looks at the interplay between perceptions and the larger structures of the human mind. Gestalt psychology (the word Gestalt translates as 'form') was largely developed by German psychologists Max Wertheimer (born 1880, died 1943), Wolfgang Köhler (born 1887, died 1967) and Kurt Koffka (born 1886, died 1941) as a reaction to the behaviourist theories of their day. These men argued that human perception could best be understood in the context of the larger structure of the human mind. This stood in contrast to other psychological approaches of that time period that placed greater emphasis on the individual perceptions themselves. As noted by Wertheimer.

> The fundamental 'formula' of Gestalt theory might be expressed in this way: There are wholes, the behaviour of which is not determined by that of their individual elements, but where the part-processes are themselves determined by the intrinsic nature of the whole. It is the hope of Gestalt theory to determine the nature of such wholes. (1938: 2)

Thus said, Gestalt theorists saw perceptions as guided by the structure of the mind, that is, the 'whole' of the mind mattered more to these thinkers than the individual parts of the mind or individual perceptions.

This focus on the interplay between perceptions and the larger system/structure of the mind influenced Moreno's own interest in understanding the psychological well-being of individuals. While a student at the University of Vienna, Moreno became interested in how the psychological well-being of individuals was linked to the social relations in which they were embedded. When Moreno immigrated to America, he began a close working relationship with Helen Hall Jennings, a student at Columbia University, whose background in research design, methods and statistics complemented the more theoretical leanings of

Moreno. Together, Moreno and Jennings explored how social relations affected psychological well-being, and in the process, they developed a technique they called 'sociometry'. This technique used quantitative methods for studying the structure of groups and the positions of individuals within groups (Moreno and Jennings, 1934). The approach also made use of 'sociograms', which were visual depictions of individuals (or any social unit) and their relationships to others in a group. Here, individuals are portrayed as points, and the relationship linking the individuals together are portrayed as lines. Figure 2.1 is an example of a sociogram.

These sociograms generated a great deal of interest and media attention when Moreno first presented them to the public in 1933 (Wasserman and Faust, 1994). Part of the appeal lay in the simple, yet powerful way in which sociograms communicated a new way of conceptualizing social relationships. They were also useful for illustrating certain network concepts, ones moreover that are still used today; these included a 'star', which is a sociogram depicting an individual at the centre of a network, and an 'isolate', which refers to an individual actor who is wholly disconnected from the rest of the network (Leinhardt, 1977; Scott, 2000).

As the popularity of sociometry quickly rose, Moreno used this momentum to start a journal called *Sociometry*. This journal became a space for exploring further developments and applications of the technique, and Moreno's writings in this journal are numerous (e.g. Moreno, 1943, 1945, 1950, 1952, 1954). However, a real synthesis of his arguments and the techniques he and Jennings developed together can be found in his book entitled, *Who Shall Survive?* (Moreno, 1953). In spite of these publications, however, the 1950s was a period in which the academic community began to slowly drift

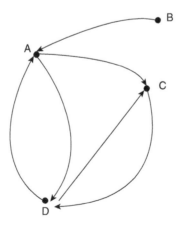

Figure 2.1   Example of a sociogram

away from Moreno and sociometry, and this shift was seen as resulting from Moreno's reputation for being a difficult person (Freeman, 2004). Moreno's last publication in *Sociometry* was in 1955, and while he continued to publish on sociometry until 1960 (Moreno, 1960, 1978), interest in the topic had largely shifted elsewhere. In 1978, the journal he founded changed its name from *Sociometry* to *Social Psychology Quarterly*. Sociometry, it seems, largely died as a disciplinary pursuit.

Beyond sociograms: matrices and graph theory

As described earlier, the field of 'sociometry' began to lose popular support within the academic community not too long after the journal *Sociometry* was founded. One frustration and shortcoming that many researchers experienced was the difficulty in uncovering any meaningful patterns in sociograms, once the network in question reached beyond a certain size. Thus, early on, scholars began publishing papers within *Sociometry* on the possibilities of using matrices for structuring and analysing network data (see for example, Dodd, 1940a, 1940b, Forsyth and Katz, 1946). These early accounts spent much time outlining what social network data looked like in matrix form, and there were also some illustrations for how they could be used to analyse sociological concepts pertaining to isolates, reciprocated and non-reciprocated relations, groups and community (Dodd, 1940a, 1940b) as well as subgroups within a network (Forsyth and Katz, 1946).

Forsyth and Katz were among the first ones to use matrices as an alternative to the sociogram. They argued that matrices could present social network data more 'objectively' (1946: 341). They proposed analysing the matrix by a systematic process of rearranging the columns and rows to reveal more visibly the subgroups, stars and isolates found within the network. Festinger (1949) and Luce and Perry (1949) built on this work, demonstrating how matrix algebra could be used in conjunction with matrices to uncover the path-lengths connecting actors together, and the presence of cliques.

Another improvement on the sociometric approach emerged from social scientists who adapted graph theory to social network data. Graph theory, a sub-field of mathematics, makes use of notation, visual graphs and a number of theorems for discussing, theorizing and analysing networks. Graph theory originated with Euler (1736), yet this branch of mathematics did not really begin to gain notice until König's (1936) paper was translated into English in 1956. Subsequently, within social psychology, Harary and Norman (1953) were among the first to begin specifying how graph theory could be used as a model for the social sciences and social networks in particular.

Kurt Lewin

Working nearly the same time period as Moreno was another European-trained scholar named Kurt Lewin. Like Moreno, Lewin had studied the Gestalt theorists, and he brought this knowledge with him when he too immigrated to the US in the 1930s. Although Lewin and Moreno did meet in 1935 (Freeman, 2004: 72), there is little evidence of the two actively collaborating with one another, and neither seems to have cited the other's work.

Lewin is most well-known for developing a theoretical framework called 'field theory', which describes and explains human behaviour and perception from a structural perspective (Lewin et al., 1936, 1951). Lewin saw behaviour as embedded within a 'field', which he defined as 'the totality of coexisting facts which are conceived of as mutually interdependent' (Lewin, 1951: 240). He argued that to truly understand perception and behaviour, one needed to understand this larger context of 'coexisting facts'. Lewin (1951) also made methodological suggestions for conducting studies from a field theory perspective: he argued that individuals and groups could be represented in topological terms, where different spaces, such as one's family, their work and so forth, could be displayed as vectors within a space. Finally, Lewin argued for mathematical techniques to analyse social space with the aim of exploring the system of relations in which a group and its environment were situated (Lewin, 1951).

In 1945, Lewin became the director of the Research Center for Group Dynamics at MIT, and it was here that his influence was most keenly felt amongst students and colleagues. These included Alex Bavelas, Dorwin Cartwright and Leon Festinger. Unfortunately, Lewin died shortly after establishing his centre at MIT, and as a result, a re-shuffling of his research team occurred, splitting the team into two new centres, one at MIT and a second at the University of Michigan. These are discussed below.

Alex Bavelas and centrality

The first centre, lead by Lewin's former student Alex Bavelas, was located at MIT and called The Group Networks Laboratory (Freeman, 2004). Here, Bavelas and his team designed a number of experiments centred around issues of communication and information diffusion within small groups (Bavelas, 1948, 1950). In particular, this work focused on how information travelled within a small group of actors, and Bavelas' team looked to see which kinds of network structures affected the speed and efficiency of this information diffusion. The experiments lead by his team resulted in an important concept for network analysis, this being centrality (Freeman, 1978; Wasserman and Faust, 1994). For Bavelas, centrality rested on the notion of distance, i.e. that a central actor was relatively close to other actors in the network, and Bavelas argued that such 'central' actors would be optimally positioned for integrating information from the dislocated parts of a network (Bavelas, 1948, 1950). In addition, Bavelas' work resulted in a global index for centrality, which looked at the overall distance of actors from the most central actor in the network (see, for example Leavitt, 1951 for a discussion on centrality index). This more global property of a network could be used as an indicator for how quickly information could travel through the network, and thus potentially solve problems more efficiently (Bavelas, 1948, 1950). Currently, this global index for centrality is more commonly referred to as 'centralization', and you can read more about centrality in Chapter 4 and centralization in Chapter 8.

Bavelas' group also used mathematics to formalize their definitions of centrality. A key contributor to this process was R. Duncan Luce, a mathematician who joined Bavelas' group after first coming into contact with Leon Festinger,[1] another former student of Lewin. Festinger taught a course at MIT on social psychology, and through a mutual acquaintance, Festinger and Luce became acquainted. Luce became interested in Festinger's ideas regarding communication networks and structure, and he thus began developing a formal, mathematical definition of a clique with the aid of his fellow student Perry (Luce and Perry, 1949). In particular, Luce and Perry used mathematical notation to specify cliques as consisting of three or more actors who were all mutually related to each other member in a subset (1949: 97). This definition was also present in an article written the same year by Festinger (1949), although neither article cites the other. Festinger's (1949) article is written in less technical terms, but he makes many of the same points: like Luce and Perry (1949), Festinger (1949) demonstrates how matrices and matrix algebra could be used to uncover cliques within a social network.

Luce (1950) also introduced the idea of an 'n-clique', which offers a broader definition of a clique. Luce (1950) argues that confining the location of cliques to subsets of actors where all actors are connected to one another is overly stringent, and does not capture the intuitive notion of a 'clique'. To remedy this problem, the authors relaxed the 'rule' that all actors need to hold mutual ties to all others, and instead, actors could be considered members if they held indirect ties of *n* length to others in the subset. Here, the analyst could specify the value for *n*, thus offering yet more flexibility for conceptualizing and measuring cliques (Luce, 1950; Luce and Perry, 1949). In Chapter 7, you will find more discussion regarding the differences between cliques and n-cliques and how to analyse for these.

---

[1]Festinger (1987) went on to develop his theory of Cognitive Dissonance, for which he is most well-known. This theory in many respects reflects his and Cartwright's earlier concerns regarding the cognitive states of individuals, although less emphasis is placed on the role of social relations and their structures.

The work of Bavelas' team was thus important for making use of mathematics to formalize fundamental concepts regarding network structure, and for developing the concepts of centrality and centralization. Furthermore, their work influenced the work of their colleagues Festinger and Cartwright,[2] who had moved Lewin's original research centre from MIT to the University of Michigan.

Festinger, Cartwright and Harary: structural balance

Shortly after arriving at the University of Michigan, Festinger was able to recruit a mathematics PhD student, named Frank Harary, to his and Cartwright's centre. As a mathematician, Harary was interested in applying graph theory to social relations and structural concepts (Cartwright and Harary, 1956; Harary, 1955–6; Harary and Kabell, 1980; Harary and Norman, 1953; Harary et al., 1965). Towards this end, he set out the possibilities of graph theory in a monograph (Harary and Norman, 1953), and shortly thereafter, he co-authored a paper with Dorwin Cartwright on the uses of graph theory for expanding upon a popular social psychology theory of the time, i.e. Heider's (1946) theory of balance (Cartwright and Harary, 1956).

The introduction of Cartwright and Harary's (1956) paper on a balance theory offers a simple, historical account of the intellectual influences felt in social psychology at that time. The authors position Heider's (1946) balance theory within the larger Gestalt tradition, and they note Kurt Lewin (Lewin et al., 1936) and Jacob Moreno as two such Gestalt theorists. In keeping with the general tenets of Gestalt and field theory, Cartwright and Harary (1956) outline the basic ideas of Heider's (1946) balance theory; here, individual cognitive states were classified as either balanced or unbalanced, and this distinction depended upon whether a person's views on a topic were in agreement or conflict with others' perceptions on that same topic.

One interesting aspect of this theory was Heider's (1946) discussion on relations connecting an individual to others as being either positive (+) or negative (−). Positive relations reflected notions of liking or agreement, and negative ones referred to feelings of dislike, conflict or even the absence of a tie. These 'signed' relations join individuals into social configurations of two or three actors, and the structure of these configurations defined whether the individual experienced a balanced or unbalanced state (Heider, 1946).

These ideas from balance theory intrigued Cartwright and Harary (Cartwright and Harary, 1956), and they used graph theory to develop a formal structural definition for balance, which they referred to as 'structural balance'. As a first

---

[2] Both Festinger (1949) and Cartwright (Cartwright and Harary, 1956) cite Bavelas (1948) as a precursor to their own work.

step, the authors translated Heider's diagrams and language into graph theoretic terms: entities became 'points', relations became 'directed lines', signed relations became 'signed directed lines', and all of these terms were summarized through the visual representation of a graph (1956: 283).

This 'new' definition of balance enabled the authors to make some key alterations and extensions to balance theory. Primarily, Cartwright and Harary extended the phenomenon of 'balance' to a wider array of social situations: 'our definition of balance may be employed whenever the terms "point" and "signed line" can be meaningfully coordinated to empirical data of any sort' (1956: 292). The authors thus made the theory applicable to situations other than one person's cognitive state. In addition, the authors were able to demonstrate how graphs of any size, not just ones consisting of three entities, could be categorized as being 'balanced', 'unbalanced', or somewhere in-between, i.e. as having a 'scale' of balance.

Cartwright and Harary (1956) then used graph theory to develop two theorems for formalizing the conditions needed for defining graphs as balanced or unbalanced. The first theorem states that a signed graph could only be considered balanced if all paths joining the same pair of points held the same sign. The second theorem – what the authors termed their 'structure theorem' – states that a signed graph of any size can be considered balanced if the points can be separated into two mutually exclusive subgraphs. These subgraphs would contain only positive ties, and the ties between the subgraphs would be negative or absent.

Thus, within the confines of one paper, these authors made significant progress on both theoretical and methodological grounds. Wasserman and Faust (1994) note that structural balance, and the work of Cartwright and Harary (1956) in particular, has generated hundreds of articles across four disciplines. In addition, their work launched a stream of research focusing on the use of triples for understanding local and more global network structures. Most relevant for the purposes of this book include the work of James Davis (Davis, 1967) on *clustering*, and of the work done on triads and *transitivity* (Davis, 1977; Davis and Leinhardt, 1971; Holland and Leinhardt, 1970, 1972). All of these topics will be covered in Chapter 5, and the concepts clustering and transitivity will be more fully discussed in further sections of this chapter.

The use of graph theory for developing formal definitions for concepts such as cliques, centrality and balance, were important early advances in the field of social network analysis that social psychology offered. Many of these contributions are still very much part of the current field of social network analysis; Bavelas' work on centrality was later extended and popularized by Freeman (Freeman, 1978), and centrality remains one of the key fundamental concepts in network analysis. In addition, cliques and n-cliques are still regularly used as measures for cohesive subgroups. Structural balance and balance theory is still being cited and used today. Taken together, the work of these early, Lewin-inspired researchers continues to influence the social network discipline today.

Current and ongoing work on social psychology and networks

The concern for cognition and perception shared by early social psychology network analysts is still present in more recent advances in the field. For example, Friedkin's (1998) social influence network theory examines the role networks play in shaping and influencing actor's perceptions, behaviours and attitudes. Simply put, Friedkin (1998) argues that actors who are similar according to attitudes, values and behaviours are likely to be socially tied to one another. Further, it is through this social tie that these actors mutually influence one another and become similar to one another over time. Social influence theory is seen as closely tied to ideas of homophily and social selection (Lazarsfeld and Merton, 1954a; McPherson et al., 2001; Mercken et al., 2009; Robins et al., 2001), and in later sections of this book, you will have further opportunities for learning about these intertwined concepts.

Another recent network theory that has emerged from social psychology is that of social exchange theory (Cook et al., 1983). This theory is based on the idea that exchanging social and material resources is fundamental to all human interaction, and that such interactions are shaped by unequal power relationships between individuals, which in turn are influenced by the network structure in which actors are found. This work currently inspires much research in both social psychology and sociology (see Molm, 2003 for a review). Thus, social psychology continues to contribute to the social network discussion in emphasizing the interplay between cognition and social relations.

Although this section has emphasized the contributions of key social psychologists, I would also like to take a moment to mention one of the sorts of cross-disciplinary interactions that took place during the time Festinger and Cartwright were leading their research centre. Festinger and Cartwright, during their time at Michigan, developed a formal collaboration with the Tavistock Institute for Human Relations, located in London, UK. In 1947, this institute, with the help of Festinger and Cartwright's group in Michigan, founded the journal *Human Relations*, which was co-published by Tavistock and the University of Michigan. Through this journal, an exchange of ideas occurred between the two countries, a collaboration that proved instrumental in influencing the thinking of one social anthropologist stationed in London by the name of Elizabeth Bott. Bott's contribution to the field of SNA is covered under the social anthropology trajectory (see next section), but it is important to note here that her involvement with Tavistock brought her, and her colleagues, into contact with the thoughts and research of the American social psychologists.

SOCIAL ANTHROPOLOGY TRAJECTORY

A common theme of the history of social network analysis, especially in the early days, is that many researchers were working separately from each other, without knowledge of one another's existence. Thus, during the time Moreno and Jennings were developing sociometry, social anthropologists in both Britain and the US were also starting to explore new ways for studying structural issues.[3] One social anthropologist in particular has had enormous influence on scholars on both sides of the Atlantic during the first half of the twentieth century. This person was Alfred Radcliffe-Brown, a social anthropologist from Britain whose thoughts regarding social structure proved to be very influential to early network analysts. Radcliffe-Brown travelled a great deal during his career; in 1920 he moved from England to teach in Australia. From 1930–1937, he was stationed at the University of Chicago, where he interacted with Warner and Davis, two important early network analysts. Thereafter, he moved to Oxford, where he interacted with a number of British social anthropologists, chief among these being Max Gluckman. By the end of his career, Radcliffe-Brown had taught at Cambridge, London, Birmingham, Pretoria, Johannesburg, Cape Town, Sydney, Oxford, Sao Paulo and Alexandria (Freeman, 2004; Radcliffe-Brown, 1952).

At each location he visited, Radcliffe-Brown lectured on social relations and the structuring of those relations. In addition, he supervised a number of studies, where data on kinship and other social relations were gathered. His contact with these different datasets led Radcliffe-Brown into making a number of generalizations about the nature of social relations, social structure and society. In particular, Radcliffe-Brown argued that society developed certain structures naturally in efforts to fulfil certain functions (Radcliffe-Brown, 1952, 1957, 1958). As such, Radcliffe-Brown's work has often been linked to the work on structural functionalism as discussed by Radcliffe-Brown's contemporaries, Talcott Parsons (Parsons, 1937, 1951) and Bronislaw Malinowski (Malinowski, 1944; Malinowski et al., 1945). Radcliffe-Brown, however, differed from these colleagues by placing more emphasis on the role of social relations. In particular, Radcliffe-Brown argued that society could be seen as a 'complex network of social relations' that he labelled a 'social structure' (Radcliffe-Brown, 1940b, 1952), and this structure could be uncovered through the development of a

---

[3] I am aware that some readers will be disappointed by the fact that I am not including a discussion regarding the work of ethnographer and philosopher, Claude Lévi-Strauss. Lévi-Strauss' (1949/1969) work on the structures of kinship set out a theoretical approach to understanding the structured patterns of kinship, and his collaboration with André Weil on this topic helped to bring formal mathematical methods to this approach. Nonetheless, this work only informed the anthropology literature on kinship, and further, his methods/techniques are not central to this book.

particular branch of mathematics that would focus on quantifying and analysing relations as units of analysis (Radcliffe-Brown, 1957).

Although Radcliffe-Brown did not go on to develop this branch of mathematics, his arguments did provide other kinds of practical, methodological advice for anthropologists. In particular, Radcliffe-Brown argued that networks could help anthropologists move beyond abstract categories of 'culture' and 'class'. He noted:

> we do not observe a 'culture', since that word denotes, not any concrete reality, but an abstraction. But direct observation does reveal to us that ... human beings are connected by a complex network of social relations. I use the term 'social structure' to denote this network of actually existing relations. (Radcliffe-Brown, 1940b: 2)

Thus, rather than use an a priori concept such as culture, the anthropologist's job was to draw abstractions from these concrete data, versus assuming notions such as culture or class exist a priori. This emphasis on 'concrete data' did receive some criticism for being overly objective in orientation (Leach, 1984), yet such a criticism did not disway many followers of Radcliffe-Brown from seeing value in this empirically oriented 'network' focus to studying culture.

During Radcliffe-Brown's time in Australia in the 1920s, he supervised a student named W. Lloyd Warner on a study pertaining to kinship patterns. When Warner completed this study in 1929, he moved to the US to become an instructor at Harvard's Department of Anthropology. There, Warner immediately began to lead anthropological studies that adopted a structural orientation (Freeman, 2004; Scott, 2000). In particular, Warner began collaborating with Elton Mayo, a trained psychologist located in Harvard's Business school, who was researching work productivity within the Western Electric company in Illinois. Prior to meeting Warner, Mayo's focus had been on the psychological characteristics of workers. However, Mayo saw Warner potentially widening the scope of the project to include a concern for the social context and structures surrounding workers (Mayo, 1933), and he thus hired Warner in 1930 as a consultant for the project. Here, the two researchers led an anthropological study (1931–1932) on interpersonal interactions among 14 workers at the Hawthorne factory in Cicero, Illinois.

The Hawthorne study involved a careful recording of all group behaviour in a bank wiring room of the factory, and the research team used graphic images of network ties to describe the group structure. In doing so, their study was the first major study, within a natural setting, to use a sociogram to describe the relations observed by the field workers (Freeman, 2004; Scott, 2000). These sociograms showed various relations such as 'horseplay' among employees, conflicts and friendships. Through careful observation, the researchers were able to detect the existence of informal groups, which they referred to as cliques (Roethlisberger et al., 1939). This use of the term clique, however, was limited to mere description, i.e. it was not like the formal mathematical model proposed by Luce and Perry (1949), and it was not used to explain any of the observed behaviour of the workers (Scott, 2000: 19).

While Warner was still at Harvard, he also launched a second study focusing on a New England town that he referred to as Yankee City. In this study, Warner conducted a full anthropological study of a modern, urban setting. In outlining the conceptual framework guiding his study, Warner describes society and communities as composed of 'a group of mutually interacting individuals', whereby each relation is 'part of the total community and mutually depended upon all other parts' (Warner and Lunt, 1941: 13–14).

In analysing and displaying the data gathered for this study, Warner's team used various sociograms to illustrate notions of cliques (Warner and Lunt, 1941). They then attempted to explain the structuring of ties through looking at other actor attribute data, in particular, socio-economic class. In addition, there was some discussion on the constraining and enabling influence of cliques on the behaviour of individuals. Finally, they also made use of matrices to uncover both cliques and positions to show how individuals belonged to different groupings (Scott, 2000; Warner and Lunt, 1941).

By the time Yankee City was completed, Warner had left Harvard for Chicago. Here, Warner supervised a number of studies emphasizing the structural aspects of social ties. Among these was the study *Deep South*, which looked at the impact of race differences on social stratification in the town of Natchez, Mississippi (Davis et al., 1941). To conduct the study, Warner hired a black couple, Allison and Elizabeth Davis, and a white couple, Burleigh and Mary Gardner, to do fieldwork in Mississippi to investigate how social relations were related to social class. Thus, they collected data on the co-attendance of black men to various social events as well as the co-attendance of white women to social events. These data are still considered a fine example of two-mode network data, where the matrices used to structure the data consisted of columns that represent events and rows that represent actors. In analysing the structural patterns in the data, Warner and his team again employed the notion of a clique, using this concept to describe levels of intimacy among actors. The *Deep South* book still remains a hallmark in the social networking literature, and the data from this study are available through the UCINET software package.

As mentioned earlier, Warner's initial interest in, and perspective of, social structural came largely from his time as a student under Radcliffe-Brown's supervision. Yet the influence of Radcliffe-Brown was even more strongly felt amongst social anthropologists in the UK, where his ideas helped shape the direction of a small group of social anthropologists situated at Manchester and London. The leader of this effort was Max Gluckman, the first Chair of Manchester's Department of Social Anthropology and Sociology, whose series of seminars on social structure brought together the likes of George Homans and Talcott Parsons, two well-known American sociologists of the day, with social anthropologists from London and Manchester. The work produced by Gluckman and his Manchester colleagues during the 1950s and 1960s has since become known for a distinctive style of social anthropology known as the Manchester School (Werbner, 1984).

Gluckman originally came from South Africa, where he had studied anthropology at the University of Witwatersrand in Johannesburg. In the early 1930s, Gluckman joined Oxford University as a Transvaal Rhodes Scholar, and he received his PhD from Oxford in 1936. During this time at Oxford, Gluckman came into contact with Radcliffe-Brown's ideas regarding structure as well as Oxford's own pre-War form of structural functionalism (Leach, 1984).

Upon completing his PhD, Gluckman returned to Africa to conduct fieldwork in Zululand. This fieldwork resulted in two books, *The Kingdom of the Zulu of South Africa* (1940b) and *Analysis of a Social Situation in Modern Zululand* (1940a). This last book, in particular, became a foundational text for Gluckman's group of social anthropologists at Manchester (Werbner, 1984). In this book, Gluckman lay the groundwork for an anthropological approach to studying social processes that emphasized the detailed description of particular social events in order to theorize aspects of society at large. In doing so, Gluckman's work demonstrated how local, specific events shed light on macro-level social processes of a larger social system (Gluckman, 1940a).

The events that most interested Gluckman were ones pertaining to conflict, and he found that understanding conflicts involved a close look at the different kinds of social relations knitting a particular group together. Thus, in his fieldwork in Africa, Gluckman (1940a) found that close kin would unite against distant kin, yet all would unite together against non-kin groups. This interplay of different relations developed into the notion of 'cross-cutting ties' (Gluckman, 1940a, 1963, 1968): here, allegiances found within one set of social relations could cut across or transcend a conflict or cleavage in a different set of relations. Thus, this interdependency of relations would allow for conflict and resolution, which in Gluckman's mind, were normal and healthy aspects of a social system's functioning (Gluckman, 1968). However, Gluckman (1968) also saw the study of these personal relations and their structuring as limited to the realm of social networks, and could not generalize to or replace an institutional analysis.

These views regarding structure, the role of cross-cutting ties, and the attention to micro events for building generalizations about more global ones, heavily influenced the group of social anthropologists surrounding Gluckman during his time at Manchester. Reference to cross-cutting ties, for example, can be found in Barnes (Barnes, 1972) and Mitchell (Mitchell, 1974). In addition, Mitchell (1969) credits Gluckman (Gluckman, 1955) for focusing the group's attention on multiplex ties as a means for looking at how ties, in different normative contexts, can link actors together into different institutional arrangements.

The Manchester school, as it became known, not only reflected this method-ological focus on social networks, but also, in making use of social networks as both a metaphor and analytical concept, this group became known as a critical tradition, in the sense that they were reacting to current trends of that time in sociology and social anthropology (Mitchell, 1974; Wellman, 1988; Werbner, 1984). In particular, they disagreed with Parson's argument that institutions and norms derived from internalized values of individuals. Instead, these social anthropologists emphasized interpersonal relations and how these relations could develop into structures and patterns that could, in turn, give rise to group norms, i.e. larger social institutions. In this way, studying social relations helped fill a gap to explain norm consensus, the rise of particular institutions, and norm-based behaviour that structural functionalism, especially the kind promoted by Parsons, failed to explain (Mitchell, 1969, 1974).

Methodologically, this group emphasized the use of ego network data that were gathered primarily through ethnographic approaches such as participant-observation and loosely structured interviewing (Barnes, 1954; Bott, 1955, 1957; Harries-Jones, 1969; Mitchell, 1969). Such ego networks acted as the empirical anchor that could ground abstract notions of networks and how they influence individual behaviour. In addition, graph theory was drawn upon as a means to formalize sociological concepts, as Mitchell explains: 'The use of graph theory ... holds considerable promise for stating the properties of networks in formal terms which should enable sociological deductions to be tested more rigorously than previously' (1969: 34).

Closely associated to the Manchester school was another group of social anthropologists located down in London, at the London School of Economics (LSE). This group consisted of Elizabeth Bott, John Barnes and Siegfried Nadel. Elizabeth Bott, a student at that time at LSE, was also working as a hired researcher at the Tavistock Institute in London at the time of her studies. As described earlier, Tavistock co-published the journal *Human Relations* with the University of Michigan, where Festinger and Cartwright were situated. As such, through this Tavistock connection, Bott was in contact with the ideas of American social psychologists, in particular the work of Moreno and Lewin.

While at Tavistock, Bott conducted an anthropological study of 20 London households and their personal networks to uncover an interesting relationship between the conjugal roles of married couples and the structure of these indi-viduals' personal networks (Bott, 1955, 1957). As she notes in her article (Bott, 1955), Bott's previous attempts to derive explanations for differences in conjugal roles were not very successful, and researching the social relations of respondents proved a more fruitful direction. In particular, she uncovered that married couples who held more 'connected' networks tended to have more segregated conjugal role-relationships, i.e. they would have strict divisions of labour and spent very little of their leisure time together. In contrast, couples with 'dispersed' networks were more likely to have more joint conjugal role-relationships, i.e. they tended to share many of the same activities and tended to spend much of their leisure time together. Thus, once again, the empirical grounding of anthropological fieldwork led to the development of a structural concept pertaining to networks.

This discussion of a network's 'connectedness', and Bott's use of the term, is seen as the first formal use of a network measure now referred to as *density* (Wellman, 1988). In discussing the relative density of networks, Bott also made use of sociograms to illustrate the difference between dispersed and connected networks. Later, Bott's colleague John Barnes (Barnes, 1969) developed a mathematical measure for 'connectedness' by measuring the density of ties. This mathematical measure is inherently the same as the one in use today.

Although Barnes helped to formalize Bott's notion of connectedness, he is best remembered as the first person to use the term 'social networks' in a field study (Scott, 2000; Wasserman and Faust, 1994). Barnes defined a network as 'a set of points some of which are joined by lines. The points of the image are people, or sometimes groups, and the lines indicate which people interact with each other. We can of course think of the whole of social life as generating a network of this kind' (1954: 237). He used this idea of a network to help explain certain behaviours within the fishing village. In doing so, Barnes (1954) raised the idea of a social network from metaphor to a theoretical concept (Mitchell, 1974). In addition, his use of the term 'social network' is also seen as a critique to contemporary social theory (Mitchell, 1974). Another important member of this British group was SN.

Siegfried Nadel, an anthropologist from LSE, gave a series of lectures on social structure, and his lecture on role analysis is perceived as one of the earliest formal treatments of the topic within network analysis. Here, Nadel describes social structure as a 'pattern or network (or "system") of relationships obtained between actors in their capacity of playing roles relative to one another' (1957: 12). This relational approach to social structure thus informed Nadel's notion of a social role. Nadel saw society as composed of relations, and social structure as composed of the relations among roles. This definition of social structure, society and roles influenced the work of Harrison White and his colleagues in developing a formal definition and analytical procedure for studying the role structure of networks (see discussion below).

Taken together, the work of these social anthropologists was important for moving social anthropology beyond discussions of culture to an empirical focus on social relations. In addition, important theoretical concepts derived from this approach: the notion of 'connectedness', which network analysts now refer to as 'density'; the idea of multiplex relations; and the use of the term 'social network' as both metaphor and analytical concept all came from these anthropologists' work. These anthropologists' work can also be seen as early examples of a qualitative form of ego network anlaysis: Bott's work in particular stands out as a fine example of this mixed-methods approach. At the head of this group's work was Max Gluckman, whose own thinking about structure influenced these anthropologists' approach to thinking about social relations and gathering such data, yet equally as important was Gluckman's role in bringing people together through his seminars. He was not the only influence however; through The Tavistock Institute and the work of Bott in particular, the ideas of social psychologists such as Lewin and Moreno were brought into the discussion.

In spite of this important early work in network analysis, scholars tend to agree that the impact of the British school of anthropology basically died out after the 1960s. One reason given is the anthropologists' own restraint in linking social networks into a larger theoretical framework (Scott, 2000). Indeed, many of these anthropologists seemed to resist the idea altogether: Mitchell notes that anthropologists' focus on social networks came largely as a reaction to institutional analyses that failed to account for the 'the relatively unstructured quality of social relationships in large-scale societies' (1974: 281). As such, a social networks approach 'supplements rather than supplants approaches which seek to circumvent the inadequacies of structural approaches; the notion itself does not compete with or replace these different approaches' (1974: 281). In that same article, Mitchell quotes Barnes (Barnes, 1972) as saying 'there is no such thing as a theory of social networks; perhaps there will never be' (1974: 2). This avoidance of expanding social networks beyond that of an 'analytical concept' applicable to rural and urban settings, is probably the main reason that social network analysis, as developed by this group of British social anthropologists, never infiltrated other disciplines (Scott, 2000).

This is not to say that social network analysis, outside of social anthropology, died out in England. In the late 1970s, Mitchell moved to Oxford and while there, he supervised a PhD student named Martin Everett, a mathematician by training, on a dissertation focused on social network analysis. After finishing his PhD, Everett moved to the University of California, Irvine, where he taught for six months and interacted with a number of early social network analysts such as Linton Freeman, John Boyd, Bill Batchelder, Kim Romney and Doug White. There, he also began working on alternatives to structural equivalence, most importantly, the idea of regular equivalence, a concept rooted in the work of Sailer (1978) and White and Reitz (1983). Examples of Everett's work on regular equivalence include Everett 1985, and a number of co-authored papers with Stephen Borgatti (Everett and Borgatti, 1988, 1990, 1993). After leaving Irvine, Everett took up a position at the University of Greenwich, where he continued his research interests and in the 1980s, began collaborating with Stephen Borgatti on re-building and extending Linton Freeman's UCINET software package. Today, Everett is leading an effort to re-establish the legacy of Clyde Mitchell at the University of Manchester's Sociology department, where he is currently director of the Clyde Mitchell Centre.

In addition to Martin Everett, there were other British network scholars in the 1970s and 1980s who continued developing and making use of social network analysis. These included a number of academics at the University of Essex during the 1970s and 1980s, who were not formally organized, yet nonetheless shared similar interests regarding networks and structure. This group included Pat Doreian, a mathematical sociologist who produced his book on *Mathematics of Social Relations* (Doreian, 1970).[4] In addition, there was Ronald Atkin, a mathematician who worked on Q-analysis and produced a book called the *Multidimensional Man* (Atkin, 1981). Other members included Professor Tony Coxon, who did work on multidimensional scaling, Charles Jones and Peter Davies.

In addition to the above, the British Sociological Association (BSA) had a study group entitled the Quantitative Sociology Group. It was through this group that John Scott first became acquainted with SNA. John Scott, probably best known in the SNA field for his handbook on social network analysis (Scott, 2000), became interested in social network analysis through his research on corporations and interlocking directorships (Hughes et al., 1977; Scott, 1977, 1979). Scott joined the Sociology department at Essex in the 1990s, but by that time, the group of network analysts who had previously been there had largely disbanded.

Currently, there is a resurgence of interest in England in social network analysis, as is demonstrated by the Nuffield Network of Network Researchers (NNNR), a multidisciplinary group of researchers interested in social networks, situated at Oxford University, and the growing social networks group at Manchester University.

THE SOCIOLOGY TRAJECTORY

It is surprising that, while many early sociological thinkers had an impact on social network analysis, sociology, as a discipline, did not start having an impact on social network analysis until the 1950s, and more prominently, in the 1970s during Harrison White's stay at Harvard. Why did it take so long for sociology to start contributing to the field of social network analysis? In a classic article on block modelling, White and colleagues (1976) note that sociologists always had an eye for structure, yet their operationalization of that structure took the form of aggregating attribute data of individuals; thus, for example, actors are grouped together according to their age, socio-economic class, or religion, without any attention to the role social relations play in grouping these actors. Thus, the influence of sociological thinkers such as Simmel, Durkheim and Weber

---

[4]In 1972, Patrick Doreian joined the University of Pittsburgh, in the United States. He has remained there, actively contributing to the mathematical sociology community, in particular, social network analysis.

were primarily felt on the emerging field through the work of Radcliffe-Brown, Warner, and other social anthropologists.

Nonetheless, ideas relating to social networks were present early on in socio-logical thought; the works of Ferdinand Tönnies (1855–1936) relied heavily on the importance of relationships in his distinction between Gemeinshaft (com-munity) and Gesellshaft (society), two ideas relating to community life for which Tönnies is best remembered. Tönnies argued that the relationships found within large, industrial cities were more transitory than those found in rural communi-ties, and as a result, the people living in cities tended to be more isolated, and less involved with their neighbours than those found in rural villages.

Another important early social thinker for social network analysis was Émile Durkheim (1858–1917), a French sociologist who argued that society was more than simply a sum of various parts. In particular, Durkheim argued that any social phenomenon (what he referred to as 'social facts') could only be under-stood in relation to others and to the wider social context. In his famous study on suicide (Durkheim, 1897), Durkheim argued that suicides were less frequent amongst those individuals who were well-integrated into society, and as such, suicides formed an example of how one particular social phenomenon, i.e. 'suicide,' could only be understood by looking at how individuals were embedded within a larger social system.

These thinkers proved influential to early network analysts, in particular the social anthropologists discussed in the previous section such as Radcliffe-Brown and Lloyd Warner. Yet when one considers current-day social network analysis, probably the most significant of these early social theorists was Georg Simmel (1858–1918), a German sociologist whose work contrasted sharply with the large-scale, macro-level theories of his contemporaries, notably, Weber and Marx (Ritzer and Goodman, 2004). One of Simmel's main arguments was that macro-level structures and social phenomena could be understood by focusing one's attention on micro social interactions among individuals and small groups. In his work, *Philosophy of Money* (1978/1907), Simmel discussed the distinc-tion between a *dyad* (a relationship between two persons) and a *triad* (a group composed of three persons), noting that the simple addition of a third person transforms the social dynamics in crucial ways, and that understanding this transformation could shed light on society at large, e.g. how larger structures constrain individuals. With dyads, each individual still maintains his or her own identity, yet this situation shifts with the introduction of a third member. With a triad, a group effect or structure is more likely to occur, and in doing so, con-strain or undermine the individuality of each person. Thus, for example, a third person can mediate between two individuals and benefit from that position, a situation Simmel (1922) referred to as *teritus gaudens*, and one current social network analysts refer to as the benefits of a 'broker' position (Burt, 1992, 2001, 2004, 2005; Gould and Fernandez, 1989).

Triads also introduce the possibility to form alliances and the possibility for coercion through group pressure. Finally, Simmel (1978/1907) argued that these group dynamics within triads could help explain how larger structures, e.g. institutions and cultures, could dominate and constrain individuals. Taken together, Simmel's attention to small structures such as dyads and triads, and his arguments for how such structures could explain group behaviour and societal norms have proven to be very influential to the field of social network analysis, and his work is still cited today.

Finally, there is one last social theorist that influenced early social network analysts (although his contribution to sociological thought, at large, is not seen as being very significant, see e.g. Freeman, 2004). This was Vilfredo Pareto (1848–1923), an economist-turned-sociologist whose systems orientation inspired early sociological work on social networks. Pareto's book, *Mind and Society* (1935), outlines a view of society that balanced the actions and abilities of individuals with opportunities and constraints of the larger class system. He argued that the elite classes in society are constantly reformed and maintained by the individual efforts of individuals who are themselves embedded in a larger class system.

In the 1920s, Pareto's work was popular amongst a small group of academics at Harvard, and it is here, at this point in time, that the story of sociology's trajectory and contribution to social network analysis begins. When Lloyd Warner moved to Harvard's anthropology department in the early 1930s (see previous section on social anthropology), a professor of medicine by the name of Lawrence Henderson began running a seminar on Pareto's work out of Harvard's School of Business Administration. This seminar was open to all Harvard members, and it formed the backbone of a new policy in Harvard to support young scholars as Junior Fellows, the purpose being to encourage an interdisciplinary approach to scholarship guided less by home disciplines and more by research questions.

Regular attendees of this seminar included Warner and members of Warner's research team, as well as sociologists Talcott Parsons and Robert Merton, who were both members of Harvard's sociology department at that time. The organizer of these seminars was George Homans, a recent graduate of Harvard who became one of Harvard's Junior Fellows in 1934. Homan's involvement in organizing Henderson's seminars led Homans' own research interests in social relations, structures, sentiments and interactions, and as such, he was one of the first to synthesize early research on social networks pertaining to small group interaction (Freeman, 2004).

As a Junior Fellow, Homans was given two supervisors, these being Henderson and Elton Mayo. Here, primarily through his contact with Elton Mayo, Homans encountered the works of Radcliffe-Brown and Malinowski, and he also became acquainted with Lloyd Warner. Based on these influences, Homans' research interests became focused around ideas of systems, social relations, and their structures. Upon completing his studies in 1939, he became an instructor for Harvard's Sociology Department, where he began to review all the research that had been done, up until that point, on small groups. This review included work done in social psychology and social anthropology, and it aimed to reach a synthesis regarding the various insights gained from these different disciplinary efforts to understand small group interactions.

The research output that emerged from this review was his classic work, *The Human Group* (Homans, 1950), a work that primarily offers key theoretical insights pertaining to social relations, and one that has gone on to influence other relevant theories in the field, such as James Coleman's (1990) theory of social action and social capital. Here, Homans argues that human interaction can be conceptualized as two different systems, an external system, composed of a set of relations among group members, and an internal system, which emerges out of the external system and which reacts to that system (see Ritzer and Goodman, 2004 for a summary of this work). Homans, in constructing these arguments, brings together insights from the likes of Warner (Roethlisberger et al., 1939; Warner and Lunt, 1941), Davis (Davis et al., 1941), Lewin (Lewin, 1951), Radcliffe-Brown (Radcliffe-Brown, 1940a, 1952, 1957; Radcliffe-Brown and Forde, 1950), Malinowski (Malinowski, 1944; Malinowski et al., 1945) and Moreno (Moreno and Jennings, 1934). As such, his book is the first comprehensive account of small-group research that combines the insights from psychology and social anthropology. In this review, he shows examples of matrices, sociograms and kinship diagrams. In short, Homans' book describes and synthesizes all the techniques, methods and theoretical insights that were currently being used in his day.

Homans' book is also important for social network analysis, in that it offers a theoretical framework linking social relations with sentiments, a framework that later developed into what has come to be known as exchange theory (Cook and Whitmeyer, 1992; Cook et al., 1983; Emerson, 1972a, 1972b). Exchange theory, mentioned earlier in relation to social psychology, remains an important theory in social network analysis that still generates a great deal of academic interest (Molm, 2003). (More discussion on this theory can be found in Chapters 3 and 5.)

At roughly the same time that Homans was studying at Harvard, Robert Merton was also studying for his PhD within Harvard's sociology department. Robert Merton, a sociologist best known for his work on functional sociology (Merton, 1968), was an important influence on early network analysts during his tenure at Columbia University's sociology department. He, alongside Paul Lazarsfeld, trained a number of PhD students who went on to become leaders in the field of social network analysis. These included James Coleman, Peter Blau and Charles Kadushin.

Robert Merton, while a student at Harvard, took part in the seminars organized by Homans, but his main interest in structure derived primarily from his reading of Georg Simmel. Shortly after completing his PhD at Harvard, Merton joined Columbia University's Sociology department in 1941, and there, he quickly began collaborating with his colleague Paul Lazarsfield. This collaboration resulted in some publications pertaining to research on social processes (e.g. Lazarsfield and Merton, 1954b; Lazarsfield et al., 1979), but more importantly, it was a collaborative relationship that resulted in training a number of PhD students in a particular style of structural thinking. Freeman (2004) notes that this period at Columbia, roughly the 1950s, was the first significant sociological effort in social network analysis.

Whereas Merton's background was in sociology, with an emphasis on sociological theory, Paul Lazarsfield's background and training were in mathematics. In the 1930s, Lazarsfield helped Moreno and Jennings to develop a mathematical, structural model of interpersonal choice (Freeman, 2004). During the 1940s, Lazarsfield's research developed a strong empirical emphasis, focusing particular on the consumption of mass media (Katz and Lazarsfield, 2006; Katz et al., 1955). This combined background in mathematics and empiricism complemented Merton's more theoretical sociological background (Freeman, 2004). The fact that the two shared an interest in structure and social relations provided a foundation for focusing PhD students' interests around social relations and structural issues.

Many of the students supervised by Merton and Lazarsfield have become famous names in the field of social network analysis. For example, James Coleman (with colleagues Katz and Mentzel), conducted a diffusion study that heavily relied on the systematic gathering and analysis of social network data (Coleman et al., 1966). Although these data have since been criticized, primarily on the basis of having been gathered through a fixed-recall procedure (Valente, 1995), they are still considered one of the earliest examples of systematic, empirical research on diffusion from a social network approach, and their insights into the relationship between diffusion and the role of personal relations still gets cited today.

In addition to this empirical work, Coleman's treatise, *Foundations of Social Theory* (Coleman, 1990), outlines an expansive theory of social action, where social networks and the structuring of those networks play a prominent role. Within this book, one chapter describes Coleman's (1990) view of social capital, and it is this chapter in particular that has been widely cited by social capital scholars working within and outside the social networks tradition (Burt, 2005; Lin, 2001b; Portes, 1998; Putnam, 1993, 2001).

Another prominent student of Merton and Lazarsfield was Charles Kadushin. Kadushin (1966) built upon Simmel's idea of a social circle through combining this idea with notions of personal influence. This work thus stands out as another early example, similar to Homans, of a sociologist combining the insights from social psychology with those of sociology. Finally, Peter Blau, another PhD student, went on to develop an important core concept within the social network field, i.e. that of homophily (Blau, 1977; Blau et al., 1982). Blau later moved to the University of Chicago, where he came into contact with James Davis (see below).

Thus, the combined efforts of Merton and Lazarfeld's students made important contributions to the field of network analysis. More importantly for the present discussion, these were the first sociological efforts made on the emerging field.

The story of this sociology trajectory, however, continues with following Blau, who upon completing his PhD at Columbia in 1952, moved to the University of Chicago, where he began interacting with another sociologist, James Davis. Davis did not have a strong background in structural theories or concepts, and it was mainly through his contact with Blau and Blau's students that he became sensitized to their importance (Freeman, 2004). At one point, Davis became interested in the work of Cartwright and Harary (Cartwright and Harary, 1956), which inspired Davis to start teaching himself graph theory. This interest in graph theory led to a paper, 'Clustering and structural balance in graphs' (Davis, 1967), where Davis built upon the findings of Cartwright and Harary (1956) by asking under what conditions can a network be split into more than two subgroups. Davis argued that a signed graph, consisting of two or more subgroups, can be called a *clusterable* graph if it contained no cycle holding a negative tie. Davis' (1967) theorems thus showed that all balanced graphs, as defined by Cartwright and Harary (1956), were in essence clusterable ones, but this did not imply that the reverse was also true, i.e. that clusterable graphs were balanced. Davis' (1967) paper has since come to be seen as translating a social psychological phenomenon, i.e. 'balance' to the sociological concern of subgroup formation, i.e. clustering (Freeman, 2004; Wasserman and Faust, 1994).

Davis' work on networks and signed graphs did not end with this paper. Davis began collaborating with a PhD student, Sam Leinhardt, who wrote a thesis on the structuring of interpersonal ties amongst children. Together, the two wrote a paper (Davis and Leinhardt, 1972) that modified Davis' (1967) earlier paper on clustering in a few important respects. First, Davis and Leinhardt (1972) noted that in the majority of cases, relations among actors were directional, and that the direction of these ties was often times not reciprocal. That is, when an actor would nominate another actor as a friend, this other would often not reciprocate the nomination. In addition, they found that signed relations were not so common. In bringing these two insights together, Davis and Leinhardt (1972) argued that current theories of structural balance and clustering needed to accommodate for the direction of ties, yet pay less attention to the sign of the relation. This argument led Davis and Leinhardt (1972) to develop a technique and concept that focused on the direction of ties, i.e. the idea of *ranked clustering*. In addition, ranked clustering was quickly modified to address digraphs that contained no signs, i.e. digraphs consisting only of positive or no relational ties.

In ranked clustering, actors in one cluster are seen as selecting actors in a second cluster, who in turn selected actors in a third. In this way, clusters were joined together in a hierarchical ranking system, whereby actors at the bottom of the hierarchy would choose actors in a higher rank, but not vice versa. Actors within clusters would still maintain positive ties to one another, and actors in different clusters (but the same rank) would hold no tie. Finally, actors in differently ranked clusters would hold a negative tie.

This idea of ranked clusters was then expanded upon to ignore the sign of a relation. To explore this, Davis, along with Leinhardt and Holland, began examining the presence of unsigned directional triads and develop the notion of *transitivity*, which is now considered an all-encompassing structural concept that considers notions of balance, clustering and ranked clustering (Wasserman and Faust, 1994).

Simply stated, transitivity refers to the idea that 'a friend of my friend is also my friend'. Intransitivity refers to instances where this simple rule is broken. Transitivity was seen as building upon Heider's (1958) discussion of cognitive balance; Heider (1958) called the case of three positively tied actors as being, in psychological terms, a 'transitive' situation. Holland and Leinhardt (Holland and Leinhardt, 1970, 1971, 1972) extended this idea of cognitive transitivity to that of interpersonal relations. In particular, they were interested in seeing the extent to which an entire network composed of social relations could be labelled 'transitive,' i.e. characterized by groupings of actors according to mutual liking. Towards this end, they developed a *triad census* (Holland and Leinhardt, 1970) for analysing a graph according to its transitive or intransitive triads (Chapter 6 looks at triad census and transitivity in greater detail). Thus, the 1950s in Columbia produced a group of students who went on to publish and develop ideas and theories still very much in use today.

While Lazarfeld and Merton's former students were publishing these works in the 1960s and 1970s, Harrison White at Harvard University's sociology department was producing, along with his students, a stream of research combining mathematical techniques (primarily matrix algebra) with sociological concepts pertaining to social relations, e.g. social roles and positions.

Harrison White and Harvard Sociology

Harvard's sociology department became a centre of social network analysis under the leadership of Harrison White. This time period at Harvard has been highlighted by many as the critical moment in social network analysis, where the efforts of Harrison White and his students culminated in a break through in terms of consolidating and pushing forward a number of previous efforts to establish a research programme centred around social network concepts, the application of mathematical techniques, and the testing of empirical data (Freeman, 2004; Scott, 2000; Wellman, 1988).

White had originally studied mathematical physics at MIT. In 1960, he earned a second PhD in sociology at Princeton. This mixed background in maths, physics and sociology influenced White's research and teaching early on. For example, his PhD thesis at Princeton involved applying algebraic models to organizational behaviour (Freeman, 2004). Soon afterwards, White moved to join Harvard's sociology department, where he continued pursuing his interest in applying algebraic models to a range of problems, primarily structural in nature. For example, in his book, *Chains of Opportunity* (1970), White made use of algebraic models to analyse how vacancy chains are created when employees near the top of an organization's hierarchy vacate their jobs, thus creating promotion opportunities for individuals lower down the ladder.

Although *Chains of Opportunity* demonstrated the use of mathematics for analysing structural problems, White's real contribution to network analysis came from his research conducted with students, in particular, his work on roles and positions (Boorman and White, 1976; Heil and White, 1976; Lorraine and White, 1971; White et al., 1976). Here, the previous work of social psychologists and social anthropologists were brought together to lay the foundation for a new rendering of the sociological concepts of positions and roles, based on a social networks approach. In particular, White et al. (1976) discussed the work of British social anthropologists Mitchell (1969) and Barnes (1972), noting the significance of these scholars' work in focusing attention to the importance of multiple relations, and on moving the term 'social network' from a metaphor to an analytical concept. In addition, they use these social anthropologists to mark a point of departure; in particular, White et al. (1976) distinguish their work from Mitchell's (1969) and others (Barnes, 1972; Bott, 1955) as an approach to viewing networks as complete networks, whereas the British anthropologists opted to 'anchor' their observations of networks in individuals, what current social network analysts would call 'ego networks'. This distinction, they note, implies the kinds of analyses that are possible; whereas the anthropologists' attention to ego networks highlighted issues of multiple relations and how such relations enabled or constrained individuals, White et al.'s (1976) attention to complete networks would enable the analysis of individuals within the context of the overall social network, thus allowing for a wider range of analytical possibilities.

White et al. (1976) also situate their work alongside the previous work of social psychologists, in particular the work on balance theory; whereas they share social anthropologists' concern that balance theory and much of the work on networks emanating from psychology takes place inside a 'sociological vacuum' (1976: 735), they do not dismiss the theory or its insights, and actually position balance theory as one of the structural 'hypotheses' that block modelling can test for.

Block modelling, and positions and roles analysis in general, are discussed in detail in Chapter 9. However, it is worth outlining a few basics here to draw attention to how this technique built upon and extended previous work on social networks. Block modelling makes use of matrices and matrix algebra to uncover a number of structural features of networks. In particular, the matrices are re-structured in such a way so that actors who share a similar set of ties to others are grouped together into one 'block' in a matrix. For example, if actor A is in contact with the same (or many of the same) others as actor B, then both actor A and B can be said to occupy a similar position within the network. This similarity, or in its extreme instance, *exactness* in position was given the label of 'structural equivalence' by Lorraine and White (Lorraine and White, 1971), and in later publications, White and his colleagues demonstrated how block models could be used to uncover similar (as opposed to exact) positions within networks (Boorman and Harrison, 1976; White et al., 1976).

By uncovering these shared or similar positions of actors across a number of different relations (e.g. marriage, descent, like and dislike), White and his colleagues argued that a complete picture of individual roles and the overall role-structure of a network can be uncovered. This contribution to social network analysis and sociology in general was quite significant; as noted by White et al. (1976), the idea of social roles had a long history in sociology and in the work of British anthropologist Nadel (1957), the concept was developed as a means for understanding how culture systems emerged. White and his team, however, were the first ones to fully develop a systematic means for uncovering positions and roles from social network data.

White's research was thus influential in developing new mathematical techniques for uncovering structures in social relations, yet he was also an influential teacher. Freeman (2004) and Wellman (1988) note that White's years of teaching at Harvard influenced and shaped a generation of social network scholars, and this influence is what made the difference in cementing the future direction in the field. Nearly all of White's PhD students have published in social network analysis, and many have become quite famous.[5] For example, Mark Granovetter, a student of White, has written one of the most cited articles within and outside sociology pertaining to social networks, i.e. the famous 'The strength of weak ties' article (Granovetter, 1973). In this paper, Granovetter reports findings of an empirical study where sampled individuals are asked how they had acquired information on new job opportunities. His results showed that, in those cases where a respondent used a personal contact for acquiring the information about

---

[5]I realise that I am only offering a few descriptions of the many students of White. This has been done primarily through interest of space, and as the names described here are the most relevant for this book.

a new job opening, the contact tended to be *weakly tied* to the respondent. In this context, weak ties referred to relations between individuals in which not much contact occurred between the two, and where neither could be considered part of the others' social circle (see Chapter 6 for more discussion on weak ties). Granovetter's research subsequently launched much interest in the topic of social networks and weak ties in particular, and his article has informed research on social capital and small worlds, both popular topics in social network analysis (see section below on 'Topical Advances').

Another student of White's was Philip Bonacich. Bonacich's contributions to social network analysis are numerous, yet his work on centrality measures is probably the most well-known contribution. Bonacich developed two new measures for centrality, the first being eigenvector centrality and the second an extension of eigenvector centrality, referred to as Bonacich's power centrality measure. Both of these measures are discussed in detail in Chapter 4, and as such, I shall avoid offering details about these here.

Finally, Barry Wellman, whose empirical research on community studies, social support, and the Internet have been widely cited and have contributed to popularizing social network analysis, has also been an important contributor to the field for having founded the International Network for Social Network Analysis (INSNA). This organization was housed at Wellman's university, the University of Toronto, and was run pretty much by his graduate students for a number of years. As part of the formation of INSNA, Wellman began publishing a newsletter called *Connections*. This newsletter slowly developed into a peer-reviewed journal, and today's version of the journal acts as both a journal and newsletter for the organization. Wellman has also published a textbook with Stephen Berkowitz, *Social Structures: A Network Approach* (1988), which still gets cited today.

Thus, the situation at Harvard was unique in that many (if not all) the PhD students studying with White went on to publish social networks research, and further, this research shared a coherence in background and training provided by these students' exposure to White's concern with mathematics and the use of matrices. As a consequence, a large body of work emerged that helped to establish social network analysis as a formal, systematic method and field for studying a wide array of social phenomena.

MODERN DEVELOPMENTS

While the students emerging out of Harvard in the 1960s helped to forge the field of social network analysis, there have been more recent developments in the field that need mentioning. These include the popularization of social network analysis through social capital and small worlds research, and the recent development in social network analysis to build stochastic models, and the use of computer simulation to explore network evolution. These are briefly addressed below.

Topical advances: social capital and small worlds

Social network analysis' popularity increased dramatically with the publication of Robert Putnam's (1993, 2001) books on social capital. Putnam's discussion on the role of networks in defining what constitutes a healthy community caught the imagination of a number of scholars and policy makers. Putnam's (2001) distinction between bridging and bonding social capital relates directly to particular network structures – bridging social capital constitutes weak ties and open network structures while bonding social capital constitutes strong ties and dense network structures. The amount of research focused on social capital has been enormous (see Kadushin, 2004 and Portes, 1998 for reviews), and the topic has likewise stimulated a new generation of researchers into studying social networks through use of social network analysis. These so-called 'network capitalists' (Wellman and Frank, 2001) demonstrate, theoretically and empirically, the relationship between social networks, network structure, and a range of beneficial outcomes (both material and non-material). Well-known network capital researchers include Ron Burt (Burt, 1997a, 1997b, 2001, 2004, 2005) and Nan Lin (Lin, 2001a, 2001b, forthcoming; Lin et al., 2001).

Alongside the social capital discussion, the research pertaining to 'small worlds' has also generated a great deal of interest in social network analysis (Milgram, 1967; Newman et al., 2006; Pool and Kochen, 1978; Watts, 1999, 2003). With small worlds, the focus is on the social phenomena many people experience of encountering a stranger for the first time, only to discover in the course of conversation that both oneself and the stranger share a friend or acquaintance in common ('What a small world!). Thus, small worlds tend to refer to large networks of heterogeneous actors who are linked together through a small number of intermediaries. This tension between distance and closeness is of particular interest in the discussion, i.e. how two people appear to be far apart (geographically or socially), but who are in reality quite closely linked to one another. Earlier research was empirical (Milgram, 1967; Pool and Kochen, 1978), focusing on chains of acquaintances. More recently, the work of Watts (1999) and Strogatz (Watts and Strogatz, 1998), have re-invigorated the discussion through using computer simulation as a way to explore how networks can evolve and change overtime, giving rise to a small-world structure. As with social capital, the research on small worlds quickly grew in number (see Newman et al., 2006; Schnettler, 2009a, 2009b) and with this attention came a subsequent interest in social network analysis and the use of computer simulation for exploring network evolution (Goyal et al., 2006; Hummon, 2000; Pujol et al., 2005).

Methodological advances: ERGMs and network dynamics

The 1980s and 1990s saw an increased interest in developing statistical models for the analysis of social network data, the most famous of these being the family of models referred to as exponential random graph models (ERGMs). This family of models include the p1, p2, and p* models, and in this book, you will be introduced to the p* model (see Chapter 10).

With ERG models, the social network is treated as the dependent variable, and the analyst is looking to explain the network structure. The challenge addressed by this family of models is how to define a probability distribution for a given network so that one can determine whether an observed network deviates significantly from chance? Given the issue of interdependency amongst network actors, one can not make use of theoretical distributions such as a normal curve, for example. The exponential random graph family of models addresses this issue by making use of an exponential function of a linear set of parameters. Such a strategy had been used in mathematical statistics in the past, and is referred to as an exponential family of distributions (Balakrishnan and Basu, 1995).

Holland and Leinhardt (1981) proposed one of the earliest models, the p1 model, which looked at the role of sender and receiver effects, including reciprocity. This was considered a log-linear graph model, with parameters that represented certain network effects such as actor indegree, outdegree and reciprocity. Here, the authors made the assumption that all pairs of actors are independent of one another, i.e. dyads were considered to be independent. Extensions were made by Wasserman and Faust, 1994, which made use of Markov processes for estimating the parameters. Here, the network structure is not explained through this model so much as the differences amongst actors in the network. Again, each dyad in the network is assumed to be independent from one another, and as such, researchers generally conclude that this model is an unrealistic reflection of network data. For example, if you were to think about friendships in real life, many such friendships depend on who else is present in the network, e.g. who else is friends with whom in the network.

The p2 model expanded upon the p1 model by making a multilevel version of the p1 model (Van Duijn and Lazega, 1997; van Duijn et al., 2004). As with the p1 model, the p2 model does not explain too much network structure, i.e. it is very limited. The model looks to explain how the number of ties found in a network (i.e. the network density), and how outdegree, indegree and reciprocity, can be explained by actor and dyadic covariates. Although the p2 model does not model network structure, it does control for it through controlling for differences between actors' degree scores and reciprocity.

A big leap came with the publication of Frank and Strauss' (1986) article on Markov graphs. Here, the authors introduced the idea of Markov dependence, and made use of the Hammersley-Clifford theorem (Besag, 1974) as the 'link between dependence structures and interactions' (1986: 833). Frank and Strauss (1986) defined Markov dependence as an assumption regarding the way in which ties are interdependent within a given network. Here, a possible tie between two actors (i, j) is seen as contingent on any and all other possible ties involving i or j. More specifically, if i and j have another actor k in common, their relationship is considered to be *conditionally dependent* on the relationship each shares with k.

The Markov dependency graphs thus inspired Wasserman and Pattison (1996) to extend Frank and Strauss' (1986) model to make a more general formula that could allow for a wider array of network statistics in the equation than those specified by Frank and Strauss (1986). This more general equation was called the p* model (Wasserman and Pattison, 1996). The probability distribution for the p* model can be expressed as an exponential function containing a number of different network statistics such as reciprocity, the presence of edges, the number of closed triads (or transitive triads), and number of two-paths or two-stars. In addition to creating this more general model for networks, the idea of Markov dependence was relaxed to create a new notion of dependence referred to as 'partial conditional independence' (Pattison and Robins, 2002). Here, the assumption is that two possible edges in the graph are dependent, conditionally on the rest of the graph, when they are incident with a common actor (this is Markov dependence), or when the presence of these edges would create a 4-cycle. An example of a 4-cycle would be actor A connecting to B, B connecting to C and C connecting to D. (for digraphs, directionality is not considered in this respect.)

The p* model is considered the most 'famous' of the exponential random graph models (Frank and Strauss, 1986; Pattison and Wasserman, 1999; Robins et al., 1999; Wasserman and Pattison, 1996). It is the preferred model to use for making statistical inferences about cross-sectional network data.

Growing in both significance and popularity is the suite of actor-based models developed for longitudinal network data by Tom Snijders and colleagues (Huisman and Snijders, 2003; Snijders, 2005, 2008). Here, changes in network structure are analysed over time, where each actor in the observed network is assumed to be evaluating his/her position and striving to find the best, i.e. optimum, configuration of relations. In doing so, all actors are assumed to have complete knowledge of the network, and to act independently of each other. This evaluation process on the part of the actor happens via an exponential function of the actor's position, in a very similar way as the p* model (see Chapter 10 for more details). The distribution of possibilities for an actor, and the actor's evaluation of the network, happens via a stochastic simulation model, i.e. computer simulation is used to generate a distribution of possible new network states for a given actor (such a simulation model is, incidentally, also used in the context of p*).

There are a number of key benefits of using these statistical models for network data over other forms of network analysis (although they do not necessarily replace the need to use other methods and approaches introduced in this book). These include the following: if you are interested in micro–macro linkages, then the p* and actor-based models can help you determine whether lower-level network configurations (such as reciprocity or transitivity) are more commonly observed in a given, observed network than might be expected by chance. Thus, an observed network with high density and centralization, two features that can be located on the macro level, might contain a high number of transitive triads, and through use of these models, you can see whether or not such a tendency is statistically significant. Often, a global network structure can result from a combination of local, sub-structures in a network. The p* and Siena models help one assess these relative contributions. In addition, one can see the relative contribution of different substructures and actor attributes to the overall network structure. For example, is the level of clustering in the network a result of reciprocity between actors, or the similarity of actors' attributes, or both? Readers should also note that the journal *Social Networks* has published special issues on the topic of p* (see volume 29 in *Social Networks*) and actor-based models (see volume 32 in *Social Networks*).

Computer simulations and network formation

Increasingly, computer simulations are being used with network analysis for a number of purposes; for example, for estimating parameter values in statistical models, and also for theory-building exercises related to network formation and emergence.

In 2005, the *American Journal of Sociology* put out a special issue on the use of agent-based modelling and computer simulation, and several of the articles within that special issue focused on the use of computer simulations for modelling networks. Here, the primary interest was in moving beyond the static view of networks that is often portrayed through the use of sociograms (Scott, 1988), to show how a network structure can evolve and change overtime through specifying certain 'rules' of behaviour amongst a group of actors. For example, Robins et al. (2005) simulated networks through use of the p* model, demonstrating how certain parameter values would lead to certain network structures, such as small worlds.

This special issue in *AJS*, however, was only one indicator of the rising interest in computer simulation and network formation. Economists and economic sociologists have, for quite some time, been interested in exploring network formation, through both computer and mathematical models (Doreian, 2002, 2006; 2008; Goyal et al., 2006; Hummon, 2000; Jackson and Watts, 2002; Jackson and Wolinsky, 1996; Tomochi, 2004). Here, the emphasis has been on devising utility functions that calculate the cost and benefit of a tie for individual actors, and then tracing what global network structures evolve from individual tie choices. More recently, simulation research on network formation has also started looking at the role spatial influences play on network formation (Wong et al., 2006).

THE NEXT STEPS: A LOOK FORWARD

Theoretically, social network analysis can still do more. Social capital, thus far, has provided the 'richest' social theory for network analysts, yet it has been criticized on a number of levels (e.g. Portes, 1998), and more recently, the theory is seen as needing 'updating' in view of the work being done on network evolution and small worlds in particular (Prell et al., forthcoming). The statistical models found in p* and Siena are a rich hybrid of traditional SNA concepts with techniques for uncovering statistical significance. Even here, though, some SNA approaches are being lost. For example, the positional and role analyses described in this book, which are fundamental approaches to social network analysis, are not incorporated within either p* or actor-based models. In addition, these models make some significant simplifying assumptions, such as the idea that actors can have 'complete knowledge' of a network or that actors all share the same tendency to form network ties (i.e. the homogeneity constraint). Finally, computer simulations of network evolution often make a similar set of simplifying assumptions regarding network dynamics. Thus, to gain a more realistic view of network formation, promise lies in the analysis of large network datasets, although gathering network data at this level can be problematic.

Taken together, social network analysis has travelled far, and yet the field still offers a number of opportunities for future research directions. In order to get started, however, one needs a good foundation in the basic concepts and procedures, which is the primary intention of this book. Without saying more, then, I shall move onto the main sections of this book, namely, introducing you to the basic concepts and methods for social network analysis.

REFERENCES

Atkin, R. (1981) *Multidimensional Man*. Harmondsworth/New York: Penguin Books.
Balakrishnan, N. and Basu, A. P. (1995) *The Exponential Distribution : Theory, Methods, and Applications*. Amsterdam: Gordon and Breach.

Barnes, J. A. (1954) 'Class and committees in a Norwegian island parish', *Human Relations,* 7: 39–58.

Barnes, J. A. (1969) 'Networks and political process', in J. C. Mitchell (ed.), *Social Networks in Urban Situations.* Manchester: University of Manchester Press.

Barnes, J. (1972) *Social Networks.* Reading, MA: Addison-Wesley.

Bavelas, A. (1948) 'A mathematical model for group structures', *Applied Anthroplogy,* 7: 16–30.

Bavelas, A. (1950) 'Communication patterns in task-oriented groups', *Journal of Accoustical Society of America,* 57: 271–82.

Besag, J. (1974) 'Spatial interaction and the statistical analysis of lattice systems', *Journal of the Royal Statistical Society,* 36: 192–236.

Bidart, C. and Lavenu, D. (2005) 'Evolutions of personal networks and life events', *Social Networks,* 27: 359–76.

Blau, P. M. (1977) *Inequality and Heterogeneity : A Primitive Theory of Social Structure,* New York: Free Press.

Blau, P., Blum, T. and Schwartz, H. (1982) 'Heterogeneity and intermarriage', *American Sociological Review* 47: 45–62.

Boorman, S. A. and Harrison, C. W. (1976) 'Social structure from multiple networks. II. Role structures', *The American Journal of Sociology,* 81: 1384–446.

Bott, E. (1955) 'Urban families: Conjugal roles and social networks', *Human Relations,* 8: 345–83.

Bott, E. (1957) *Family and Social Network; Roles, Norms, and External Relationships in Ordinary Urban Families.* London: Tavistock Publications.

Burt, R. S. (1992) *Structural Holes: The Social Structure of Competition.* Cambridge, MA: Harvard University Press.

Burt, R. (1997a) 'The contingent value of social capital', *Administrative Science Quarterly,* 42: 339–65.

Burt, R. S. (1997b) 'A note on social capital and network content', *Social Networks,* 19: 355–73.

Burt, R. (2001) 'Structure holes versus network closure as social capital', in N. Lin, K. Cook and R. Burt (eds), *Social Capital: Theory and Research.* New York: Aldine de Gruyter.

Burt, R. S. (2004) 'Structural holes and good ideas', *American Journal of Sociology,* 110: 349–99.

Burt, R. (2005) *Brokerage and Closure: An Introduction to Social Capital.* Oxford: Oxford University Press.

Cartwright, D. and Harary, F. (1956) 'Structural balance: A generalization of Heider's theory', *Psychological Review,* 63: 277–92.

Coleman, J. S. (1990) *Foundations of Social Theory.* Cambridge: Belknap Press of Harvard University.

Coleman, J. S., Katz, E. and Menzel, H. (1966) *Medical Innovation: A Diffusion Study.* New York: Bobbs-Merrill.

Cook, K. S. and Whitmeyer, J. M. (1992) 'Two approaches to social structure: Exchange theory and network analysis', *Annual Review of Sociology,* 18: 109–27.

Cook, K. S., Emerson, R.M., Gilmore, M.R. and Yamagishi, T. (1983) 'The distribution of power in exchange networks: Theory and experimental results', *American Journal of Sociology,* 89: 275–305.

Davis, A., Gardner, B. B., Gardner, M. R. and Warner, W. L. (1941) *Deep South: A Social Anthropological Study of Caste and Class*. Chicago, IL: The University of Chicago press.

Davis, J. A. (1967) 'Clustering and structural balance in graphs', *Human Relations,* 20: 181–7.

Davis, J. A. (1977) 'Sociometric triads as multi-variate systems', *Journal of Mathematical Sociological,* 5: 41–60.

Davis, J. A. and Leinhardt, S. (1971) 'The structure of positive interpersonal relations in small groups', in M. Berger, J. Zelditch and B. Anderson (eds), *Sociological Theories in Progress*. New York: Houghton-Mifflin.

Davis, J. A. and Leinhardt, S. (1972) 'The structure of positive interpersonal relations in small groups', in M. Berger, J. Zelditch, and B. Anderson (eds), *Sociological Theories in Progress*. New York: Houghton-Mifflin.

Dodd, S. C. (1940a) 'Analyses of the interrelation matrix by its surface and structure', *Sociometry,* 3: 133–43.

Dodd, S. C. (1940b) 'The Interrelation Matrix', *Sociometry,* 3: 91–101.

Doreian, P. (1970) *Mathematics and the Study of Social Relations*. London: Weidenfeld and Nicolson.

Doreian, P. (2002) 'Event sequences as generators of social network evolution', *Social Networks,* 24: 93–119.

Doreian, P. (2006) 'Actor network utilities and network evolution', *Social Networks,* 28: 137–64.

Doreian, P. (2008) 'A note on actor network utilities and network evolution', *Social Networks,* 30: 104–6.

Durkheim, E. (1897) *Le suicide; étude de sociologie*. Paris: F. Alcan.

Emerson, R. (1972a) 'Exchange theory, Part II: Exchange relations and networks', in J. Berger, J. Morris Zelditch and B. Anderson (eds), *Sociological Theories in Progress, Vol. 2*. Boston: Houghton-Mifflin.

Emerson, R. M. (1972b) 'Exchange theory, Part I: A psychological basis for social exchange', in J. Berger, J. Morris Zelditch and B. Anderson (eds), *Sociological Theories in Progress, Vol. 2*. Boston: Houghton-Mifflin.

Euler, L. (1736) 'Solutio problematis ad geometriam situs pertinentis'. *Commentarii Academiae Scientiarum Imperialis Petropolitana,* 8: 128–40.

Everett, M. G. (1985) 'Role similarity and complexity in social networks', *Social Networks,* 7: 353–9.

Everett, M. G. and S. Borgatti (1988) 'Calculating role similarities: An algorithm that helps determine the orbits of a graph', *Social Networks,* 10: 77–91.

Everett, M. G. and Borgatti, S. (1990) 'A testing example for positional analysis techniques', *Social Networks,* 12: 253–60.

Everett, M. G. and Borgatti, S. P. (1993) 'An extension of regular colouring of graphs to digraphs, networks and hypergraphs', *Social Networks,* 15: 237–54.

Festinger, L. (1949) 'The analysis of sociograms using matrix algebra', *Human Relations,* 2: 153–8.

Festinger, L. (1957) *A Theory of Cognitive Dissonance*. Evanston, IL: Row.

Forsyth, E. and Katz, L. (1946) 'A matrix approach to the analysis of sociometric data: Preliminary report', *Sociometry,* 9: 340–7.

Frank, O. and Strauss, D. (1986) 'Markov graphs', *Journal of the American Statistical Association,* 81: 832–42.

Freeman, L. C. (1978) 'Centrality in social networks: Conceptual clarification', *Social Networks*, 1: 215–39.

Freeman, L. C. (2004) *The Development of Social Network Analysis: A Study in the Sociology of Science*. Vancouver, BC/North Charleston, SC: Empirical Press/BookSurge.

Friedkin, N.E. (1998) *A Structural Theory of Social Influence*. Cambridge and New York: Cambridge University Press.

Gluckman, M. (1940a) 'Analysis of a social situation in modern Zululand', *Bantu Studies*, 14: 1–30.

Gluckman, M. (1955) *The Judicial Process among the Barotse of Northern Rhodesia*. Manchester: Manchester University Press.

Gluckman, M. (1963) *Order and Rebellion in Tribal Africa*. London: Cohen & West.

Gluckman, M. (1968) 'Psychological, sociological and anthropological explanations of witchraft and gossip: a clarification', *Man*, 3: 20–34.

Gould, R. V. and Fernandez, R. M. (1989) 'Structures of mediation: A formal approach to brokerage in transaction networks', *Sociological Methodology*, 19: 89–126.

Goyal, S., Van Der Leij, M. J. and Moraga-Gonzalez, J. L. (2006) 'Economics: An emerging small world', *Journal of Political Economy*, 114: 403–12.

Granovetter, M. (1973) 'The strength of weak ties', *American Journal of Sociology*, 78: 1360–80.

Harary, F. (1955–6) 'On the notion of balance of a signed graph', *Michigan Mathematics Journal*, 2.

Harary, F. and Kabell, J. A. (1980) 'A simple algorithm to detect balance in signed graphs', *Mathematical Social Sciences*, 1: 131–6.

Harary, F. and Norman, R. Z. (1953) *Graph Theory as a Mathematical Model in Social Science*, Ann Arbor, MI: University of Michigan.

Harary, F., Norman, R. Z. and Cartwright, D. (1965) *Structural Models: An Introduction to the Theory of Directed Graphs*. New York: Wiley.

Harries-Jones, P. (1969) '"Home-boy" ties and political organization in a copperbelt township', in J. C. Mitchell (ed.), *Social Networks in Urban Situations*. Manchester: Manchester University Press.

Heider, F. (1946) 'Attitudes and cognitive organization', *Journal of Psychology*, 21: 107–12.

Heider, F. (1958) *The Psychology of Interpersonal Relations*. New York: Wiley.

Heil, G. H. and White, H. C. (1976) 'An algorithm for finding simultaneous homomorphic correspondences between graphs and their image graphs', *Behavioral Science*, 21: 26–35.

Holland, P. and Leinhardt, S. (1970) 'A method for detecting structure in sociometric data', *American Journal of Sociology*, 76: 492–513.

Holland, P. W. and Leinhardt, S. (1971) 'Transitivity in structural models of small groups', *Small Group Research*, 2: 107–24.

Holland, P. W. and Leinhardt, S. (1972) 'Some evidence on the transitivity of positive interpersonal sentiment', *American Journal of Sociology*, 72: 1205–9.

Holland, P. W. and Leinhardt, S. (1981) 'An exponential family of probability distributions for directed graphs', *Journal of the American Statistical Association*, 76(373): 33–50.

Homans, G. C. (1950) *The Human Group*. London: Routledge and Kegan Paul.

Hughes, M., Scott, J. and Mackenzie, J. (1977) 'Trends in interlocking directorships: An international comparison', *Acta Sociologica*, 20: 287–92.

Huisman, M. and Snijders, T. (2003) 'Statistical analysis of longitudinal network data with changing composition', *Sociological Methods and Research*, 32: 253–87.

Hummon, N. P. (2000) 'Utility and dynamic social networks', *Social Networks*, 22: 221–49.

Jackson, M. O. and Watts, A. (2002) 'The evolution of social and economic networks', *Journal of Economic Theory*, 106: 265–95.

Jackson, M. O. and Wolinsky, A. (1996) 'A strategic model of social and economic networks', *Journal of Economic Theory*, 71: 44–74.

Kadushin, C. (1966) 'The friends and supporters of psychotherapy: On social circles and urban life', *American Sociological Review*, 31: 786–802.

Kadushin, C. (2004) 'Too much investment in social capital?', *Social Networks*, 26: 75–90.

Katz, E. and Lazarsfeld, P. F. (2006) *Personal Influence: The Part Played by People in the Flow of Mass Communications*. New Brunswick, NJ: Transaction Publishers.

Katz, E., Lazarsfeld, P. F. and Columbia University Bureau of Applied Social Research (1955) *Personal Influence: The Part Played by People in the Flow of Mass Communications*, Glencoe, IL: Free Press.

Kónig, D. (1936) *Theorie derendlichen and unendlichen Graphen*. Leipzig: Akademische Verlagsgesellschaft.

Lazarsfeld, P. F. and Merton, R. K. (1954a) 'Friendship as social process: A substantive and methodological analysis', in P. L. kendall (ed.), *The Varied Sociology of Paul F. Lazarsfeld*. New York: Columbia University Press.

Lazarsfeld, P. F. and Merton, R. K. (1954b) 'Friendship as social process: A substantive and methodological analysis', in M. Berger, T. Abel and C. Page (eds), *Freedom and Control in Modern Society*. New York: Octagon.

Lazarsfeld, P. F., Merton, R. K., Coleman, J. S. and Rossi, P. H. (1979) *Qualitative and Quantitative Social Research: Papers in Honor of Paul F. Lazarsfeld*. New York: Free Press.

Lazega, E. and Van Duijn, M. (1997) 'Position in formal structure, personal characteristics and choices of advisors in a law firm: A logistic regression model for dyadic network data', *Social Networks*, 19: 375–97.

Leach, E. R. (1984) 'Glimpses of the unmentionable in the history of British social anthropology', *Annual Review of Anthropology*, 13: 1–23.

Leavitt, H. (1951) 'Some effects of certain communication patterns on group performance', *Journal of abnormal and social psychology*, 46: 38–50.

Leinhardt, S. (1977) *Social Networks: A Developing Paradigm*. New York: Academic Press.

Lévi-Strauss, C. (1949/1969) *The Elementary Structures of KInship (Les structures élémentaires de la parenté)*. London: Eyre & Spottiswoode.

Lewin, K. (1951) *Field Theory in Social Science; Selected Theoretical Papers*. New York: Harper.

Lewin, K., Heider, F. and Heider, G. M. (1936) *Principles of Topological Psychology*, New York London: McGraw-Hill.

Lin, N. (2001a) 'Building a network theory of social capital', in N. lin, K. Cook and R. Burt, (eds), *Social Capital: Theory and Research*. New York: Aldine De Gruyter.

Lin, N. (2001b) *Social Capital: A Theory of Social Structure and Action*. Cambridge, UK New York: Cambridge University Press.

Lin, N. (forthcoming) 'A network theory of social capital', in D. Castiglione, J. V. Deth, and G. Wolleb, (eds), *Handbook on Social Capital*. Oxford: Oxford University Press.

Lin, N., Fu, Y. and Hsung, R. (2001) 'The position generator: Measurement technique for investigations in social capital', in N. lin, K. Cook and R. Burt (eds), *Social Capital: Theory and Research*. New York: Aldine de Gruyter.

Lorraine, F. and White, H. C. (1971) 'Structural equivalence of individuals in social networks', *Journal of Mathematical Sociology*, 1: 49–80.

Luce, R. (1950) 'Connectivity and generalized n-cliques in sociometric group structure', *Psychometrika*, 15: 169–90.

Luce, R. and Perry, A. D. (1949) 'A method of matrix analysis of group structure', *Psychometrika*, 14.

Malinowski, B. (1944) *A Scientific Theory of Culture*. Chapel Hill: University of North Carolina Press.

Malinowski, B., Kaberry, P. M. and Yale University Louis Stern Memorial Fund (1945) *The Dynamics of Culture Change: An Inquiry into Race Relations in Africa*, New Haven: Yale University Press.

Mayo, E. (1933) *The Human Problems of an Industrial Civilization*. New York: Macmillan.

McPherson, M., Smith-Lovin, L. and Cook, J. M. (2001) 'Birds of a feather: Homophily in social networks', *Annual Review of Sociology*, 27: 415–44.

Mercken, L., Snijders, T. A. B., Steglich, C. and Vriesa, H. D. (2009) 'Dynamics of adolescent friendship networks and smoking behavior: Social network analyses in six European countries', *Social Science & Medicine*, 69: 1506–14.

Merton, R. K. (1968) *Social Theory and Social Structure*. New York: Free Press.

Milgram, S. (1967) 'The small world problem', *Psychology Today*: 60–7.

Mitchell, J. C. (1969) *Social Networks in Urban Situations*, Manchester, UK: Manchester University Press.

Mitchell, J. C. (1974) 'Social networks', *Annual Review of Anthropology*, 3: 279–99.

Molm, L. (2003) 'Theoretical comparisons of forms of exchange', *Sociological Theory*, 21: 1–17.

Moreno, J. L. (1943) 'Sociometry and the cultural order', *Sociometry*, 6: 299–344.

Moreno, J. L. (1945) 'The two sociometries, human and subhuman', *Sociometry*, 8: 64–75.

Moreno, J. L. (1950) 'Note on cohesion in social groups', *Sociometry*, 13: 176.

Moreno, J. L. (1952) 'A note on sociometry and group dynamics', *Sociometry*, 15: 364–66.

Moreno, J. L. (1953) *Who Shall Survive? Foundations of Sociometry, Group Psychotherapy and Sociodrama*. Beacon, NY: Beacon House.

Moreno, J. L. (1954) 'Old and new trends in sociometry: Turning points in small group research', *Sociometry*, 17: 179–93.

Moreno, J. L. (1960) *The Sociometry Reader*. Glencoe, IL: Free Press.

Moreno, J. L. (1978) *Who Shall Survive?: Foundations of Sociometry, Group Psychotherapy, and Sociodrama*. Beacon, NY: Beacon House.

Moreno, J. L. and Jennings, H. H. (1934) *Who Shall Survive? A New Approach to the Problem of Human Interrelations*. Washington, DC: Nervous and Mental Disease Publishing Co.

Nadel, S. F. (1957) *The Theory of Social Structure*. Glencoe, IL: Free Press.

Newman, M. E. J., Barabási, A.-L. and Watts, D. J. (2006) *The Structure and Dynamics of Networks*. Princeton: Princeton University Press.

Pareto, V., Livingston, A., Bongiorno, A. and Rogers, J.H. (1935) *The Mind and Society, Trattato di sociologia generale*. New York: Harcourt.

Parsons, T. (1937) *The Structure of Social Action; A Study in Social Theory with Special Reference to a Group of Recent European Writers*. New York: McGraw-Hill.

Parsons, T. (1951) *The Social System*. Glencoe, IL: Free Press.

Pattison, P.E. and Robins, G.L (2002) 'Neighbourhood based models for social networks', in R.M. Stolzenberg (ed.) *Sociological Methodology*. Stolzenberg. Boston, MA: Blackwell Publishing. pp. 301–37.

Pattison, P.E. and Wasserman, S. (1999) 'Logit models and logistic regressions for social networks, II. Multivariate relations', *British Journal of Mathematical and Statistical Psychology*, 52: 169–94.

Pool, I. and Kochen, M. (1978) 'Contacts and influence', *Social Networks*, 1: 5–51.

Portes, A. (1998) 'Social capital: Its origins and applications in modern sociology', *Annual Review of Sociology*, 22: 1–24.

Prell, C., Hubacek, K., Reed, M. and Racin, L. (forthcoming) 'Competing views, competing structures: The role of formal and informal structures in shaping stakeholder perceptions', *Ecology and Society*.

Pujol, J. M., Flache, A., Delgado, J. and Sangueesa, R. (2005) 'How can social networks ever become complex? Modelling the emergence of complex networks from local social exchange', *Journal of Artificial Societies and Social Simulation*, 8. Available at: http://jasss.soc.surrey.ac.uk/8/4/12.html.

Putnam, R. D. (1993) *Making Democracy Work: Civic Traditions in Modern Italy*. Princeton, NJ: Princeton University Press.

Putnam, R. D. (2001) *Bowling Alone: The Collapse and Revival of American Community*. London: Simon & Schuster.

Radcliffe-Brown, A. R. (1940a) 'On social structure', *Journal of the Royal Anthropological Institute*, 70: 1–12.

Radcliffe-Brown, A. R. (1940b) 'On social structure', *Journal of the Royal Anthropological Society of Great Britain and Ireland*, 70: 1–12.

Radcliffe-Brown, A. R. (1952) *Structure and Function in Primitive Society, Essays and Addresses*. London: Cohen & West.

Radcliffe-Brown, A. R. (1957) *A Natural Science of Society*, Glencoe, IL: Free Press.

Radcliffe-Brown, A. R. (1958) *Method in Social Anthropology; Selected Essays*. Chicago: University of Chicago Press.

Radcliffe-Brown, A. R. and Forde, C. D. (1950) *African Systems of Kinship and Marriage*, London and New York: Oxford University Press.

Ritzer, G. and Goodman, D. J. (2004) *Sociological Theory*. Boston: McGraw-Hill.

Robins, G., Elliott, P. and Pattison, P. (2001) 'Network models for social selection processes', *Social Networks*, 23: 1–30.

Robins, G., Pattison, P. and Woolcock, J. (2005) 'Small and other worlds: Global network structures from local processes', *American Journal of Sociology*, 110: 894–936.

Robins, G., Snijders, T., Wang, P., Handcock, M. and Pattison, P. (2007) 'Recent developments in exponential random graph models for social networks', *Social Networks* 29: 192–215.

Roethlisberger, F. J., Dickson, W. J., Wright, H. A., Pforzheimer, C. H. and Western Electric Company (1939) *Management and the Worker: An Account of a Research*

Program Conducted by the Western Electric Company, Hawthorne Works, Chicago. Cambridge, MA: Harvard University Press.

Sailer, L. D. (1978) 'Structural equivalence: Meaning and definition, computation and application', *Social Networks*, 1: 73–90.

Schnettler, S. (2009a) 'A small world on feet of clay? A comparison of empirical small-world studies against best-practice criteria', *Social Networks*, 31: 179–89.

Schnettler, S. (2009b) 'A structured overview of 50 years of small-world research', *Social Networks*, 31: 165–78.

Scott, J. (1977) 'Structure and configuration in interlocking directorships', *Connections*, 1: 27–9.

Scott, J. (1979) *Corporations, Classes, and Capitalism.* London: Hutchinson.

Scott, J. (1988) 'social network analysis: Trend report', *Sociology*, 22: 109–27.

Scott, J. (2000) *Social Network Analysis: A handbook.* Newbury Park: SAGE Publications.

Simmel, G. (1922/1955) *Conflict and the Web of Group Affiliations.* Translated by Wolff, Kurt H., Bendix, Reinhard. New York: Free Press.

Simmel, G. (1978/1907) *The Philosophy of Money* trans. Tom Bottomore and David Frisby. London: Routledge.

Snijders, T. A. B. (2005) 'Models for longitudinal network data', in P. Carrington, J. Scott and S. Wasserman (eds), *Models and Methods in Social Network Analysis.* New York: Cambridge University Press.

Snijders, T. (2008) 'Longitudinal methods of network analysis', in B. Meyers and J. Scott (eds), *Encyclopedia of Complexity and System Science.* London: Springer Verlag.

Tomochi, M. (2004) 'Defectors' niches: Prisoner's dilemma game on disordered networks', *Social Networks*, 26: 309–21.

Valente, T. W. (1995) *Network Models of the Diffusion of Innovations.* Cresskill, NJ: Hampton Press.

Van Duijn, M. A. J., Snijders, T. A. B. and Zijlstra, B. J. H. (2004) 'p2: A random effects model with covariates for directed graphs', *Statistica Neerlandica*, 58: 234–54.

Warner, W. L. and Lunt, P. S. (1941) *The Social Life of a Modern Community.* New Haven: Yale University Press.

Wasserman, S. and Faust, F. (1994) *Social Network Analysis: Methods and Applications.* Cambridge: Cambridge University Press.

Wasserman, S. and Pattison, P. (1996) 'Logit models and logistic regressions for social networks: I. An introduction to Markov random graphs and p*', *Psychometrika* 61(3): 401–26.

Watts, D. J. (1999) 'Networks, dynamics and the small world phenomenon', *American Journal of Sociology*, 105: 493–527.

Watts, D. J. (2003) *Six Degrees: The Science of a Connected Age.* New York: Norton.

Watts, D. J. and Strogatz, S. H. (1998) 'Collective dynamics of small world networks', *Nature*, 393: 440–2.

Wellman, B. (1988) 'Structural analysis: From method and metaphor to theory and substance', in B. Wellman and S. D. Berkowitz (eds), *Social Structures: A Network Approach.* Cambridge and New York: Cambridge University Press.

Wellman, B. and Berkowitz, S. (1988) *Social Structures: A Network Approach.* Cambridge: Cambridge University Press.

Wellman, B. and Frank, K. (2001) 'Network capital in a multi-level world: Getting support in personal communities', in N. Lin, K. Cook and R. Burt (eds), *Social Capital: Theory and Research.* New York: Aldine de Gruyter.

Werbner, R. P. (1984) 'The Manchester school in South-central Africa', *Annual Review of Anthropology*, 13: 157–85.

Wertheimer, M. (1938) 'Gestalt theory', in W. D. Ellis (ed.), *A Source Book of Gestalt Psychology*. New York: Harcourt, Brace and Co.

White, D. R. and Reitz, K. P. (1983) 'Graph and semigroup homomorphisms on networks of relations', *Social Networks, 5*.

White, H. C. (1970) *Chains of Opportunity: System Models of Mobility in Organizations*, Cambridge, MA: Harvard University Press.

White, H. C., Boorman, S. A. and Breiger, R. L. (1976) 'Social structure from multiple networks. I. Blockmodels of Roles and Positions', *The American Journal of Sociology*, 81: 730–80.

Wong, L. H., Pattison, P. and Robins, G. (2006) 'A spatial model for social networks', *Physica A: Statistical Mechanics and its Applications*, 360: 99–120.

3

HOW TO STUDY SOCIAL
NETWORKS, FROM THEORY
TO DESIGN

Much of this book focuses on how to analyse social network data. However, many newcomers to the approach have questions about how to conduct a study of this sort, for example, how to make an SNA research design, how to gather data, and how to tackle some of the ethical, validity and reliability issues of SNA?

In this chapter, I shall walk you through the steps needed to design an SNA study of your own. As you will see, many of the same concerns and issues of doing social science research apply to an SNA study: you need to think about the wider literature surrounding your problem of interest, develop research questions, and think about the ethical issues of dealing with human subjects. However, within the context of SNA, many of these concerns are handled slightly differently. By the end of this chapter, you will understand the following:

- How to start designing an SNA study

- Theoretical frameworks, and inductive versus deductive approaches to SNA

- What kinds of research questions can be answered through an SNA study

- The different techniques used for gathering SNA data

- Issues of validity, reliability and ethics

- Structuring and inputting data for analysis

- Initial analysis of networks via visual graphs

OVERVIEW OF THE PROCESS

A quick overview of the process is found below. Keep in mind that, as with most social science research, these steps need not necessarily take place in the order I suggest here. For example, those researchers more familiar with qualitative, flexible approaches to conducting research (e.g. Robson, 2002) might find the below order a bit too proscriptive and constraining. In addition, especially when one is designing a research study, one might enter into the design process at any stage. Thus, for example, you might already have a particular theoretical framework you have done in previous research, and now you simply wish to test some of those ideas through social network data. Thus, although the steps I suggest below certainly can be followed in the order I prescribe, they need not, and it might therefore be helpful to simply think of the below steps as ones you ought to take in designing your study, but not necessarily in the order shown below.

The steps I prescribe in this chapter include the following:

1 Read up on the literature

2 Develop a theoretical framework

3 Develop research questions or hypotheses

4 Determine your population of interest, sample and network boundary

5 Gather your data

6 Some considerations in gathering data

7 Inputting and structuring your data into matrices

8 Initial visualization of the network

9 Further analysis and interpretation of results

STEP ONE: READ UP ON THE LITERATURE

Even before you start to formulate your research questions, I suggest you spend time familiarizing yourself with social network studies already conducted on a topic similar to your own (I am continually surprised as both a teacher and a reviewer how often people ignore this first important step!). You would do well to go to journals within your specific field and do key word searches for 'social networks' or 'social network analysis'. Most likely you will come across a few examples of studies that have applied the social network analytic approach.

In addition, however, there are a few journals that specialize in social network analysis, and you would do well to visit these journals. The International Network of Social Network Analysis (INSNA) keeps an up-to-date website (http://www.insna.org/) with information on journals that specialize in the topic of network analysis as well as find links to topic areas and people that use the SNA approach. The list of journals includes *Social Networks*, *Connections* and the *Journal of Social Structure*.

I encourage you to spend some time reading up on social network analysis as it applies to your subject area before attempting to design a study of your own. You might find that some of the research questions you are interested in exploring have been explored by other researchers, in which case you would need to either change your research question or improve upon the research design and/or findings found in the published article. More importantly, however, you will see examples of how previous researchers have formulated research questions, gathered data and analysed those data.

STEP TWO: DEVELOPING A THEORETICAL FRAMEWORK

The British social anthropologists in the 1950s and 1960s, and sociologist Harrison White from Harvard (see Chapter 2 on SNA's history for more details on these) shared in common an interest in building 'empirical models', meaning, they were interested in inducing theoretical concepts and frameworks based on the empirical social network data they had gathered. Such inductive research, obviously, was not theory-driven, but rather, attempted to derive theoretical concepts from the data at hand. For example, Max Gluckman's notion of 'cross-cutting ties' (Gluckman, 1940, 1963) and Bott's arguments of the role of 'connectedness' in relation to conjugal roles (Bott, 1955) are good anthropological examples of inductive research, where close explorations of social network data led to some interesting theoretical insights and conclusions. In addition, as discussed and illustrated by Mitchell (Mitchell, 1969), social network concepts guided the data explorations, which in turn shaped the kinds of theoretical concepts and models that surfaced. More commonly, however, social network studies adopt a deductive, theory-driven approach to their work. The list of examples is endless, but the study by Burt (2004) on structural holes and good ideas serves as a good illustration. Ron Burt's hypothesis regarding where good ideas come from, and how such good ideas help one perform better within a given organizational context relates to the sort of network structure surrounding an individual. In particular, Burt theorizes that an individual with an open network structure is more likely to be in touch with diverse forms of knowledge, and hence, be in a strategically advantageous position for developing innovative, 'good' ideas. His findings show how managers within a particular firm were rewarded for occupying a 'broker' role in the sense that positive performance evaluations and promotions were disproportionately given to managers who brokered connections across structural holes. Furthermore, such managers tended to get higher scores for measures on creativity and good ideas.

The above example illustrates how the analyst, when conducting a deductive study involving social network analysis, has a clear idea of the theory he or she would like to 'test' through gathering and analysing social network (and other) data. Common theories that are 'tested' in a deductive approach to social network analysis include the following: social capital, network exchange, biased net theory, social influence, and social selection. These are covered elsewhere in the book, but a brief summary of these theories are found below:

- *Social capital*   Social capital refers to the value found within social networks as well as the value one gains access to through social networks. As such, social capital tends to have both an intrinsic and instrumental notion of the value of social networks. Research on social capital from a social networks perspective tends to focus on how certain structural features of the social network, for example weak, bridging ties or strong ties and dense structures, correspond to a variety of different outcome variables, for example, one's ability to 'get by' as compared to 'getting ahead'. Well-known social network analysts who research social capital include Ron Burt (1997, 2001, 2005); Nan Lin (2001a, 2001b; Lin et al., 2001); and Barry Wellman (Wellman and Frank, 2001).

- *Network exchange or social exchange theory*   This theory is generally considered a social psychology theory, although numerous examples of exchange theory studies can be found in the sociology, business and management literatures. In general, this theory looks at negotiated bargaining scenarios between actors, where the terms for bargaining are known well in advance. Such bargaining scenarios involve individual decisions to give (or not to give) valued items with others, usually with the understanding that such offerings will be reciprocated. George Homans (Homans, 1958), whom you read about in Chapter 2, is generally credited with founding this theory, although his work is seen as only speaking to dyadic interactions, i.e. interactions between two people. Extensions to social exchange theory have been made by Peter Blau (1964), Emerson (1972a, 1972b), and Cook and colleagues (1983). For example, Cook and colleagues (1983) ran experiments to identify how network structure influences whom in the network emerges as powerful. Their experiments showed that certain centrality measures reflected notions of power only under certain network structural conditions.

- More recently, Molm (2003; Molm et al., 2000) has looked at the role of trust and altruism in the context of exchange relations, noting that negotiated kinds of exchange are possible without considerations for reciprocity or trust, but in many real-life scenarios, the terms of agreement and 'rules of engagement' are not generally known, and thus in such scenarios the role of trust looms large.

- *Biased net theory*   This theory considers the extent to which observed social networks deviate from random ones. Rapoport (1957) is considered the founder of this theory, whereby ties are seen as deriving from a mixture of both random and non-random influences. The non-random influences are discussed in terms of 'biases', i.e. that observed networks tend to have a bias towards reciprocity and transitivity. Although problems in parameter estimation remain for those wishing to make use of this approach (Skvoretz, 1990; Skvoretz et al., 2004), the theoretical ideas continue to inspire a number of disciplines, most recently the academic community interested in the topic of small worlds and scale-free networks (Newman et al., 2006).

- *Social influence and social selection network theory*   Social influence network theory considers how actors influence one another's thoughts and behaviours. The theory, rooted in social psychology, developed into a network theory through the work of Friedkin (1998). Here, actors are seen as involved in a process, whereby, in the first stage of the process, actors start out with their own opinions or behaviours, and in each successive stage, they are seen as altering their opinion or behaviour to the group 'norm', which in essence is a (weighted) average of the other opinions of actors found in the network. Social influence is typically measured through an autocorrelation procedure (Leenders, 2002), and is generally seen in close relation to social selection network theory (Erickson, 1988; Leenders, 1997).

- Social selection network theory looks at how pairs of actors are attracted to one another based on certain characteristics (or behaviours) they possess. In general, similarity is seen as the main basis upon which selection processes occur (Byrne, 1997), and more recently, research has extended social selection research to look at structures beyond the dyadic level, e.g. triads (Robins et al., 2001), and Snijders and colleagues (Huisman and Snijders, 2003; Snijders, 2005; Snijders et al., forthcoming) have developed statistical, actor-based models that aim to explore this tension between social selection and social influence processes. (Please note that social influence and social selection are closely related to the concept of homophily, and homophily will be introduced to the reader at different points throughout this book.)

- *Social networks and diffusion of innovations*   Diffusion of innovations looks at the process by which a new technology or idea gets adopted by a given community (Rogers, 1995). In social network analysis, diffusion scholars look at how an innovation gets communicated through the network, and how individual actors are influenced by the network to adopt or reject a given innovation. The earliest example of a social network diffusion study was conducted by Coleman et al. (1966), where the authors showed how doctors' willingness to prescribe a new antibiotic coincided with the kind of social network surrounding each doctor. The work of Tom Valente and colleagues (Valente, 1995; Valente and Davis, 1999), in particular, has focused attention on the ways network analysis can be used for identifying the most central individuals in a diffusion network.

STEP THREE: DEVELOPING A RESEARCH QUESTION OR HYPOTHESIS

With regards to deductive research inquiries, where you are guided by certain theories or theoretical frameworks, your research questions or hypotheses flow from the theories of interest. Nonetheless, when constructing research questions pertaining to the study of social networks, I often tell students that it is helpful to think about how a social network (as one variable) relates to, affects, or is affected by another variable or set of variables. The list for possibilities of course is endless, but here are just a few examples to help you get started:

- How does an individual's personal network affect that person's ability to access certain kinds of resources?

- How do individuals gain access to social support through their personal networks?

- How does the structure of a given social network affect the formation (or maintenance) of collective norms?

- To what extent are particular behaviours, such as smoking or academic performance, influenced by one's friendship ties to others?

The above questions pose social networks and/or their structure as affecting variables, yet you could also reverse this order, i.e. ask what kinds of variables affect the development, maintenance, structuring or dissolution of social networks or features of that network. Examples of these kinds of questions include the following:

- How does membership in an organization affect the likelihood of social ties forming amongst individuals?

- What role does geographical proximity play in the formation?

- Are actors who are similar to one another on some characteristic more likely to form a tie?

- Are two people more likely to form ties with one another, based on them sharing a common friend?

All of the above questions are examples of sorts of general research questions you might be interested in exploring through social network analysis. If you were interested in testing hypotheses, however, then you would need to make predictive statements about how you envision social networks affecting a particular outcome variable, or alternatively, how some particular variable (say gender) affects the way ties form and/or are structured.

In addition to the above examples of how social networks affect (or are affected by) some other kind of variable, you might also be interested in studying how two different types of social networks, e.g. friendship and advice, relate to one another, or affect one another in some way. The below questions are again examples of the kinds of questions you might want to ask at this level:

- Do friends (relation 1) tend to offer advice (relation 2) on personal matters?

- Do colleagues (relation 1) tend to trust (relation 2) one another?

Thus, I have just offered you some possible ways you can start to think about the role of social networks in relation to other variables (or to other social networks), and how to structure such relationships as research questions.

STEP FOUR: WHO IS YOUR POPULATION? WHAT IS YOUR NETWORK BOUNDARY?

Thus far in your research design, you have done some background reading, and you have developed some research questions or hypotheses that might explore or test some theoretical perspective. Now your next step pertains to whom you plan to study. In deciding whom you plan to study, the issues of sampling, population and network boundary are important. As you noticed in Chapter 1, you have the choice in network analysis for studying ego networks or complete networks. With ego networks, the issue of population and sampling are the same as in standard survey methods: you randomly sample a given number of egos from a given population. In traditional survey research, this is the same as, say, randomly sampling a given number of respondents or individuals from a given population. Once you have your sample of egos (e.g. individual respondents), you gather ego network data for each of your respondents. Thus, the network data is not complete network data, and one can not use analyses designed for complete network data, such as centralization and density. Instead, the network data gathered are the immediate, personal networks surrounding each respondent, i.e. ego, and thus the analyses you can perform are limited to those of ego network measures. In this book, I shall go over analyses you can use for both ego networks and complete ones, although most of the attention will be given to complete networks.

With complete networks, the issue of population and sampling becomes more complicated, as they are intrinsically linked with the notion of a network boundary. A network boundary, you may recall, refers to the boundary around a set of actors that the researcher deems to be the complete set of actors for the network study. Identifying the boundary of the network therefore is equivalent to identifying the study's population. Sometimes identifying a network boundary is fairly straightforward: an analyst is interested in studying how employees within a given workplace relate to one another. Here, the boundary is specified by who is considered an employee at this particular organization or business. Yet often defining the network boundary is more complicated: if I were to use a classroom as my boundary and ask students to tell me who their friends are, I am surely ignoring other important friends they might have within the school, or even outside of the school.

There are no perfect solutions to this issue of network boundary, but there are a variety of options in trying to approximate what the boundary might be.

Option 1: The realist (or reputational) approach

The realist approach, as described by Laumann et al. (1989) and Wasserman and Faust (1994) advocates allowing actors to define the boundary; here, membership is identified by the actors themselves in much the same way that one can identify members of a club. All members of a club can identify and name other members; although no one particular member may be able to identify all others, through asking enough members of your target population, you ought to be able to identify pretty accurately the network boundary.

The key aspect of the realist approach is identifying, early on, who are the key informants for your target population. You need to be confident that the informants you speak with are ones who have a good understanding of the network in question and can offer an accurate picture of the members of this network. Thus, locating who is a 'key informant' might be a tricky process in itself.

Option 2: The nominalist approach

Rather than rely on the actors, the nominalist approach relies on theoretical (or other) justifications of the researcher for defining the network boundary. A researcher might decide, for example, to include in the network only those actors who participate in organizing a particular social event. The justification might be that this social event is the main focus of your study, and you want to see how the social ties occurring through this event influence the way the event unfolds.

However, in defining your boundary in this way, you would be potentially ignoring important ties that influence the behaviours of each participant in your study. There might be, for example, another event that you ought to be observing. Thus, you need to be able to fully justify your reasons for drawing a boundary around a network based on this approach (Laumann et al., 1989; Wasserman and Faust, 1994).

Option 3: Snowball sampling

You have probably come across snowball sampling before. This method of sampling involves asking an initial group of respondents to nominate others. These others are then approached by the researcher, and in turn, are asked to nominate, again, others for the study. This procedure continues until names start to repeat, and the researcher feels he or she has saturated the possible list of nominations (Bryman, 2008).

The problem with this approach is that the sample is biased by whom the researcher initially approaches (Scott, 2000). Had the researcher initially approached another set of respondents, the sample could have looked different. In addition, not all researchers have the time to continue 'rolling a snowball' until a complete, well-defined network boundary has formed. For this reason, Knoke and Kuklinski (1982) recommend a researcher think of a snowball sample in terms of 'zones', where the first zone is formed from the initial set of respondents' nominations, the second zone formed out of the first set of nominees' nominations, and so on. Given that any number of zones is possible with a snowball sample, the authors recommend going as far as the second zone for most social network studies (although the number of zones is something that should ultimately be decided based on the research questions and theoretical interests of the researcher).

There are no perfect solutions for determining a network boundary. Indeed, this is an issue that network analysts have yet to fully resolve (Granovetter, 1976; Knox et al., 2006) and statisticians are currently exploring ways of modelling social networks when the sampling frame or population is not fully known (David and Snijders, 2002). This is not to discourage you from attempting to try and be a rigorous as possible in identifying your network boundary. The above strategies will hopefully help you get started. Finally, becoming sensitive to this complicated issue, and making good judgements based on an understanding of the possible alternatives, is generally considered the best means forward for conducting good practice.

STEP FIVE: GATHERING THE DATA

Now that you know your network boundary, it is time to gather data on your variables of interest, where at least one of your data include information on how the social actors in your network relate to one another. Your research questions are critical here: are you primarily interested in how friendship ties affect certain behaviour, for example? Or are you interested in seeing how people acquire various types of resources through different kinds of relational ties to others? The clearer the picture you can have of what data you are interested in gathering, the stronger the likelihood that you can develop the measurement instrument or methodological approach that will enable you to gather good network data.

Qualitative and quantitative data gathering

I would like to say a few comments about the suitability of gathering (or not gathering) qualitative data alongside your quantitative social network data. If you have a clear theoretical perspective guiding your research study, then you can probably proceed to gather social network data more or less immediately. However, a number of good network studies, i.e. ones primarily using quantitative data and making use of the concepts and analyses presented in this book, either take place after an initial phase of qualitative research, or are done in tandem with the gathering of qualitative data. For example, Uzzi (1996), who is well-known for his study on embedded ties, spends the first half of his article describing ethnographic field work he conducted to illustrate the ways respondents thought about and characterized the social ties in which they participated. From this rich account, he then moves onto devising a series of precise, quantitative measures of network ties. The qualitative research therefore informed and helped shape the quantitative work that followed. In my own research, I often make use of data gathered through qualitative interviews and focus groups to inform questionnaire design for gathering my social network and other data (Prell et al., 2008, 2009). Thus, even though I spend most of my time here describing how to develop measures for gathering quantitative data on social networks, you should be aware that qualitative work can be a useful compliment and helpful precedent to designing a quantitative SNA study. Qualitative research is also used in the social network field for understanding network evolution (Bidart and Lavenu, 2005), for uncovering more subtle processes of friendship dynamics (e.g. Bellotti, 2008); and as a means for triangulation or measurement error (Lubbers et al., in press; Lievrouw et al., 1987). Finally, in the annual INSNA Sunbelt conference, workshops are now offered, looking at the combination of qualitative and quantitative social network data.

Option 1: The questionnaire and/or structured interview

You are probably already well familiar with questionnaires. A questionnaire consists of either closed-ended or open-ended questions aimed at gathering data on your research question(s) of interest. In general, closed-ended questions such as Likert-scale items are preferred to open-ended ones, as such closed-ended questions lend themselves more readily to quantitative analysis. I will not review the advantages and disadvantages of administering a questionnaire, nor delve deeply into how to construct one, as these are topics for other textbooks (see for example Brace, 2008; Bradburn et al., 2004; Oppenheim and Oppenheim, 1992). Here, I shall help you think through some of the major issues in constructing a useful questionnaire for the purpose of gathering SNA data. Please keep in mind as I discuss questionnaires that many of these same sorts of suggestions can be easily applied to structured interviews. The main difference is how the questions are administered: do you hand respondents a questionnaire for them to fill in or do you have a face to face interview with a respondent and read from a structured script?

There are a number of options to think about in constructing such a questionnaire or interview script. Will you use a list of names (roster) or will you have respondents rely on their own memory (free recall)? Will you decide ahead of time how many nominations a respondent should list (fixed), or will you allow a respondent to nominate as many as he/she wishes (free)? Are you merely interested in the presence or absence of a tie (binary data), or are you interested in getting a measure of intensity for the tie (valued data)? Taken together, the issues to make decisions about questionnaire design include the use of roster, free or fixed recall questions, binary or valued data.

Roster

A roster refers to a list of all the actors in your network. Thus, with a roster, it is assumed that you already have a clear network boundary. Here, you present this roster to your respondents and ask questions about each person on the roster. For example, in one study (Prell et al., 2008), we approached a group of stakeholders with a roster (a total of 60 names). Respondents were then asked three different social network questions regarding each person on the roster. All questions were measured through use of Likert scales. Thus, we gathered valued social network data on a set of actors.

The questions we used included the following:

- How often do you communicate with this person?
- Do you feel you understand this person's views regarding (topic listed here)?
- Do you feel you agree with this person's views on (topic listed here)?

Participants thus answered each of the above questions for all 59 names (i.e. excluding the name of the actual participant).

Free and fixed recall

With the free-recall technique, you may or may not know all the actors in the network of your study, i.e. you may or may not know your network boundary. You might also use this approach if you are studying ego networks, where boundary is not an issue. Here, rather than present your respondent with a roster, you ask the respondent to 'recall' names based on the respondent's memory. You help the respondent recall who is part of their network by asking appropriate questions about their relationships (also see the discussion below pertaining to name generator questions).

For example, Wellman's (Wellman and Wortley, 1990) study on community ties and social support asked respondents free-recall questions to uncover which sorts of ties respondents would use to receive various kinds of support. For example, they asked respondents to nominate intimate others with whom they are connected, where intimate members were those whom respondents 'feel are closest to you outside your home'. In addition, they asked about 'significant network members' who were non-intimates who were 'in touch with' the respondent's 'daily life' and who were 'significant' in the respondent's life. These two types of ties, i.e. intimate and significant ties, jointly made up the respondent's set of active network members. This study was not a complete network study, but rather one focused on ego networks.

If you decide to use the free-recall approach, as opposed to a roster, you also need to decide whether you will allow respondents to list as many names as they can recall (a free-choice approach) or if you want to place an upper limit to the number of nominations your respondent can make (fixed-choice approach). If you say to your respondents that you want only three nominations in answer to your question, you are using the fixed-choice option. This option was used by Coleman et al. (Coleman et al., 1966) in their study on the diffusion of a new medicine innovation amongst physicians working within the same community. Here, the researchers asked physicians which other physicians in the community they consulted for advice, with whom they socialized, and with whom they discussed particular cases. For each question, doctors were limited to nominating three names. The authors' decisions to use this fixed-choice approach has since been criticized for offering a limited view of these physicians' personal networks (Valente, 1995), and in general, the fixed-choice method is considered rather restrictive and likely to lead towards measurement error (Wasserman and Faust, 1994). The major argument against fixed choice is that you increase the likelihood of getting incomplete or inaccurate data, as not all respondents will have networks composed of this fixed number. Some might have more and others less.

However, there might be practical reasons for making this choice. For example, if you are restricted on time and resources, or if your questionnaire is considerably long, you might be forced to constrain your respondents to a certain upper limit of nominations. Thus, be aware of the sorts of trade-offs in devising your questions.

Crafting your questions

How many social network questions do you need in order to adequately capture the important relational properties of a network? It is not an exact science, but in general, the more social network questions, the better. In doing so, you not only uncover additional actors in the network who might not be captured by just one question, but also, you uncover additional aspects of relationships between actors by gathering more network data.

For example, perhaps a teenage boy tends to socialize with the same group of people on weekends, but when it comes to advice on personal matters, he may only turn to family members. Further, although he might socialize with the same group, he might only consider a small portion of these friends 'close' friends. Finally, perhaps some of these close friends are ones that, in addition to family members, are people he turns to for advice. Thus, asking about these different kinds of networks uncovers additional actors in this boy's network, as well as which actors the boy shares a multiplex and/or stronger tie. How these questions are phrased depends on other research design criteria, such as your understanding of the research site, whether you are using a roster, and whether you are gathering ego network, as opposed to complete network data.

One way to start thinking about the phrasing of your questions is to consider *what exactly you are trying to measure*. Consider the following example: Many network scholars are interested in advice relations, i.e. who turns to whom for advice. Yet consider the below set of questions, and ask yourself how the resulting data would differ for each question?

- Whom do you turn to for advice?

- Whom do you turn to for advice when you are experiencing difficulties at work?

- Whom do you turn to for advice when you experience difficulties at work with computers?

- Whom do you turn to for advice when you experience difficulties at work with your boss?

You might notice that the first two questions are rather vague; the first question is virtually useless, given the plethora of topics one could ask advice about. The second one is not much better, as in most cases, we turn to different colleagues for advice given the nature of our problem or request. Being clear on what kinds of data you are hoping to gather, and developing questions that are specific and detailed enough to gather that kind of information, is very important for social network studies.

Each of the above questions pertaining to advice is called a *name generator* question. A name generator question is one that will, literally, generate a list of names for the researcher. Name generator questions are typically used when you do not have a roster of names for a respondent to refer to. In the case where you do have a roster, the above questions would be answered by the respondent making selections from the list of names found on the roster.

As I mentioned earlier, you may wish to ask a number of different name generator questions to uncover multiple relations existing amongst a group of actors. In addition to name generator questions, however, you might wish to simply gain additional information on the people a respondent nominated. Thus, to the last advice question listed above, i.e. 'Whom do you turn to for advice when you experience difficulties at work with your boss?', your respondent may give you two names: David and Janine. Now that you have these two names, you might wish to ask some additional questions just about these nominees. Such additional questions are referred to as *name interpreter* questions, and examples of such questions include the following:

- What is this person's gender?

- What is their age?

- How long have you known this person?

Name generator and name interpreter questions are the common means for gathering network data in instances where you are conducting an interview or administering a questionnaire. In addition, as I mentioned earlier, when a roster is being used, respondents can be asked to refer to the roster in 'generating' their names for a particular question. If you are using a roster, the nature of the questions is largely the same, it has more to do with how the question gets phrased. Thus, for example, with 'advice', the question becomes, 'which of the people on this list do you turn to for advice for _____?' Thus, the names that are *generated* are found *within* the roster itself, versus generated from a respondent's recall.

One disadvantage of gathering network data through name generator questions of this sort, especially when the data you are gathering is complete network data using a roster, is that each network question gets repeated for each actor listed on the roster. For example, if you have a network composed of 50 actors, and thus 50 names on your roster, then you wish to gather network data on all 50 of those actors. To do this, the same social network question gets repeated for each actor found on the roster (excluding, of course, the one actor in the network who is being interviewed). You thus need to be careful in constructing your questions, realising that, in the interest of potentially exhausting your respondents, you are limited in how many network questions you can ask.

Option 2: Observation

As the previous section indicates, devising accurate questions to gather network data can be tricky. You might therefore prefer to gather your data through observing your actors. Here, you do not rely on respondents' memory to uncover the social network, but rather your own observations of who interacts with whom.

To gather data through observation, you need to ensure a consistent and clear means by which you will code the various interactions amongst your actors. This is easier said than done. For example, you need to be clear what constitutes an 'interaction'. Is it when two actors talk to each other, when they look at each other, or when they are simply in the same room together? Once you have devised a means by which to define and thus observe interactions, you go to the setting in which your actors are located and observe their behaviour for a specified, extended period of time, and you count the number of times you observe interaction between the actors according to your definition. Also, keep in mind that gathering data through observation is very difficult; several interactions could happen simultaneously, and your ability as an observer to notice all of these in a reliable fashion will be a real challenge.

You may recall from Chapter 2 that one of the earliest social network studies gathered data in this way. Between 1931–1932, Elton and Warner conducted an anthropological study on interpersonal interactions among 14 workers at the Hawthorne electrical factory in Chicago. Here, they carefully observed all group behaviour in a bank wiring room of the factory, and the research team used graphs to visually display the group and their relations. UCINET has these datasets, and you can examine these datasets at your leisure.

Option 3: Diaries or archives

A wide range of archival material can be used for gathering network data: for example, diaries, newspapers, journal articles, minutes of meetings, historical texts and so forth. A famous network study that gathered data through historical archives is that of Padgett and Ansell (Padgett and Ansell, 1993). Here, the authors coded a number of historical texts pertaining to the Florentine families in medieval Italian society, and this coding scheme resulted in network data on a variety of types of relations; i) kinship, ii) joint ownerships or partnerships of businesses, iii) bank employment, iv) real estate ties, v) patronage, vi) personal loans, vii) personal friends and viii) surety ties. These relational data were compared to economic data to assess the power dynamics of the Florentine oligarchy and to explain the Medici family's rise to power.

Another popular use of archival data is found in studies that focus on citations and scientific articles (Collins, 1974; Lenoir, 1979; Small and Griffith, 1974). This are the 'who cites whom' studies, and it is a common method found in the sociology of science as a means for uncovering the way social actors interact in the creation or formation of knowledge. Block models, cluster analysis and the use of visual graphs are all used in these sorts of studies.

One benefit of using archival data is that a network boundary can be more easily traced with such data (Knox et al., 2006); the researcher does not need to rely on the memory of respondents nor on the reliability of the observer.

Option 4: Electronic sources and the Internet

An increasingly popular means of gathering social network data is through the Internet and other electronic communication technologies. One of the earliest examples is Linton Freeman's study of email exchanges among social network scholars, and how such exchanges changed over time (see a description of this study in Wasserman and Faust, 1994). Another example is the data found from such collaborative websites as Wikipedia, an online encyclopedia written, managed and run by volunteers. Contributors' entries are saved as logs, thus allowing dataminers to harvest which users contribute and comment upon which topics, thus producing a type of bipartite network (e.g. Brandes and Lerner, 2008; Tyler et al., 2003).

With the growing rise in popularity of social networking sites such as Facebook, Bebo and MySpace, social network scholars are discovering ways to harness data from these sites. For example, Lewis et al., (2008) received permission from Facebook, and a university in which a high portion of students were found to be Facebook users, to access and download over 11,000 profiles and network data on a cohort of college freshman students. Steps were taken to ensure student privacy. Bonuses of data collection of this sort included the avoidance of interviewer effects(Marsden, 2003), as well as imperfections in name recall (Brewer, 2000; Brewer and Webster, 2000), and other potential sources of measurement error that may accompany survey research (Bernard and Killworth, 1977; Marsden, 1990).

Not all data come from the Internet. For example, Eagle and colleagues (2009) gathered data from mobile phones back in 2004, demonstrating what kinds of data can be harvested in this manner. Currently, many communication providers store data for users for up to six months, in particular, data on who sends whom communication messages through use of such phone devices. Such data tends to get sold on to marketing agencies.

STEP SIX: SOME CONSIDERATIONS ON GATHERING NETWORK DATA

The above section offers you some options in ways of gathering network data. In making use of these choices, however, there are some additional issues you need to consider in gathering network data. These are discussed below.

Directed or undirected data

If you are observing people at a party, are you interested in who speaks with whom, or are you also interested in who initiated the conversation? Who approached whom at the party might be equally (or perhaps more) interesting than just recording which actors are engaged in conversation with one another. The difference in recording these kinds of observations reflects differences in gathering directed or undirected data. Directed data are data that look at how a tie is given from one actor to another. Thus, examples of directed data include who nominates whom as 'trustworthy' or who loaned money to whom. Directed data are considered richer data than undirected data, that is, more information is held within directed data as you not only have information on the tie being present or absent, but also information on who initiated the tie. Directed data, being a richer form of data, can also be converted to undirected data in situations where, for example, certain analytical procedures demand undirected data (see Chapter 1). However, the reverse is not true; if you gather undirected data, you can not retrospectively attempt to establish the senders and receivers of the tie.

The general advice is to try and gather directed data where possible, as these can always be reduced down to an undirected graph later on during analysis.

Binary versus valued data

Another choice you need to think about with regards to gathering data is the distinction between binary or valued data. With binary data, your main concern is recording the presence or absence of a tie. For example, you might wish to simply ask a respondent 'are you friends with this person? (Yes/no)'. The answer you receive would be recorded as a 1 (for yes) or a 0 (for no), depending on the response. For many data analyses, such binary data is sufficient for uncovering a lot of network patterns, and indeed, the majority of UCINET datasets contain only binary datasets.

You might wish, however, to get a deeper sense for the strength of a relationship between two actors, and how that would compare to the relationship between other actors. Such information would require gathering valued data. Valued data refers to data reflecting the relative strength, frequency or duration of a relationship between actors. For example, one can measure the duration of a friendship tie between actors, noting which actors have been friends for 1 year, 2 years, 3 years and so forth.

There are different options for gathering valued data. One option involves the use of Likert scales, such as the example shown below:

How frequently do you communicate with this person? Rarely 1 2 3 4 5 Very often

Depending on the respondent's answer, you record a 1, 2, 3, 4 or 5 to convey the frequency, and thus to some extent the strength of the tie between two actors. (Please note that only measuring the frequency of communication between actors is not enough of an indicator for measuring the strength of tie. Please see Granovetter, 1973, for more discussion.)

The Strength of weak ties

Probably the most cited social network analysis article is that of Granovetter's (1973) 'The strength of weak ties', published in *The American Journal of Sociology*. This paper, based on Granovetter's doctoral thesis, was based on data gathered on how professionals in Massachusetts used their personal networks to find out information on new job opportunities. In particular, Granovetter was interested in the nature and strength of relationship existing between the respondent and the respondent's contact person. Tie strength was thus measured through a frequency of contact question, where respondents rated their contact person as someone they met with often, occasionally or rarely.

Granovetter's findings showed a simple, yet profound pattern pertaining to personal contacts, the strength of tie, and the success of respondents in landing a new job. Of those respondents who did find new jobs through personal contacts, roughly 15 per cent said they saw these contacts on a regular basis (i.e. often), whereas 55 per cent said they saw their contact 'occasionally', and a further 29 per cent said they saw their contact 'rarely'. Granovetter concluded from these findings that weak ties, as measured through frequency of contact, were a more important resource for individuals in locating information on new jobs than were stronger ties. This conclusion rested on the idea that strong ties tend to exist among close friends and family members, and that information among such closely tied others tends to become redundant. In contrast, new information was more likely to be found via those ties that were not embedded in such tightly bound groups of friends and relatives.

Granovetter's work has since gone on to inspire a number of concepts and theories in the social network field, notably Ron Burt's notion of a structural hole (Burt, 1992); social capital (Burt, 2005; Lin, 2001a: 549); and early theorizing on small worlds (Watts, 1999).

Another method of gathering valued data would be to rank actors. Here, each actor in a network receives a rank relative to the other actors in the network. Each actor would thus receive one, and only one rank. The easiest way for you to gather ranking data is through the use of a deck of cards. Here, each name is assigned to a card, and respondents are then asked to arrange the cards in a pile with the lowest card holding the lowest rank, and the highest card holding the highest rank. For example, you might ask respondents to put the names of those they like the most at the top of the pile and the names of those they like least at the bottom of the pile. Such an approach, although helpful in making distinctions between persons of 'high rank' and 'low rank', might nonetheless result in measurement error; in essence, you are 'forcing' your research participants into placing actors into exclusive rank categories, where he or she might prefer to place several actors in the same rank category.

In UCINET, you will find an example of ranked data. These data are entitled 'Camp 92', and they were gathered by Borgatti, Bernard, Pelto and Ryan at the 1992 NSF Summer Institute on Research Methods in Cultural Anthropology. The data were collected through card sorting, where each respondent sorted the cards according to how much interaction that respondent had with each person on each card since the beginning of the summer course. The resulting data ranged from 1 to 17, with '1' indicating the most interaction and '17' the least interaction.

Reliability and validity issues

As with all research endeavours, you need to think about issues of reliability and validity in gathering your social network data. Reliability is concerned with the extent to which a measurement will yield the same results time and time again. This assumes that the variable of interest remains fairly stable over time. For social networks, such an assumption is problematic as social networks tend to change more frequently than a variable such as gender or socio-economic class. For these reasons, social network analysts think about reliability slightly differently. First, a measure is seen as being more reliable if it tends to generate reciprocal choices. By this I mean that if I were to measure friendship in a classroom by asking you 'who are you friends with in this class?' I would hope that your nominee would nominate you as well as an indicator of my measure's reliability. Here, the same measure for friendship has generated the same tie two times (two actors have commented on the same tie in the same way).

Research has shown that the reciprocation of nominations tends to occur more often for stronger or more intense relations. Thus, social network analysis tends to measure stronger ties more reliably than weaker ones (Marsden and

Campbell, 1984). Other research has shown that aggregates tend to be more reliable than individual choices. For example, as we will see later in this book, *degree centrality* is a social network measure that aggregates the ties directly received or given by an actor. Thus, in a given set of actors, some actors have higher degree centrality scores than others. Research has shown that even if individual nominations tend to differ slightly from one round of interviews to the next, the overall patterns of who has higher and who has lower degree centrality tends to remain the same (Burt et al., 1985).

Validity concerns the extent to which a measurement truly reflects the concept or variable one is trying to measure. With social network analysis, the issue of validity circles around whether questions aimed at measuring a respondent's network accurately measures that network. The accuracy of name generator questions has been well studied (Bernard and Killworth, 1977; Killworth and Bernard, 1976, 1979). Here, the communication networks, as measured by respondents' nominations through a name-recall procedure, are compared with the communication networks resulting from observations. In general, less than 50 per cent accuracy is found with regards to networks generated by respondents' responses to the question 'Who do you talk to?'. In addition, validity issues can stem from differences in senders and receivers. For example, whom I nominate as someone that I ask for advice is probably very different from someone I would nominate as a person I give advice to. Finally, some studies only consider reciprocated ties as valid ones for inclusion in a study (Krackhardt and Kilduff, 2002); here, the reasoning is that one can only be certain a friendship exists if both parties nominate the other as a friend.

Nonetheless, as network analysts tend to be more interested in the more stable patterns of networks, relying on respondents' own views of their social networks is still justifiable (Wellman and Berkowitz, 1988). You can make good choices about how to phrase your questions to improve their accuracy. For example, name generator questions that are fixed choice are less accurate than free-recall questions, or research designs that use a roster. With fixed-choice designs, you limit your respondents to a small number of choices, for example three to five choices. In doing so, you make the (most probably faulty) assumption that respondents' networks consist of three to five actors. Thus you are introducing measurement error into design and decreasing the accuracy of your measurement (Wasserman and Faust, 1994).

Missing data

As I have indicated above, it is difficult to gather social network data that is perfectly accurate in reflecting a 'real' observed network. The obstacles range from differences in respondent recall/memory, and also differences in perception of who actually constitutes being a friend. In addition to this level of data 'noise', network analysts must also contend with issues of missing data. Missing data can result from incorrect specification of the network boundary, constricting the number of nominees a respondent can name (fixed-choice design), and from respondent absenteeism during data collection (Kossinets, 2006). Statisticians are reviewing and working on methods for handling missing data (Huisman and Steglich, 2008). Some ways forward include the use and specification of ERGM models (Robins et al., 2004); developing likelihood-based estimation techniques, based on the available data (Schafer and Graham, 2002); reconstructing the data, as suggested by Stork and Richards (1992); and replacing missing data with values representing weak relations, as suggested by Burt (1987). None of these procedures are perfect, yet some yield better results than others, and readers are encouraged to explore further readings if interested (e.g. Huisman and Steglich, 2008).

Beyond these issues of validity, reliability and missing data, I suggest you consult with other texts regarding how to conduct social science research (see for example Babbie, 2008; Bryman, 2008; Robson, 2002). Here, I have simply tried to alert you to some of the specific issues of reliability and validity pertaining to social networks.

Ethical concerns

When you think about the ethics of any social research, you are primarily concerned with the potential harm to your research participants. All of the normal ethical concerns apply to social network analysis, and here I will highlight only those issues which are of unique concern to the network approach (if you would like more general advice regarding the ethical concerns of conducting social research, I suggest visiting the British Sociological Association's website, which offers detailed ethical guidelines for conducting research).

Top of the list of concerns are issues of anonymity when making use of a roster. Here, all of your respondents will be seeing who else is being studied, as well as their own name listed in the roster. This might make some respondents uncomfortable, and some might even refuse to participate in this study because they do not like the idea of their name being seen by others. In other words, they do not feel as though their participation is in anyway anonymous.

As with many ethical issues, there is no straightforward answer to how to deal with this issue. Of course, informed consent is critical: you need to explain to your respondents how you plan on using the data, and you can emphasize that once the data has been collected, it will be treated as anonymous data. You can also insure confidentiality, i.e. other respondents will see who is listed on the roster, but you will not share information gained from any one respondent with another. Finally, make sure that your respondents/participants are aware that their participation is voluntary and that they can leave the study at any time.

What if the respondent still says no to participating in your study after you have given him or her an informed consent form? Here the issue becomes whether or not that person's name (identity) should in any way be included in the study: if you are using a roster, should the name be removed from the roster? If another participant were to name that individual through free recall, should you remove the name from the dataset? Such questions circle around the notion of who 'owns' a relationship. Relationships are shared between actors, not just one actor, and thus, if an individual actor is reporting on his or her perceptions of their relations with others, should not that person be allowed to comment on their perceptions of their relations with others? If respondents own their perceptions, but not the relationship itself, a researcher may wish to argue this point in making use of a roster of names, even if not everyone on that roster has agreed to participate in the study. Alternatively, a researcher may feel that neither party ought to report on a relationship without the consent of the other (Borgatti and Molina, 2005). Whichever position you ultimately decide to take on this issue, you should be aware of the arguments and be ready to defend your position accordingly.

Another ethical issue is the use of social network analysis in the context of business management. Here the issue for the researcher is the following: will people lose their jobs, not be promoted, or be treated 'differently' as a result of your social network study (Borgatti and Molina, 2005)? Again, what is critical here is informed consent: respondents should not be deceived into thinking their answers will not be shown to management if the researcher knows that this will be the case. The researcher could also use some leverage with management and how the data will be handled, for example the researcher could strike a bargain with the manager and say that social network findings can be presented and summarized, but no names of individual actors will be given.

Finally, when I discussed the use of electronic media such as mobile phones and Internet technologies such as Facebook, I briefly commented on some of the potential threats to users' privacy. Facebook claims, for example, that it 'owns' all data users place on their accounts, and mobile phone providers, in order to offset the costs of gathering data on users' communication patterns, sells such data to marketing agencies. Clearly, threats to users' privacy exist. From a researcher's standpoint, however, such threats to privacy all exist within the normal concerns for conducting ethical social science research; participants need to either sign consent forms and/or a number of measures need to be put into place to ensure that participants' privacy is protected.

Taken together, the best advice regarding the ethics of social network research is answering the question 'To what extent will my research potentially harm my research subjects?'. In answering this question, it is a good idea to discuss the issues with colleagues or others familiar with the field, as well as refer to the ethical guidelines listed here.

STEP SEVEN: INPUTTING AND STRUCTURING DATA INTO MATRICES

Once you have gathered your data, you will want to organize those data into a suitable format to enable you to analyse that data. There are different procedures for inputting and structuring your data. Here, I will only show you one method, but this is one of the more common ways of structuring your data. This method is a case-by-case data matrix. In Chapter 1, I introduced you to case-by-case matrices; here I will simply demonstrate and walk you through how to create a matrix for your own social network data.

Below is an example of part of a questionnaire used to gather both social network data as well as attribute data on each actor in the network. The attribute data included a) which department each student came from and b) the gender of each student. Below, you will see how we gather data on the students' social networks (Prell and Haythornthwaite, 2006).

Please rate on a 5 point scale the extent to which you agree or disagree with each statement for each and every student listed. Please circle your name and please circle a number for each student where 1 = strongly disagree; 5 = strongly agree and d/k = don't know.

Student	I consider this person my friend	I think this person is fun to work with	I could depend on this person to get a job done	I like to socialize with this person
Alan	1 2 3 4 5 d/k	1 2 3 4 5 d/k	1 2 3 4 5 d/k	1 2 3 4 5 d/k
Brad	1 2 3 4 5 d/k	1 2 3 4 5 d/k	1 2 3 4 5 d/k	1 2 3 4 5 d/k
Carlos	1 2 3 4 5 d/k	1 2 3 4 5 d/k	1 2 3 4 5 d/k	1 2 3 4 5 d/k
Diane	1 2 3 4 5 d/k	1 2 3 4 5 d/k	1 2 3 4 5 d/k	1 2 3 4 5 d/k
Emily	1 2 3 4 5 d/k	1 2 3 4 5 d/k	1 2 3 4 5 d/k	1 2 3 4 5 d/k

The above questionnaire example gathers data on four different relations for this set of students. These relations include a) friendship b) fun to work with

c) dependability and d) socializing. Further, each of these relations contains valued data. I will show you how to create a matrix for social relation of friendship. This will be a *valued adjacency matrix*.

When constructing an adjacency matrix, you first enter the names of all your actors in both the rows in the columns as shown below:

	Alan	Brad	Carlos	Diane	Emily
Alan					
Brad					
Carlos					
Diane					
Emily					

Next, you enter the nominations of each respondent, starting with the row representing that respondent, and then inserting a value under the column representing that respondent's choice. For example, suppose Alan, in the role of the respondent, nominated Carlos and Diane as friends, and gave each of them a score of 5. Alan does not consider Brad and Emily friends, and so he gives each of them a score of 1. Given these nominations of Alan, you would enter these values into a matrix in the following way:

	Alan	Brad	Carlos	Diane	Emily
Alan	0	1	5	5	1

Notice that I have given a 0 under Alan's column, as Alan does not have any kind of relationship with himself that is of interest in the context of the social network study. Remember that in most cases in social network analysis the diagonal of the matrix is ignored or treated with zeros.

Your next step would be to continue entering each respondent's nominations until you have a complete case-by-case matrix (that is an adjacency matrix). Once this matrix is complete, you would create new matrices for the relation 'fun to work with', 'dependability' and 'socializing'. Each of these matrices would hold the same set of names in its rows and columns. In the end, you would have four separate matrices on the same set of actors (Alan, Brad, Carlos, Diane and Emily).

Now I will show you how to create a matrix for the actor attributes. As I said earlier, there are two attributes for these data: gender and home department. Below, you see how I structured these data into a case-by-variable matrix, where

1 = male; 2 = female for the variable Gender and 1 = sociology, 2 = economics and 3 = politics for the variable Department:

	Gender	Department
Alan	1	1
Brad	1	2
Carlos	1	1
Diane	2	1
Emily	2	3

Your dataset for this group of actors now consists of five matrices: four are adjacency matrices holding value data and one is a case-by-variable matrix containing actor attribute data.

STEP EIGHT: INITIAL VISUALIZATION OF THE NETWORK

When I bring students into the computer lab for the first time to start looking at social network data, one of the first things I ask them to do is to visualize the data as a graph in NetDraw, which is a visualization package found within UCINET (*Visualize>NetDraw*). As Moreno, the father of sociometry noted, drawing graphs of networks is a 'method of exploration' (Moreno, 1953). Thus, I see visualizing networks as graphs as an important means for students and analysts alike to get an initial, first 'feel' for the network they are studying.

Yet often, this initial look at a graph can reveal very little if the network is large and/or there are many crossover ties. At this point, what can help in visualization is including additional data into the graph, in the form of attribute data, or in the form of previous analyses conducted on the network. For example, Figures 3.1 and 3.2 below illustrate how a visualization exercise might take place. These digraphs are visual images of a network coming from the Freeman's EIES dataset in UCINET. This particular network consists of 32 actors, and shows who sent whom email messages during the course of the study. These data are asymmetric, and valued, where the values of the ties reflect the total number of messages person i sent to person j.

The first digraph shows the network in its 'raw' format. That is, I have simply brought the network data into NetDraw and run the 'draw' command without any additional manipulations or inclusions.

What we see is a large mass of ties crisscrossing one another, linking a group of actors together. There is not much we can conclude about the patterns in such

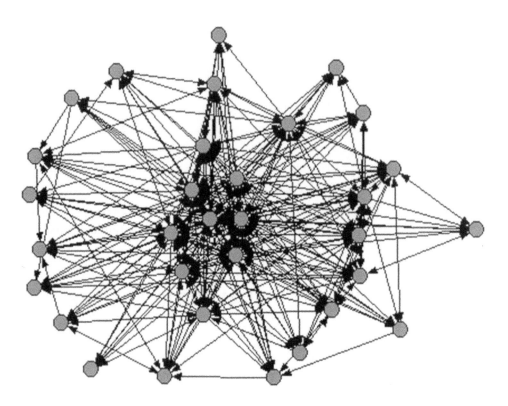

Figure 3.1   Who sent whom email messages – Digraph 1

a digraph; it appears that a few actors have more links than others, and that the network appears, overall, to be connected, i.e. that all actors are connected to one another through some kind of path.

However, this same network is again redrawn, and its image is shown in Figure 3.2. Here, I include attribute data into my digraph, and make some changes to the placement of actors in this digraph based on this new information. Thus, the shapes of the nodes have been altered to correspond with actors' disciplines, and then these disciplines grouped together accordingly. Thus, group A consists of mathematicians; group B are anthropologists; group C are 'other' disciplines; and group D are sociologists. In addition, I have also manipulated this digraph to show the strength of ties, whereby stronger ties, i.e. those consisting of a higher number of email messages, appear bolder and weaker ties, i.e. those consisting of a lower number of email messages, thinner. Finally, this second digraph shows nodes differing in size, and these size differences correspond to the 'centrality' of each actor. Thus, actors who have more ties to others, i.e. the more 'central' actors, appear larger in this digraph.

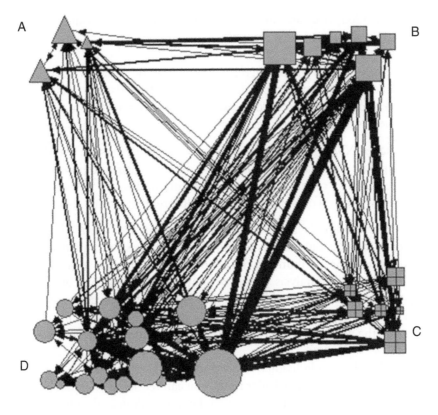

Figure 3.2 Who sent whom email messages – Digraph 2

Taken together, Figure 3.2 shows us that i) the largest group of actors in this network are sociologists (group D); ii) that certain of these sociologists (the larger circles in group D) play a more central role than any other actor in the network and iii) that anthropologists (group B) and sociologists (group D) seem to share stronger ties, whereas mathematicians (group A) seem to share weaker ties with others in the group. Thus, visualizing network data alongside other data in this way can help one develop a better interpretation or 'visual story' about what is happening in the network. In doing so, such visual displays can help you gain some initial impressions for your data and may also inspire what kind of additional analyses you would like to perform.

To access NetDraw in UCINET, simply go to *Visualize>Netdraw*. A new window will appear, launching the NetDraw application. Within this application window, go to *File>Open>Ucinet dataset* and here you will see options to select network data, two-mode network data, attribute data, or coordinates. I suggest you first open your network data, and once this is loaded in NetDraw, proceed with loading any attribute datasets. Once both the network and attribute datasets are loaded, you can start to play with the different layout features available in NetDraw. Below is just a small sampling:

- *Properties > Lines > Tie Strength:* If your network data is valued data, and you would like to display these differences in values visually, use this option. You can decide how thick you wish 'stronger' ties to be shown, and also make choices on colours of ties.

- *Properties > Nodes > Symbols > Shape > Attribute-based:* Use this option to manipulate the shape of nodes based on some attribute information, for example, gender, organizational department, political party and so forth. NetDraw will give you some options for different shapes to choose from.

- *Properties > Nodes > Symbols > Shape > Attribute-based:* Similar to the option above, you can use this option to change the size of attributes according to some actor attribute. In the example I gave in this section, I first ran a degree centrality analysis on my network data, and then I brought in the output file, named 'FreemanDegree' into NetDraw as an attribute file. Thus, many of the analyses you conduct in UCINET can be brought into NetDraw, alongside the network data, to reveal some structural features visually.

You can also click on individual nodes and drag them around the screen manually. If you right click on a particular node, you can see some additional options as well, e.g. the option to select all nodes with the same colour and so forth. I encourage you to explore and play around with the various options in NetDraw.

Visualizing networks through digraphs via the NetDraw program is not the only way you can visualize networks. Later in this book, in Chapter 9, I will introduce you to block modelling, which is an approach for locating positions and analysing roles in a network. Block modelling involves the use of block models, which are a different way to visualize networks. Finally, readers who are interested in exploring even more techniques and approaches to visualizing data might find these readings useful: Bertin (1983), and Brandes et al., (2001, 2006).

STEP NINE: FURTHER ANALYSIS AND INTERPRETATION OF RESULTS

The last phase of your research includes analysing, interpreting and writing up your results. The analysis of networks tends to focus on complete network data, although specific analyses have been designed just for ego networks as well. Chapters 4–9 focus on some of the variety of network analyses available to you. Primarily, these analyses can be compared to descriptive statistics used in more traditional social science research (e.g. mean, standard deviation, etc.). In other words, they do not offer you tests of statistical significance. In Chapter 9, however, I spend some time introducing you to analyses that involve tests of statistical significance.

SUMMARY AND CONCLUSIONS

In this chapter you learnt a number of important considerations and practical steps for thinking through how to conduct your own social network study. Practical considerations include thinking through the steps of gathering data, validity and reliability issues, structuring your data into matrices for analysis, and any ethical issues your study might involve. I introduced you to some popular theoretical approaches and frameworks used in the social network community, and I offered you some examples of each.

Let's now turn our attention to the next section of this book, which deals with social network analyses in terms of network levels.

REFERENCES

Babbie, E. R. (2008) *The Basics of Social Research*, 4th edn. Belmont, CA: Thomson/ Wadsworth.

Bellotti, E. (2008) 'What are friends for? Elective communities of single people', *Social Networks*, 30: 318–29.

Bernard, H. and Killworth, P. (1977) 'Informant accuracy in social network data II', *Human Communication Research*, 4.

Bertin, J. (1983) *Semiology of Graphics: Diagrams, Networks, Maps*. University of Wisconsin: University of Wisconsin Press.

Bidart, C. and Lavenu, D. (2005) 'Evolutions of personal networks and life events', *Social Networks*, 27: 359–76.

Blau, P. M. (1964) *Exchange and Power in Social Life*. New York: Wiley.

Borgatti, S. P. and Molina, J.-L. (2005) 'Toward ethical guidelines for network research in organizations', *Social Networks*, 27: 107–17.

Bott, E. (1955) 'Urban families: Conjugal roles and social networks', *Human Relations*, 8: 345–83.

Brace, I. (2008) *Questionnaire Design: How to Plan, Structure and Write Survey Material for Effective Market Research*. London and Philadelphia: Kogan Page.

Bradburn, N. M., Wansink, B. and Sudman, S. (2004) *Asking Questions: The Definitive Guide to Questionnaire Design for Market Research, Political Polls, and Social and Health Questionnaires*. San Francisco: Jossey-Bass.

Brandes, U., Raab, J. and Wagner, D. (2001) 'Exploratory network visualization: Simultaneous display of actor status and connections', *Journal of Social Structure*, 2.

Brandes, U., Kenis, P. and Raab, J. (2006) 'Explanation through network visualization', *Methodology,* 2: 16–23.

Brandes, U. and Lerner, J. (2008) 'Visual analysis of controversy in user-generated encyclopedias', *Information Visualization – Special issue on visual analytics science and technology,* 7(1): 34–48.

Brewer, D. D. (2000) 'Erratum to "Forgetting in the recall-based elicitation of personal and social networks": [Social Networks 22 (2000) 29–43]', *Social Networks,* 22: 367.

Brewer, D. D. and Webster, C. M. (2000) 'Forgetting of friends and its effects on measuring friendship networks', *Social Networks,* 21: 361–73.

Bryman, A. (2008) *Social Research Methods.* Oxford and New York: Oxford University Press.

Burt, R. S. (1987) 'A note on missing network data in the general social survey', *Social Networks,* 9: 63–73.

Burt, R. S. (1992) *Structural Holes: The Social Structure of Competition.* Cambridge, MA: Harvard University Press.

Burt, R. (1997) 'The contingent value of social capital', *Administrative Science Quarterly,* 42: 339–65.

Burt, R. (2001) 'Structure holes versus network closure as social capital', in N. Lin, K. Cook, and R. Burt (eds), *Social Capital: Theory and Research.* New York: Aldine de Gruyter.

Burt, R. S. (2004) 'Structural holes and good ideas', *American Journal of Sociology,* 110: 349–99.

Burt, R. (2005) *Brokerage and Closure: An Introduction to Social Capital.* Oxford: Oxford University Press.

Burt, R., Marsden, P. and Rossi, P. H. (1985) 'A research agenda for survey network data', *Columbia university workshop on survey network data.* Columbia, NY.

Byrne, D. (1997) 'An overview (and underview) of research and theory within the attraction paradigm', *Journal of Social and Personal Relationships,* 14: 417–31.

Coleman, J. S., Katz, E. and Menzel, H. (1966) *Medical Innovation: A Diffusion Study.* New York: Bobbs-Merrill Company, Inc.

Collins, H. M. (1974) 'The TEA set: Tacit knowledge and scientific networks', *Science Studies,* 4:165–85.

Cook, K. S., Emerson, R.M., Gilmore, M.R. and Yamagishi, T. (1983) 'The distribution of power in exchange networks: Theory and experimental results', *American Journal of Sociology,* 89: 275–305.

David, B. and Snijders, T. (2002) 'Estimating the size of the homeless population in Budapest, Hungary', *Quality and Quantity,* 36: 291–303.

Eagle, N., Pentland, A. and Lazer, D. (2009) 'Inferring social network structure using mobile phone data', *Proceedings of the National Academy of Sciences (PNAS)* 106: 15274–8.

Emerson, R. (1972a) 'Exchange theory, part II: Exchange relations and networks', in J. Berger, J. Morris zelditch and B. Anderson (eds), *Sociological Theories in Progress, Vol. 2.* Boston: Houghton-Mifflin.

Emerson, R. M. (1972b) 'Exchange theory, part I: A psychological basis for social exchange', in J. Berger, J. Morris zelditch and B. Anderson (eds), *Sociological Theories in Progress, Vol. 2.* Boston: Houghton-Mifflin.

Erickson, B. (1988) 'The relational basis of attitudes', in B. Wellman and S. D. Berkowitz, (eds), *Social Structures: A Network Approach.* Cambridge: Cambridge University Press.

Friedkin, N. E. (1998) *A Structural Theory of Social Influence*. Cambridge and New York: Cambridge University Press.

Gluckman, M. (1940) 'Analysis of a social situation in modern Zululand', *Bantu Studies*, 14: 1–30.

Gluckman, M. (1963) *Order and Rebellion in Tribal Africa*. London: Cohen & West.

Granovetter, M. (1973) 'The strength of weak ties', *The American Journal of Sociology*, 78: 1360–80.

Granovetter, M. (1976) 'Network sampling: Some first steps'. *The American Journal of Sociology*, 81: 1287–303.

Homans, G. C. (1958) 'Social behavior as exchange', *The American Journal of Sociology*, 63: 597–606.

Huisman, M. and Snijders, T. (2003) 'Statistical analysis of longitudinal network data with changing composition', *Sociological Methods and Research*, 32: 253–87.

Huisman, M. and Steglich, C. (2008) 'Treatment of non-response in longitudinal network studies', *Social Networks*, 30: 297–308.

Killworth, B. and Bernard, H. (1976) 'Informant accuracy in social network data', *Human Organization*, 35: 269–86.

Killworth, P. D. and Bernard, H. R. (1979) 'Informant accuracy in social network data III: A comparison of triadic structure in behavioral and cognitive data', *Social Networks*, 2: 19–46.

Knoke, D. and Kuklinski, J. (1982) *Network Analysis*. London: SAGE.

Knox, H., Harvey, P. and Savage, M. (2006) 'Social networks and the study of relations: Networks as method, metaphor and form', *Economy and Society*, 35: 113–40.

Kossinets, G. (2006) 'Effects of missing data in social networks', *Social Networks*, 28: 247–68.

Krackhardt, D. and Kilduff, M. (2002) 'Structure, culture and Simmelian ties in entrepreneurial firms', *Social Networks*, 24: 279–90.

Laumann, E. O., Marsden, P. and Prensky, D. (1989) 'The boundary specification problem in network analysis', in L. C. Freeman, D. White and A. K. Romney (eds), *Research Methods in Social Network Analysis*. Fairfax, VA: George Mason University Press.

Leenders, R. T. A. J. (1997) 'Longitudinal behavior of network structure and actor attributes: Modeling interdependence of contagion and selection', in P. Doreian and F. N. Stokman (eds), *Evolution of Social Networks*. Amsterdam: Gordon & Breach.

Leenders, R. T. A. J. (2002) 'Modeling social influence through network autocorrelation: Constructing the weight matrix', *Social Networks*, 24: 21–47.

Lenoir, T. (1979) 'Quantitative foundations for the sociology of science: On linking blockmodeling with co-citation analysis', *Social Studies of Science*, 9: 455–80.

Lewis, K., Kaufman, J., Gonzalez, M., Wimmer, A. and Christakis, N. (2008) 'Tastes, ties, and time: A new social network dataset using Facebook.com', *Social Networks*, 30: 330–42.

Lievrouw, L. A., Rogers, E. M., Lowe, C. U. and Nadel, E. (1987) 'Triangulation as a research strategy for identifying invisible colleges among biomedical scientists', *Social Networks*, 9: 217–48.

Lin, N. (2001a) 'Building a network theory of social capital', in N. Lin, K. Cook and R. Burt (eds), *Social Capital: Theory and Research*. New York: Aldine De Gruyter.

Lin, N. (2001b) *Social Capital: A Theory of Social Structure and Action*. Cambridge, UK/New York: Cambridge University Press.

Lin, N., Fu, Y. and Hsung, R. (2001) 'The position generator: Measurement technique for investigations in social capital', in N. Lin, K. Cook and R. Burt (eds), *Social Capital: Theory and Research.* New York: Aldine de Gruyter.

Lubbers, M. J., Molina, J. L., Lerner, J., Brandes, U., Ávila, J. and McCarty, C. (in press) 'Longitudinal analysis of personal networks. The case of Argentinean migrants in Spain', *Social Networks.*

Marsden, P. (1990) 'Network data and measurement', *Annual Review of Sociology,* 16: 435–63.

Marsden, P. V. (2003) 'Interviewer effects in measuring network size using a single name generator', *Social Networks,* 25: 1–16.

Marsden, P. and Campbell, K. (1984) 'Measuring tie strength', *Social Forces,* 63: 482–501.

Mitchell, C. (1969) 'The concept and use of social networks', in J. C. Mitchell (ed.), *Social Networks in Urban Situations.* Manchester: Manchester University Press.

Molm, L. (2003) 'Theoretical comparisons of forms of exchange', *Sociological Theory,* 21: 1–17.

Molm, L. D., Takahashi, N. and Peterson, G. (2000) 'Risk and trust in social exchange: An experimental test of a classical proposition', *The American Journal of Sociology,* 105: 1396–427.

Moreno, J. L. (1953) *Who Shall Survive? Foundations of Sociometry, Group Psychotherapy and Sociodrama.* Beacon, NY. Beacon House.

Newman, M. E. J., Barabási, A.-L. and Watts, D. J. (2006) *The Structure and Dynamics of Networks.* Princeton: Princeton University Press.

Oppenheim, A. N. and Oppenheim, A. N. (1992) Questionnaire Design, Interviewing, and Attitude Measurement. London and New York: Pinter Publishers.

Padgett, J. F. and Ansell, C. K. (1993) 'Robust action and the rise of the Medici, 1400–34', *The American Journal of Sociology,* 98: 1259–319.

Prell, C. and Haythornthwaite, C. (2006) 'Social ties and social identity: Looking at the roles of media and motivation in computer-mediated groups', *3rd Annual Applications of Social Network Analysis.* University of Zurich.

Prell, C., Hubacek, K., Quinn, C. and Reed, M. (2008) '"Who's in the network?" When stakeholders influence data analysis', *Systemic Practice and Action Research,* 21: 443–58.

Prell, C., Hubacek, K. and Reed, M. (2009) 'Stakeholder analysis and social network analysis in natural resource management', *Society and Natural Resources,* 22: 501–18.

Rapoport, A. (1957) 'Contribution to the theory of random and biased nets', *Bulletin of Mathematical Biology,* 19: 257–77.

Robins, G., Elliott, P. and Pattison, P. (2001) 'Network models for social selection processes', *Social Networks,* 23: 1–30.

Robins, G., Pattison, P. and Woolcock, J. (2004) 'Missing data in networks: exponential random graph (p*) models for networks with non-respondents', *Social Networks,* 26: 257–83.

Robson, C. (2002) *Real World Research: A Resource for Social Scientists and Practitioner-researchers.* Oxford, UK/Madden, MA: Blackwell Publishers.

Rogers, E. M. (1995) *Diffusion of Innovations.* New York: Free Press.

Schafer, J. L. and Graham, J. W. (2002) 'Missing data: Our view of the state of the art', *Psychological Methods,* 7: 147–77.

Scott, J. (2000) *Social Network Analysis: A Handbook.* Newbury Park: SAGE Publications.

Skvoretz, J. (1990) 'Biased net theory: Approximations, simulations and observations', *Social Networks,* 12: 217–38.

Skvoretz, J., Fararo, T. J. and Agneessens, F. (2004) 'Advances in biased net theory: Definitions, derivations, and estimations', *Social Networks,* 26: 113–39.

Small, H. and Griffith, B. C. (1974) 'The structure of scientific literatures I: Identifying and graphing specialties', *Science Studies,* 4: 17–40.

Snijders, T. A. B. (2005) 'Models for longitudinal network data, in P. Carrington, J. Scott and S. Wasserman (eds), *Models and Methods in Social Network Analysis.* New York: Cambridge University Press.

Snijders, T. A. B., Steglich, C. E. G. and Van De Bunt, G. G. (forthcoming) 'Introduction to actor-based models for network dynamics', *Social Networks.*

Stork, D. and Richards, W. D. (1992) 'Nonrespondents in communication network studies', *Group and Organization Management,* 17: 193–209.

Tyler, J., Wilkinson, D. M. and Huberman, B. (2003) 'Email as spectroscopy: Automated discovery of community structure within organisations', *Information Retrieval (SIGIR 2003):* 72–79.

Uzzi, B. (1996) 'The sources and consequences of embeddedness for the economic performance of organisations: The network effect', *American Sociological Review,* 61: 674–98.

Valente, T. W. (1995) *Network Models of the Diffusion of Innovations.* Cresskill, NJ: Hampton Press.

Valente, T. W. and Davis, R. (1999) 'Accelerating the diffusion of innovations using opinion leaders', *The Annals of the American Academy of Political and Social Science,* 566: 55–67.

Wasserman, S. and Faust, F. (1994) *Social Network Analysis: Methods and Applications.* Cambridge: Cambridge University Press.

Watts, D. J. (1999) 'Networks, dynamics and the small world phenomenon', *American Journal of Sociology,* 105: 493–527.

Wellman, B. and Berkowitz, S. (1988) *Social Structures: A Network Approach.* Cambridge: Cambridge University Press.

Wellman, B. and Frank, K. (2001) 'Network capital in a multi-level world: Getting support in personal communities', in N. Lin, K. Cook and R. Burt (eds), *Social Capital: Theory and Research.* New York: Aldine de Gruyter.

Wellman, B. and Wortley, S. (1990) 'Different strokes from different folks: Community ties and social support', *The American Journal of Sociology,* 96: 558–88.

PART II

LEVELS OF ANALYSIS

PART II

METHODS OF
ANALYSIS

4

ACTOR LEVEL IN COMPLETE NETWORKS

Chapters 4 and 5 look at individual actors in networks, what I refer to as the 'actor level'. In this chapter, I will introduce the actor level within complete networks. In Chapter 5, I will look at individual actors and their immediate, personal networks, i.e. ego networks. Throughout both chapters, you will be given instruction on how to analyse these concepts and measures within the UCINET software environment.

INDIVIDUAL ACTORS IN COMPLETE NETWORKS

Individual actor attributes, such as age, gender, and so forth, are of interest to social network analysts, and you will likely use them from time to time in your own social network studies. For example, when I discuss broker roles below, you will see how individual attributes can make meaningful contributions in the study of social networks. For now, however, when I refer to the actor level of social network analysis, I refer to an actor's position in a network, or to the actor's ego network, and how to analyse and describe this position or ego network according to particular concepts and measures developed in social network analysis.

Why look at individual actors? When you consider yourself and your own social networks, you probably feel that in certain networks you feel more at the centre of things, that is, more popular or 'in the know' of what is going on in your network; and in other networks, you feel more on the periphery, that is, more of an outsider. You might also have been in situations where, because of who you knew or who were your friends, you were able to mediate conflicts or help resolve a particular dispute. In these instances, whether you feel you are popular, peripheral or a good mediator, it is your position within the network that is contributing to how you feel about your role in that particular context. Thus, understanding how individual actors are positioned within a particular network can help us understand such questions as who is important to that network, who makes things 'happen' in the network or holds the network together in times of distress. If certain actors in the network seem to have more resources or riches than others, understanding the social network surrounding that individual might shed light as to how that person can have such an advantage.

In this chapter, I will start with measures of centrality and move on to ego networks. Measures of centrality were some of the first attempts to start uncovering this question of 'who is important in the network?' As usually happens in the social sciences, other analysts developed alternative measures that either improved upon these earlier centrality measures, or uncovered a different dimension to the notion of centrality. Although there is not space enough to address all the measures designed for analysing networks on the individual actor level, those described here, i.e. measures of centrality, are probably the most 'popular' and widely used measures for complete networks.

CENTRALITY MEASURES

Many of you already have an intuitive sense for what we mean in network analysis by 'centrality': people who occupy a central position in a network tend to be more visible, they tend to know many people and many people know them. They might be considered leaders, they might be at the centre of gossip circles, or they might be among the first to hear of any news. Social network analysts have been intrigued by this notion of central actors for quite some time, and consequently, they have developed different ways of conceptualizing, measuring and analysing centrality.

Linton Freeman (1979) was the first to draw a graph that summarized, in visual terms, the various meanings of centrality. Freeman used the figure of a 'star graph', shown in Figure 4.1, to launch his discussion on the ways in which scholars have conceptualized and measured centrality.

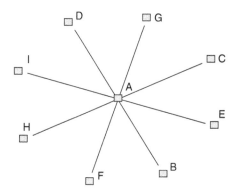

Figure 4.1   Star graph

In this star graph, the most central actor is obviously the one represented by the node in the centre. This node has the highest *degree* of ties to others; it falls *between* all the other nodes; and it has the shortest path lengths to all other actors, making it the *closest* actor to all the others. These notions of centrality – an actor's degree, betweenness and closeness – all translate into unique centrality measures, which are each explored below.

Degree, indegree and outdegree centrality

Degree centrality is generally considered the most intuitive form of centrality. It is simply the number of immediate contacts an actor has in a network. To measure degree centrality, you count the number of alters adjacent to ego, ignoring both the direction and value of the tie (see 'A note of caution!' box below). Because you are not looking at the direction of ties, degree centrality is thus seen as a measure for an actor's level of *involvement* or *activity* in the network. It does not consider whether or not an actor is seen as influential or popular. In a communication network, an actor with high degree centrality is one who can be considered to be a major channel for information in that particular network. This actor speaks with many others, and thus both hears and spreads new information quickly.

Formula for degree centrality, for actor i:

$$C_D(i) = \sum_{j=1}^{n} x_{ij} = \sum_{i=1}^{n} x_{ji}$$

Where,

x_{ij} = the value of the tie from actor i to actor j (the value being either 0 or 1). Thus, it is the sum of all ties.

n = the number of nodes in the network.

Note that degree centrality does not look at the direction of lines. Degree centrality is analysed on symmetric data, i.e. on graphs, but not on digraphs.

Formula for normalized degree:

$$C'_D(i) + \frac{C_D(i)}{n-1} \; ; \text{ where } n = \text{the number of nodes.}$$

An example of degree centrality can be seen in Figure 4.2.

With the friendship graph in Figure 4.2, node A has the highest degree centrality, as this node has a total of 4 direct links with other nodes. In comparison,

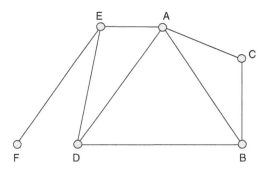

Figure 4.2   Friendship graph

node F has a degree centrality of 1. Node A is thus seen as being *involved* in more friendship ties than Node F. In both these cases, degree centrality was calculated simply by counting the number of actors adjacent to the focal actor, or rather, counting the number of alters adjacent to ego.

A note of caution! Calculating centrality and some data considerations

The degree centrality scores are calculated on matrices holding binary, symmetrical network data. This means, specifically, that the matrix cells hold either 1s or 0s, and that the upper half triangle of the matrix matches the lower half. I have already mentioned that symmetric matrix data, when displayed visually, is referred to as a graph.

Because of this concern for symmetric, binary data, you need to ensure your data are both binary and symmetrical before calculating degree centrality. You can transform your data to binary, symmetric matrices in UCINET. Go to *Transform > Dichotomize* to convert data to binary data (1s and 0s). Then convert your dichotomized matrix to a symmetrical one by going to *Transform > Symmetrize*.

Degree centrality can be calculated on valued data, but one must do so with care: one must consider the values attached to the lines, and realize that the resulting degree centrality score will bias toward stronger ties, i.e. those ties with a higher value. Thus, actor *i* might have a higher degree centrality score than actor *j*, but this would not necessarily be reflective of how many ties are directly tied to actor *i*. Actor *i* might have fewer ties, but each are of a higher value, thus inflating actor *i*'s score.

With degree centrality, one ignores the direction of the tie. However, the direction of the tie can often reveal some interesting insights into group structure and the placement of individuals within this structure.

For example, if I asked you, 'who do you consider to be your friend in this particular class?' you might nominate three individuals, yet not all of these same three may nominate you, and another two might! Thus, when you perceive the direction of ties as important to the network you wish to study, you might prefer using indegree and outdegree centrality. Indegree and outdegree centrality are computed on digraphs, i.e. networks holding directional data.

Indegree centrality is the number of ties received by an actor from others, and *outdegree* centrality is the number of ties given by that actor to others. Indegree centrality is often used as a measure for *prestige* or *popularity* and outdegree centrality as a measure of *expansiveness*. For relations based on exchange, indegree may be seen as a measure for 'receiving' and outdegree a measure of 'giving'. To illustrate indegree, and outdegree centrality, look at Figure 4.3.

In Figure 4.3, node A has an outdegree of 3, and indegree of 2. Node F has an outdegree of 1 and an indegree of 0. Whereas with degree centrality, node A held the highest score, and was thus seen as being involved in the most amount of friendship ties in the network, here the picture changes: node A is no more 'prestigious' than nodes B, D or E. All of these nodes hold an indegree centrality of 2.

Comparing actors in different networks: Some considerations

A disadvantage of degree, indegree and outdegree is that these centrality measures can only be used to make meaningful comparisons among actors in the same network. If you want to compare actors in two different networks, *then the two networks need to be the same size, i.e. they both need to hold the same number of actors.* When networks differ in size, measures of degree, indegree and outdegree cannot be compared. This is because these measures are based on the size of the network (i.e. size *g*), and so comparison is therefore difficult. Realizing this constraint, Freeman (1979) developed a way to convert degree, indegree and outdegree centrality scores into proportions. This converted form of these centrality measures are called 'normalized' centrality measures. In converting

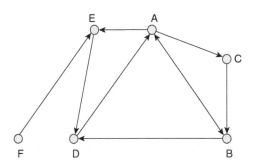

Figure 4.3   Friendship digraph

these centrality measures into normalized centrality measures, Freeman enabled an analyst to compare the centrality of actors from one network to the next.[1]

For example, the normalized degree centrality for actor A is 80 per cent, the normalized outdegree centrality for actor A is 60 per cent and the normalized indegree centrality for actor A is 40 per cent. UCINET will compute these normalized values for you.

Taken together, degree, indegree and outdegree are simple measures of centrality that can nonetheless communicate well notions of involvement, prestige or dependence.

1. Comparing networks of a different size

Please note that networks that differ greatly in size should never be compared, as the size of a network can bias measures such as degree and density. For example, an actor in a small network will, by virtue of the small number of actors in the network, have a greater chance of connecting to a higher proportion of these actors than someone embedded in a larger network. Thus, smaller networks tend to have higher density scores than larger networks, and as such, comparison of the two should be avoided.

Equation for indegree centrality, for actor i:

$$C_I(i) = \sum_{j=1}^{n} x_{ji}$$

Equation for outdegree centrality, for actor i:

$$C_O(i) = \sum_{j=1}^{n} x_{ij}$$

where

x_{ji} = the value of the tie from actor j to actor i (the value being either 0 or 1); and
n = the number of nodes in the network

Equation for normalized indegree centrality (not allowing for self-loops):

$$C'_I(i) = \frac{C_I(i)}{n-1}$$

Equation for normalized outdegree centrality (not allowing for self-loops):

$$C'_O(i)_i = \frac{C_O(i)}{n-1}$$

Where n = the total number of nodes in the network.

Analysing for degree, indegree and outdegree centrality

If you are investigating degree centrality, you need to first make sure that your data are symmetrical and binary. UCINET has a command for transforming data from valued to binary (*Transform > Dichotomize*) and another for symmetrizing your data (*Transform > Symmetrize*). Perform one command, save the resulting data as a new data file and then perform the second command on this new data file. Depending on your data, you may need to use both commands. Once your data is in the appropriate format, go to *Network > Centrality > Degree*. Input your data and click OK. The output gives you observed counts and normalized degree scores for each actor in the network.

For indegree and outdegree centrality, the procedure is quite similar. Here, you need to make sure your data are in binary form, but you want to make sure the data are asymmetric. Next, go to *Network > Centrality > Degree*. Input your data and under the option 'treat your data as symmetric?' select No. Click OK, and the output gives you observed counts and normalized scores for each actor in the network.

Eigenvector centrality

In the last section I introduced three forms of degree centrality. Degree centrality focuses on the size of a focal actor's local network, i.e. the number of alters directly tied to a focal actor. Eigenvector centrality expands on this notion of degree centrality. It is the sum of an actor's connections to other actors, weighted by their degree centrality. With eigenvector centrality, you are looking at the local network of actors *immediately adjacent* to your focal actor (Bonacich, 1987, 2007; Bonacich and Lloyd, 2001). Your attention encompasses a wider view of the network when computing this score. Thus, eigenvector centrality can be seen as a more refined version of degree centrality (Borgatti, 1995).

Let's start with an example: if you have just started a new job, you most likely want to get to know your new colleagues relatively quickly. If your job is in a large company, then there are many new colleagues to get to know. One way you could quickly get to know these new colleagues would be if you could locate someone who knows many people in the company, i.e. someone who has a lot of degree centrality. The person may have acquired these many ties to colleagues as a result of having worked there a long time, or of the nature of his or her role in the company, or maybe because he or she organizes a lot of social activities for the colleagues. In any case, by locating this person and forming a tie with this person, you stand a high chance of being introduced to many people in your new job, many more than you would have met had you tried to form ties with others one by one on your own. In addition, when you have a problem or a new idea, this new contact of yours would probably know whom you should approach for advice. Thus, through forming a tie with this one particular colleague, you have dramatically increased your access to new ties, and thus your eigenvector centrality.

This reliance on other actors' ties lies behind the concept of eigenvector centrality. In essence, you are measuring the degree centrality of an actor's alters, and if these alters have high degree centrality, then your focal actor has high eigenvector centrality.

To calculate eigenvector centrality, your network may hold valued data, but it must be undirected, i.e. symmetric. The box below shows how one calculates eigenvector centrality, which is different from using a simple formula. In essence, each actor's eigenvector score is weighted by the sum of degree centralities of the alters to whom he or she is connected (Bonacich, 1987, 2007; Bonacich and Lloyd, 2001).

Rather than a formula for eigenvector centrality, one is making use of an algorithm to search for the largest eigenvalue of an adjacency matrix.

Thus, $C_E(i)$ = the eigenvector centrality for actor i, which is the ith entry of the unit eigenvector e. Here, e refers to the largest eigenvalue of the adjacency matrix.

The value of e is the solution to the equation $Ae = \lambda e$. Here, the value of e is such that the square of its entries sum to unity. In addition, A represents an adjacency matrix, and λ represents the array of eigenvalues in the matrix. In this context, e is a positive value, and consequently, the greatest eigenvalue would be the centrality score for actor i.

Again, UCINET calculates these scores for you, and thus, it would be more helpful (initially) to see an example in action. Figure 4.4 shows a graph holding 15 nodes. By now, your understanding of degree centrality should allow you to guess which nodes are the most 'central' ones in this graph: nodes A and O have

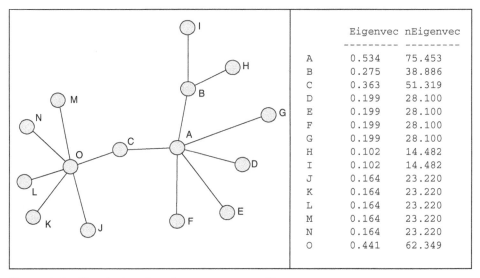

	Eigenvec	nEigenvec
A	0.534	75.453
B	0.275	38.886
C	0.363	51.319
D	0.199	28.100
E	0.199	28.100
F	0.199	28.100
G	0.199	28.100
H	0.102	14.482
I	0.102	14.482
J	0.164	23.220
K	0.164	23.220
L	0.164	23.220
M	0.164	23.220
N	0.164	23.220
O	0.441	62.349

Figure 4.4   Graph showing eigenvector centrality

the highest degree centralities (they both have a degree centrality of 6). The rest of these nodes have a degree centrality of either 1 or 2 at the most.

Eigenvector centrality, however, changes these centrality scores. Because we are taking into consideration not just how many ties a focal actor has, but also how many ties each of his or her alters have, the centrality score becomes weighted towards those actors who have alters with high degree centralities. Thus, look at node C: this node has a degree centrality of 2, but its eigenvector centrality is the third highest (normalized eigenvector score = 51.3 per cent)! This is because node C, although only having two ties in this network (i.e. a degree centrality of 2), has these two ties with the two most central nodes in the network! Thus, node C's alters have dramatically increased node C's eigenvector centrality score as a result.

These results show how eigenvector centrality is an extension of degree centrality. As such, there are times when eigenvector centrality will yield the same results as degree centrality (Bonacich, 2007). For example, if each actor in a network has the exact same degree centrality, they will also have the same exact eigenvector centrality. Eigenvector is based on the notion of differences in degree centrality among actors. If all actors have the same degree, then eigenvector centrality will not be able to capitalize on any differences. Eigenvector is sensitive to instances where an actor with low degree centrality can be connected to someone with high degree centrality, or vice versa. In such instances, it is the degree of one's contacts that influence one's centrality. Thus, when differences in degree are found in a network, an analyst would do well to also check for eigenvector.

Analysing for eigenvector centrality

First, be sure that your data are symmetric. UCINET has a command for symmetrizing your data (*Transform > Symmetrize*). Once your data is in the appropriate format, go to *Network > Centrality >Eigenvector*. Input your data and click OK. The output gives you observed counts and normalized scores for each actor in the network.

Betweenness centrality

Degree, indegree and outdegree centrality might be the most intuitive forms of centrality and thus the easiest to both calculate and understand. However, they are not considered the most powerful measures of centrality. For one thing, these measures of centrality do not consider the rest of the network; they only look at the immediate ties of each actor. Thus, if centrality is about an actor's position within a network, not just his or her own ego network, these measures of centrality ignore some important pieces of information, namely, the other actors and ties in the network!

Betweenness centrality, like eigenvector centrality, takes into consideration the rest of the network when computing a score for an individual actor. In addition, however, betweenness captures a slightly different dimension of the notion of centrality: as many of you have probably experienced, sometimes it is not so important *how many people* you know in a network, but rather where you are *placed* within that network. With eigenvector centrality, the idea of 'placement' had to do with whether you were connected to someone who was well-connected. With betweenness, the thinking is if you are placed *between* two disconnected actors, then this placement of betweenness affords you certain advantages. Actor C, in Figure 4.5 is an example of a *between* actor. Remove actor C, and the network falls apart.

In Chapter 1, we already discussed such an actor, calling this actor a 'cut-point'. This term reflects the notion of the graph being cut in two if this point (i.e. node) were removed. Within the discussion of centrality, however, we focus on more than just the role of being a cut-point. We also look at the strategic and other advantages such an actor gains from occupying this position.

Betweenness centrality, as the name implies, thus looks at how often an actor rests *between* two other actors. More specifically, betweenness centrality calculates how many times an actor sits on the *geodesic* (i.e. the shortest path) linking two other actors together. This measure is considered one of the more 'demanding' measures of centrality because it requires that you not only look at more information in the network (e.g. the length of geodesics linking pairs of actors together), it also requires that an actor be an intermediary if you are to give this actor any points for being a central actor.

In communication networks, betweenness centrality measures how much potential control an actor has over the flow of information. If an actor rests between many other actors in the network, then this actor can greatly influence the network by choosing to withhold or distort information she or he receives.

In the friendship graph shown in Figure 4.6, actor E sits between actor F and the rest of the network. In particular, E connects F to actors A and D,

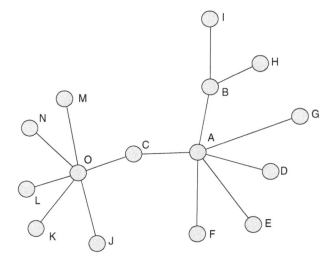

Figure 4.5   Betweenness graph

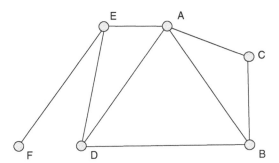

Figure 4.6 Friendship graph

and vice versa. Node E thus performs an important role in connecting two segments of the network, and allowing information to flow from node F to the rest of the network and vice versa. Without node E, the network would fragment into two different components. In addition, node E also is seen as gaining power by holding this between position: node E can control or influence the flow of information from node F to nodes A and D, and vice versa. Node E, in this instance, is seen as a broker between node F and nodes A and D. Conversely, actor E might also encounter a great deal of stress, as this actor must also respond to the needs of these different segments of the network.

The formula for betweenness centrality:

$$C_B(k) = \Sigma \partial_{ikj} / \partial_{ij}, i \neq j \neq k$$

∂_{ikj} = the number of geodesics linking actors i and j that pass through node k;

∂_{ij} = the number of geodesics linking actors i and j;

Thus, the betweenness centrality calculated by the above formula is for actor k.

Normalized betweenness centrality (not allowing for self-loops):

$$C'_B = C_B(k) / [(n-1)(n-2)/2]$$

Betweenness centrality can be calculated on directed or undirected data, but the data should be binary, i.e. the ties are recorded as either 1s or 0s. Thus, if you have a network holding valued data, it is recommended that you first convert these data to binary format.

Once you have ensured that you have binary network data, you compute betweenness centrality by counting the number of times actor i rests on a geodesic for actors j and k.

With the current example, actor E's betweenness score is '4', because actor E sits on the geodesic from actor F to four other actors in the network. The other betweenness scores for the other actors are shown below:

E   4.0
A   3.5
D   1.0
B   0.5
C   0.0
F   0.0

In looking at the rest of the betweenness scores for actors in Figure 4.6, you will notice that actors A and B each have a ½ value for betweenness. In this case, both A and B sit on two different geodesics linking D and C. That is, D or C could reach one another either through A or B, and the path length would be the same. Thus, the score of '1' for sitting 'between' two nodes must be divided equally between nodes A and B. This proportionality of each actor's betweenness centrality score, determined by whether or not the focal actor rests on the only geodesic linking two others together, is reflected in the denomination of the formula found in the above figure.

Because nodes must sometimes receive partial scores for betweenness, these partial scores can be seen as probabilities for control. In the above example, actors A and B each have a 50–50 probability of being able to control the flow of information from D to C.

Normalized betweenness centrality

Again, if you wish to compare betweenness centrality scores of actors from one network to those actors' scores in another network, you need to compute the normalized betweenness centrality score. As with degree centrality, you would normalize betweenness centrality by making the betweenness centrality score a proportion. With the above example, the normalized betweenness scores are the following:

E   40 per cent
A   35 per cent
D   10 per cent
B   5 per cent
C   0 per cent
F   0 per cent

Research has shown that betweenness centrality best captures the most important actors in the network, i.e. the leaders or the most influential network members. This may be because betweenness centrality results in a higher amount of variance among actors, as compared to other measures of centrality. By this I mean that the differences (i.e. the variances) in betweenness scores among a group of actors in a network are greater than those generated by other measures centrality (Freeman, 1979; Wasserman and Faust, 1994). Thus, who is more important to the network stands out much more clearly in using betweenness centrality than other forms of centrality.

Analysing for betweenness centrality

You need to first make sure that your data are binary. UCINET has a command for transforming data from valued to binary (*Transform > Dichotomize*). Once your data is in the appropriate format, go to *Network > Centrality > Betweenness*. Input your data and click OK. The output gives you observed counts and normalized scores for each actor in the network.

Closeness centrality

Like betweenness and eigenvector, closeness centrality is considered a more global measure of centrality, as compared with degree, indegree or outdegree. That is, closeness centrality takes into consideration the entire network of ties when calculating the centrality of an individual actor. Closeness centrality differs from the other forms of centrality in some important ways: for example, whereas degree centrality emphasized *activity*, and betweenness centrality emphasized *potential control* over information flow, closeness centrality emphasizes an actor's *independence*. The logic of closeness centrality can be summarized as follows: if an actor is not central, she generally needs to rely on others to relay messages through the network (Bavelas, 1950; Freeman, 1979). Thus, an actor who is close to many other actors is a very independent actor. He or she can quickly reach others without having to rely much on intermediaries. An actor with high closeness centrality would also be seen as someone who could more easily mobilize a network, as she or he can more easily reach out to everyone in the network.

But closeness centrality is not just used as a measure for independence within a communication network: researchers have linked closeness centrality with an actor's ability to easily access information in the network (Leavitt, 1951), with power (Coleman, 1973) and with influence (Friedkin, 1991).

Closeness is determined by the short path lengths linking actors together: it measures centrality as the *distance* between actors, where actors who have the *shortest distance* to other actors are seen as having the most closeness centrality.

Formula for closeness centrality, for actor i:

$C_C(i) = \sum\limits_{j=1}^{n} d_{ij}$ where d_{ij} = the distance connecting actor i to actor j.

Please note, the above calculation is in essence the *farness* score.

Normalized closeness centrality (not allowing for self-loops):

$C'_C(i) = [C_C(i)]^{-1}(n-1)$

For example, in Figure 4.6, node A is relatively close to all the other nodes in the network and node F is relatively far away. This is because node A has a path length of 1 to most of the other nodes, whereas F has longer geodesics of 2 or 3 to the other nodes. Thus, node A is seen as the node who would most likely hear about new information early on. He or she would also be seen as someone who could quickly diffuse information through the network.

To calculate closeness, you start by ensuring that your data matrix holds binary data. In addition, you need to remove any isolates from your network, as closeness centrality can only be calculated on fully connected networks. Finally, it is not only that the network needs to be fully connected, but also strongly connected. By this I mean that, in a directed network, all the actors can reach one another by virtue of some path, paying attention to the direction of the arcs. A weakly connected graph, in contrast, would be one where all actors are connected by some path, ignoring the direction of the arcs.

If you were to leave isolates in a graph, these isolates would hold an infinite distance from all other actors in the network, as there would be no ties upon which to calculate closeness centrality. In a similar way, if you were to have a weakly connected digraph, then some actor i may never reach an actor j.

Next, you begin calculating closeness centrality by calculating its *opposite*, meaning each actor's farness score. This involves calculating the distance between actor i and actor j, which translates as actor i's *farness score.*

In UCINET, you will notice that the raw closeness scores are conveyed as farness scores. This has been done to remind the analyst that, unlike the other centrality scores computed by UCINET, closeness centrality is a reversed score, i.e. higher scores are less close and therefore low scores are more central. Normalized closeness scores are also given in the UCINET output, for example, for actor F, the farness score is 11, and the normalized closeness centrality score is 45.45 per cent. Thus, node F is only 45.45 per cent as close to the other nodes as he or she could be. Compare this with the normalized closeness score of node A, which is 83.33 per cent. Below you will see the other farness and normalized closeness scores for each actor found in the above graph.

	1	2
	Farness	nCloseness
	------------	------------
A	6.000	83.333
E	7.000	71.429
D	7.000	71.429
B	8.000	62.500
C	9.000	55.556
F	11.000	45.455

Taken together, closeness centrality can be seen as a measure for an actor's independence, as well as a means for uncovering how a network can quickly and efficiently relay messages through the group.

Analysing for closeness centrality

You need to first make sure that your data are binary. In addition, your data can not contain any isolates. UCINET has a command for transforming data from valued to binary (*Transform > Dichotomize*). Once your data is in the appropriate format, go to *Network > Centrality > Closeness*. Input your data and click OK. The output gives you observed counts and normalized scores for each actor in the network.

Beta-centrality: A look at the relationship between centrality and power

Up until now, we have looked at the most common measures of centrality in social network analysis. These measures emphasize different aspects of the notion of centrality: degree focuses on an ego's immediate contacts; eigenvector on the degree centrality of one's alters; betweenness on the focal actor resting on geodesics; and closeness on the path lengths connecting actors together. Although each measure offers a slightly different interpretation on what it means to be central, all the measures are designed to highlight which actors are important to the network and/or important because of their network position.

Phillip Bonacich (Bonacich, 1987) developed a measure of centrality, called 'beta-centrality', that simultaneously critiques these other measures as well as provides an alternative. Bonacich realized that previous research into the different centrality measures offered up conflicting evidence: in some cases, the centrality scores would reveal the most important, or powerful, actor in a network, but in other situations, the most powerful actors would be the semi-peripheral ones, not the central ones (Cook et al., 1983). Furthermore, these differences had to do largely with the nature of the relational context: if the social network

were composed of 'positive' relations such as communication, then the traditional centrality measures would, for the most part, consistently coincide with
the most powerful actor in the network. If the social network were composed of
'negative' relations, then centrality measures would often fail.

In addition, Bonacich recognized that centrality measures differed in the extent
to which they considered the entire network structure in calculating a focal
actor's centrality score. Did an actor derive more power from his or her immediate contacts, or did an actor derive power from the wider network structure?
This concern for wider network structure was already an interest of Bonacich:
as you will recall, Bonacich was the one who developed the eigenvector form of
centrality discussed earlier (Bonacich, 1972).

Equation for beta-centrality (not allowing for self-loops):

$$C_\beta(i) = \sum_{j=1}^{n} A_{i,j}(\alpha + \beta C_\beta(j)); \text{ where}$$

α = a scaling parameter, which is set to normalize the score.

β = a value selected by the analyst to reflect the amount of dependence
of actor i's centrality on the centralities of the alters to whom actor i
is directly tied. This must be smaller than the reciprocal of the largest
eigenvalue.

$A_{i,j}$ = the adjacency matrix (which can be binary or valued);

x_j = the centrality of j, i.e. the centrality of actor i's partners.

To address these issues regarding the relationship between centrality and
power, Bonacich developed what he called 'beta centrality', which makes use
of a parameter (called 'beta' or β) that can be controlled by the analyst. The
parameter β reflects the extent to which power is linked to the centrality of others. Thus, if an analyst assigns small values of β to the equation, the analysis
is weighted towards the local structure surrounding ego. Larger values weight
the equation towards the wider network structure. In addition, whether β is
assigned a positive or negative value holds some importance; a positive value
indicates that it is good for the focal actor to be connected to highly central
people. This is very similar to the idea of eigenvector centrality discussed earlier
(and indeed, Bonacich makes it clear he sees beta-centrality as an extension to
eigenvector!). However, a negative β implies that it is to your disadvantage to
be connected with others who are themselves well-connected. If β is assigned
positive value, then the network under question is considered a 'positive'

network. If β is negative, then the network is considered 'negative' (see text box for definitions of positive and negative relations).

Positive and negative relations in social network analysis

Centrality measures are partially dependent on whether relations are negative or positive. Negative relations are ones where power rests on a zero-sum basis. That is, one actor's gain results in another actor's loss. In addition, negative relations are ones where actors gain power when they connect to others who have a lower status than themselves; or others who are not very well connected. Examples of negative relations include exchange networks or networks based on bargaining. Here, it is to one's advantage to be well-connected in an environment where people tend to not know one another, i.e. it is to your advantage to be in the position of a 'hub' or 'star'.

Positive relations are not based on these zero-sum exchanges: an actor can be powerful through gaining contacts with others without inflicting a loss on another actor. In addition, positive relations are ones where actors receive power when connected to others who have higher status than themselves. Examples of positive relations include communication networks or influence networks.

Negative and positive relations are an important component of social exchange theory. You can read more about this theory and the descriptions of positive and negative relations in the following sources: Bonacich (1987); Cook et al. (1983); Cook and Whitmeyer, (1992); Klein Ikkink and van Tilburg (1999); Willer (1992).

To compute beta-centrality, you start with either a valued or binary network of symmetrical ties. Next, you determine a value for β: lower values give weight to the local structure of ego and higher values give weight to the centrality of others to whom ego is connected. UCINET will automatically select the value of a for you: this parameter, used to normalize the equation, is selected so that the sum of squares of the node centralities is the size of the network.

Let's consider the following example: if you were studying a communication network, and you knew that communication tended to travel long distances through this network, then in analysing for beta-centrality, you would assign a high positive value to β. In contrast, if you were studying a network based on exchanges and bargaining, where actors are influenced by their immediate neighbours, you would assign a low negative value to β.

Let's consider another example. Figure 4.7 represents an exchange network studied by Cook and colleagues (1983). It is thus a negative relation. In their study, Cook et al. found that although actor A was the most central actor in the network, the more powerful actors were actors C, B and D. In this study, power was measured by how many profits an actor gained through bargaining with his/her immediate neighbours. Thus, centrality in this study failed to reflect power. Bonacich (Bonacich, 1987) used this same network and analysed for centrality using his beta-centrality measure. The table to the right of the graph show a summary of Bonacich's (Bonacich, 1987) findings. Basically, when β was given a negative value, the actors B, C and D held high centrality scores. Their centrality, then, reflected their power in this particular context.

Thus, Bonacich's measure offers some flexibility in analysing centrality, especially when an analyst is looking at centrality as an indicator of power. The measure lets you choose if you want to assess the centrality of an actor based on the actor's direct ties to others, or assess centrality based on the wider network structure. In addition, beta-centrality allows you to choose whether it is to one's advantage to be connected to high-status or low-status individuals (or well-connected or poorly connected others).

Analysing for Bonacich's power centrality

You may use valued, directed date for Beta centrality. Once your data is in the appropriate format, go to *Network > Centrality > alpha centrality (Bonacich).*

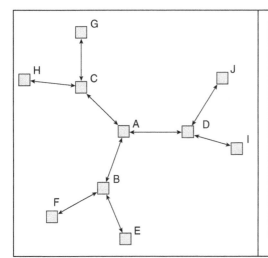

B values	Actor A	Actors B, C and D
−0.5	.....	....
−0.4	−1.00	1.67
−0.3	0.36	1.81
−0.2	1.00	1.67
−0.1	1.30	1.55
0	1.46	1.46
0.1	1.57	1.40
0.2	1.63	1.36
0.3	1.68	1.33
0.4	1.72	1.30
0.5	....	......

Figure 4.7   Power centrality digraph and values

Input your data and click OK. The output gives you observed counts and normalized scores for each actor in the network.

SOME CONCLUDING MARKS COMPARING THE DIFFERENT MEASURES

To compare the different centralities, I have compiled for you a brief list. This list summarizes many of the points made earlier in this chapter, as well as some of the points made by others, notably Freeman (1979), Wasserman and Faust (1994), Mizurchi and Potts (1998) and Valente et al., 2008:

- Eigenvector and Beta-centrality consider the degree centrality of other actors in the network. Degree, betweenness and closeness do not.

- Degree centrality does not consider the direction of ties. Indegree and Outdegree centrality do take into consideration the direction of a tie. Closeness, eigenvector and betweenness centrality can also be calculated on directional data.

- Betweenness centrality draws attention to who is critical for a network's information flow, i.e. who connects different segments of the network together and is an important intermediary or broker. The distribution of betweenness centrality scores in a network is also considered better at capturing the variation in actors' centralities (Wasserman and Faust, 1994). Thus, the contrast between central and non-central actors are more highly contrasted when one makes use of betweenness.

- In contrast to betweenness, degree-based measures are considered less capable for unveiling stark differences/variations in centrality scores among actors.

- Degree centrality measures an individual's *involvement* in the network. Indegree centrality reveals '*popular*' actors and outdegree centrality focuses on the *expansion* of a focal actor's network.

- Eigenvector is sensitive to instances where an actor with low degree centrality can be connected to someone with high degree centrality, and gain an advantage from that connection.

The relationship between centrality and power depends not only on whether the relation is positive or negative, but also on the structure of the network: if peripheral actors are embedded in their own cliques, they can shift power away from the central actor. In addition, the number of subgroups can influence centrality and power relationships: if a central actor plays the role of tie-breaker among an even number of subgroups, this increases the central actor's power.

RESEARCH EXAMPLES AND EXTENSIONS

The two research summaries below provide you with an example of centrality measures being applied to the context of students, and the centrality measure being applied to a different kind of network structure, i.e. two-mode networks.

The social networks of academic performance in a student context of poverty in Mexico (Ramirez Ortiz, 2004)

This study looked at how students' social networks influenced the marks they received. In particular, the research team predicted that centrality scores would be related to students' academic performance. The team surveyed, between November 1999 and January 2000, a total of 523 male and female, second-and third-year students at a public junior high school in Zapopan, Jalisco, Mexico. Each student sampled was asked the following questions:

'Who do you communicate with to improve your academic performance?' (a list of peers with names, surnames and grades)
'How often do you communicate with them?' (with numbered answer options: 'often', 'sometimes', and 'a little').
'What do you think about your grade average?' (with answer options of: 'good', 'fair', or 'bad').

Academic performance was defined as the grade average obtained by students during the fourth two-month period of the school year (that went from September 1999 through to May 2000). In general, the researchers found that greater communication among students coincided with high academic performance. With regards to centrality, the researchers found that eigenvector and closeness centrality were the main predictors of high academic performance. The high closeness score suggested that those students who were well-integrated within the student social network were ones able to easily communicate with others how to improve academic performance. In addition, the eigenvector centrality scores implied that a central actor could communicate how to improve academic performance to other members with central positions who then spread the word to all the network members.

Centrality in two-mode networks

Here, I shall briefly describe two articles in *Social Networks* that pay special attention to how centrality can be computed on two-mode networks, which are also referred to as bipartite networks or affiliation networks. The first article, by Katherine Faust (Faust, 1997), looks at the mathematical and conceptual considerations for measuring centrality on two-mode networks. In particular, Faust (1997) re-examines each of the centrality formulas proposed by Freeman (1979), taking into account the duality inherent in two-mode networks, and she proposes new equations that this duality takes into consideration. Some points she highlights include the following:

- There should be centrality scores for both actors and events, and there should be a clearly specified relationship between these two quantities (1997: 162).

- The centrality of an actor should depend on the collection of events to which it belongs, and similarly, the centrality of an event should depend on the centrality of its members (1997: 162).

- Actors create links between events and events create links between actors. Thus, some form of betweenness centrality ought to be appropriate for studying affiliation networks (1997: 163).

- In affiliation networks, actors and events are typically structured in terms of subsets. For example, less central actors participate in events only when more central actors are also present. Similarly, events to which less central actors belong are a subset of the events attended by more central actors. Thus, centrality measures should be able to extend to subsets of actors and events (1997: 165).

In the same issue of *Social Networks*, Borgatti and Everett (1997) discuss, in more general terms, a number of considerations in analysing two-mode networks, and like Faust (1997), they highlight some important considerations in thinking about centrality in the context of two-mode networks. The considerations they raise are on how to compute raw and normalized scores for the different centrality measures, and as it is these sorts of computations that are used in UCINET, I shall briefly discuss them here, and I shall refer to two-mode data as actor-by-event networks, for purposes of illustration.

For degree centrality, in the context of two-mode data consisting of actors and events, the degree of a given actor would be the number of events that actor attended. Normalized degree centrality would need a special adjustment to Freeman's (1979) normalization equation, whereby each raw score would need to be divided by the size of the opposite set of nodes. For example, the normalized degree of an actor would entail dividing that score by the total number of events found in the network.

For closeness centrality, the shortest possible path linking an actor to another actor would automatically entail at least one intermediary event. That is, the path linking actors together would take the form of a-e-a-e and so forth, where an actor is represented as a and events are represented as e. Because an actor can only be a distance of 1 to an event, and distance of 2 from another actor, this implies another adjustment to the normalization formula provided by Freeman (1979). Thus, rather than taking the total distance score and dividing the quantity by n − 1 (Freeman's suggestion), one would need to divide the distance score by $n_i + 2n_o − 2$, where n_i = the size of the node set of the focal actor and n_o = the size of the other node set (e.g. events). For example, if the score being normalized is an actor's score (as opposed to an event's), then n_i would refer to the size of the actor-set of nodes and n_o to the size of the events set of nodes.

For betweenness centrality, the shortest path on which a node rests can originate and end with a node from either set, e.g. the betweenness of an actor could be based on looking at the path from actor to actor, actor to event (or vice versa) or event to event. Again, in computing the normalization score, consideration needs to be given to both nodal sets in computing a theoretical maximum score for the size of the network.

Finally, for eigenvector centrality, the centrality of an actor would rest on the centralities of the events that actor attended; for an event's centrality, the centrality score would depend on the sum of the centralities of the actors attending that event. Once again, normalized scores would need to consider the size of both node sets.

You can make use of these centrality measures for two-mode networks by simply going to *Network > Centrality > 2-mode Centrality*. There, the various centrality measures discussed above are calculated for your two-mode network data.

CONCLUSIONS AND SUMMARY

This chapter looked at actor-level concepts for complete networks, and at the end of the chapter, for complete bipartite or two-mode networks. In particular, we looked at a number of centrality measures, i.e. degree, betweenness, eigenvector and beta-centrality. I also introduced you to normalized centrality measures. In the next chapter, I shall continue discussing actor-level concepts and measures for ego networks. These will include ego network size and density, as well as some social networks concepts such as homophily, brokerage and structural holes.

REFERENCES

Bavelas, A. (1950) 'Communication patterns in task-oriented groups', *Journal of Accoustical Society of America,* 57: 271–82.

Bonacich, P. (1972) 'Factoring and weighting approaches to clique identification', *Journal of Mathematical Sociology,* 2: 113–20.

Bonacich, P. (1987) 'Power and centrality: A family of measures', *The American Journal of Sociology,* 92: 1170–82.

Bonacich, P. (2007) 'Some unique properties of eigenvector centrality', *Social Networks,* 29: 555–64.

Bonacich, P. and Lloyd, P. (2001) 'Eigenvector-like measures of centrality for asymmetric relations', *Social Networks,* 23: 191–201.

Borgatti, S. P. (1995) 'Centrality and AIDS', *Connections,* 18: 112–15.

Borgatti, S. P. and Everett, M. G. (1997) 'Network analysis of 2-mode data', *Social Networks,* 19: 243–69.

Coleman, J. S. (1973) *The Mathematics of Collective Action.* Chicago: Aldine.

Cook, K. S. and Whitmeyer, J. M. (1992) 'Two approaches to social structure: Exchange theory and network analysis', *Annual Review of Sociology,* 18: 109–27.

Cook, K. S., Emerson, R. M., Gilmore, M. R. and Yamagishi, T. (1983) 'The distribution of power in exchange networks: Theory and experimental results', *American Journal of Sociology,* 89: 275–305.

Faust, K. (1997) 'Centrality in affiliation networks', *Social Networks,* 19: 157–91.

Freeman, L. C. (1979) 'Centrality in social networks', *Social Networks,* 1: 215–39.

Friedkin, N. E. (1991) 'Theoretical foundations for centrality measures', *American Journal of Sociology,* 96: 1478–504.

Klein Ikkink, K. and Van Tilburg, T. (1999) 'Broken ties: Reciprocity and other factors affecting the termination of older adults' relationships', *Social Networks,* 21: 131–46.

Leavitt, H. (1951) 'Some effects of certain communication patterns on group performance', *Journal of Abnormal and Social Psychology,* 46: 38–50.

Mizruchi, M. S. and Potts, B. B. (1998) 'Centrality and power revisited: Actor success in group decision making', *Social Networks,* 20: 353–87.

Ramírez Ortiz, M. G., Caballero Hoyos, J. R. and Ramírez López, M. G. (2004) 'The social networks of academic performance in a student context of poverty in Mexico', *Social Networks,* 26: 175–88.

Wasserman, S. and Faust, F. (1994) *Social Network Analysis: Methods and Applications.* Cambridge: Cambridge University Press.

Willer, D. (1992) 'Predicting power in exchange networks: A brief history and introduction to the issues', *Social Networks,* 14: 187–211.

5

ACTOR LEVEL IN EGO NETWORKS

The previous section looked at the centrality of individual actors in complete networks. Complete networks are ones where all actors in the network are known beforehand and where the ties linking these actors together are then measured. For example, an organization and its employees could be studied as a complete network, where the researcher gathers data on the various relational ties linking these employees together. To gather these data, we would ask people to look at a list of names (what we call a roster) and ask: 'with whom on this list are you friends with?' or similarly, 'whom in this organization do you turn to for advice?' – in both cases, the list of names we provide to respondents defines the boundary of the network we are interested in studying.

However, for many social settings, it is difficult to know beforehand all the actors in a given social network (Wellman and Berkowitz, 1988). Finding a network boundary can, in itself, be a difficult task (see Chapter 3), and if the researcher is not studying a setting where a boundary can arguably be drawn in a relatively straightforward manner, for example, by studying a school, an organization or club, it will be difficult for a researcher to outline a network boundary within a reasonable amount of time (again, see Chapter 3 for suggestions and guidelines for dealing with problems in network boundaries).

Thus an alternative approach to studying social networks is to study the personal, immediate networks surrounding an ego, and these are often referred to as *ego networks*. Ego networks refer to networks that are defined as they are perceived and reported by respondents (Wellman, 1983). With ego networks, each respondent is seen as the centre of his or her own network. This respondent is referred to as an 'ego' and its immediate contacts as 'alters'. In studying ego networks, we are interested in looking at how egos make use of or are influenced by their alters.

Here is some terminology to get us started:

- An ego is an individual actor or node. An ego is at the centre of an ego network.

- An ego's network is composed of itself, the ego, and its immediate contacts, referred to as alters. Ties are measured between ego and alters, as well as between the alters.

- An ego and its alters, and the ties connecting these together, make up an ego-centric network, also referred to as personal network or simply ego network.

The properties of ego networks that are typically studied include the *size* of an ego-network, i.e. how many alters an ego is tied to; the *density* of the network, i.e. the extent to which ego's alters are also tied to one another; and the *strength of ties* connecting ego to alters. These properties will be covered in detail in this chapter.

Three popular research areas involving the analysis of ego networks include *structural holes* of an ego, the *broker* roles of an ego, and the *homophilous* ties connecting egos and alters together. These three research areas will be discussed in detail in this chapter.

HOW TO GATHER EGO NETWORK DATA

Many of these issues were discussed in Chapter 3; however, I feel it useful within the context of the discussion of ego networks to revisit some of these (and other) issues. In an ego network study, a set of respondents are sampled (usually through either random sampling techniques or snowball sampling techniques) and are asked a name-generator question or questions. A name-generator question is one designed specifically for the purpose of generating a list of names according to a particular social relation. Examples of name-generator questions include the following:

- Whom do you turn to for advice regarding routine work matters?

- Whom do you turn to for advice regarding issues dealing with promotion?

- Whom would you turn towards in the event of a personal crisis?

- Whom would you turn towards if you needed to borrow a large sum of money?

- Whom do you normally socialize with on weekends?

As you can imagine, the answers to the above questions could easily result in a number of different names. The different names offered for each question result in different ego networks for the respondent, where each ego network represents a particular social relation linking the respondent (ego) to a list of others (ego's alters).

For example, a respondent might turn to one person for advice on work matters, but would not typically socialize with that same person on weekends. In general, it is a good idea to have more than one name-generator question when you interview respondents about their ego networks, as doing so will reveal a more complete view of the respondents' ego network. However, determining which name-generator questions to use should be guided by your research questions and the literature search you conduct prior to initiating your study.

Although ego networks focus on the ties linking ego to alters, you can also gather data on how an alter links to another alter. To gain information on how the alters are tied to one another, you would ask a follow-up question to your name-generator question. This follow-up question would ask the respondent to comment on his/her perception of how alters are linked to one another. An example of such a follow-up question is the following: 'To the best of your knowledge, does [alter 1] ask [alter 2] for advice on work matters?' This follow-up question could then be repeated for each alter the respondent had listed for the original name-generator question.

Once you have gathered data on all your egos and egos' alters, you are ready to analyse these data for a variety of ego-network properties. Typical ego-network properties include size and density.

EGO NETWORK SIZE AND DENSITY

The below figure shows the ego network graph for Sophia, based on the name-generator question, 'Whom do you turn to for advice on work matters?' Sophia lists two names, Anna and George, and based on a follow-up question, Sophia states that Anna and George do not ask advice from each other. Thus, Sophia is the ego, Anna and George are her alters, and Anna and George are not tied to one another. Figure 5.1 shows the graph for Sophia's ego network.

Looking at Figure 5.1, you can deduce a lot of information about Sophia's ego network. Because she has 2 alters, the network size of her ego network is 2.

The density score is also easily deduced from this graph. The density of an ego network refers to the percentage of all possible ties in the ego network that

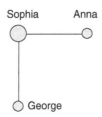

Figure 5.1 Advice graph on work matters

are actually present, excluding the ego. It is essentially the same as the network density score explained in Chapter 7, but on the ego network level. To compute Sophia's network density score, you would first count the number of ties present in the network that do not involve Sophia (in this case 0) and divide this number by the number of pairs of alters in Sophia's network. In this example, there is one pair: Anna and George. Next, you would divide the number of ties (0), by the number of pairs (1). In this example, the resulting value is 0.

Ego density for an ego network (with ego as actor i) is calculated as follows (not allowing for self-loops):

$$d_i = \frac{L}{n(n-1)/2};$$

where n refers to the number of alters ego is connected to and L refers to the number of lines between the alters.

In calculating ego density, you need to calculate the number of maximum possible ties in the ego network. This is done by counting how many alters an ego is connected to; each alter can potentially be connected to all other alters, except oneself, and so an undirected graph with n nodes could contain a maximum number of $n(n-1)/2$ lines.

For digraphs, the formula is slightly altered, as follows: $d_i = \frac{L}{n(n-1)}$

Let's look at a second example, to compare our findings with the previous one. Figure 5.2 shows an ego network graph for Jim, based on the question, 'With whom do you normally socialize on weekends?' Using a follow-up question on Jim's knowledge of his alters' ties to one another, data on Jim's alters were also gathered.

Here, you can see that Jim's ego network size is 3, as there are 3 alters in his network. The number of ties not involving Jim is 1, and the total number of potential pairs of alters in this ego network is 3. These include: i) Al and Liam, ii) Frank and Liam, iii) Al and Frank.

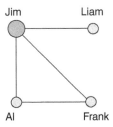

Figure 5.2   Socialize on weekends graph

Thus, to compute the density score for Jim, you divide the number of ties (1), by the number of potential pairs (3), and you get 0.33. So 33 per cent of the potential ties in this ego network are actually present. (Please note that I have calculated ego network density on graphs, i.e. undirected data. You could also adjust the formula to consider directional data, as shown in the box above.)

As mentioned in Chapter 2, Elizabeth Bott's (1955, 1957) research on conjugal roles is considered a classic example of an ego network study, and her main finding in that study was the role of density in relation to conjugal roles. Her findings showed that couples who had more dense personal networks tended to divide household work and socializing according to more traditional gender roles. Another famous early study on personal networks was that of Claude Fischer (1982), whose work on Californian's personal networks showed the importance of geographical proximity in forming and maintaining friendship ties. In a latter study, Fischer and Shavit (1995) compared the data from Fischer's earlier study to data gathered in Haifa, Israel. This comparison showed that the personal networks in Israel were denser than the Americans', which the authors concluded as being partially a result of the cultural frameworks of the two respective countries, where Israelis tend towards a group orientation and Americans toward individualism.

Analysing size and density

These basic properties of ego networks can be easily assessed in UCINET. Simply go to *Networks > Ego networks > Egonet basic measures*. The output gives you, among other things, the size and density of each ego network in your dataset. For fuller explanation of the UCINET output, please refer to the UCINET helpfile.

Analysing these basic properties of ego networks can answer a number of potential research questions relating to how social networks might affect individuals' behaviour, attitudes, performance or beliefs. For example, are individuals with larger advice networks more likely to get higher salaries in the workplace? Or would density play a role here, meaning that individuals with larger denser networks are paid less than individuals with larger, less dense networks? Asking such questions implies, first of all, that you also have data on individuals' salaries, but these questions also point towards an important research area in social network analysis involving ego networks, that of structural holes.

STRUCTURAL HOLES

Ron Burt developed the notion of a structural hole to discuss how certain network structures can give individuals a strategic advantage over others. Burt refers to structural holes as 'the empty spaces in social structure' (2005: 16).

These empty spaces result from actors not having a tie between them. Figure 5.3 helps to illustrate this idea.

The graphs in Figure 5.3 represent the advice-on-work-matters network for Sophia and Jim, respectively. Both networks are the same size (four), yet they differ in terms of their density: none of the pairs of alters in Sophia's network share a tie (graph a), whereas all pairs share a tie in Jim's network (graph b). Sophia bridges four structural holes in her ego network, whereas Jim does not bridge any structural holes.

Burt would argue that Sophia's network holds a greater diversity of information than Jim's network. This conclusion is based on the idea that information becomes redundant when many of the same actors have ties with one another. For example, the fact that Mary, Lois, Alex and Rose all turn to one another for advice suggests that much of the same information and advice circulates among these four individuals. The fact that Alex goes to each of them suggests that Alex is probably hearing the same sort of advice again, and again. In contrast, none of Sophia's contacts turn to one another for advice; because they are not in contact with each other, the chances are more likely that they each offer Sophia a different view or piece of advice from one another.

Thus Sophia, in connecting to individuals who are unconnected themselves, is connecting to non-redundant pieces of information. None of Sophia's alters are in contact with each other, and so the likelihood that they know the same information is much less. For Jim, the situation is the exact opposite: because all of his alters are connected to each other, the likelihood is high that these alters recycle the same pieces of information over and over again. Thus, Jim is probably not receiving as much advice, or as diverse advice, on work matters as Sophia. This difference in diversity of sources of advice would enable Sophia, on the whole, to make better decisions about her work than Jim, simply because she is exposed to a richer pool of information.

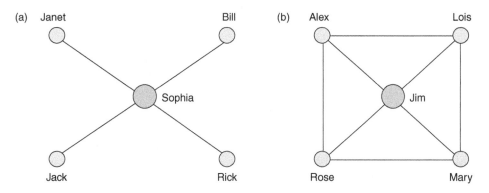

Figure 5.3   Advice on work graph

This idea of structural holes, and the benefits of structural holes, is one you may have come across in other sociological research. For example, Simmel (1922) and Merton (1957) discuss *teritus gaudens*, the idea that someone who brokers between others benefits from that broker role. In addition, the betweenness centrality measure I discussed earlier is also similar to this notion of structural holes: once again, the focus is on the actor that rests between disconnected others.

Burt, however, highlights different aspects of this simple idea. For one thing, he bases the idea of a 'broker' or 'between' actor on an ego network. In contrast, betweenness centrality is typically used on complete networks. This difference between an ego network and a complete network is significant. As you may recall, betweenness centrality counts how many times an actor rests 'between' two other actors by calculating the lengths and number of geodesics the 'between' actor rests upon. As such, a betweenness score might become high for some actors simply because a few geodesics are very long, and not because the actor is brokering between numerous other actors. Thus, having a high betweenness score does not necessarily reflect the fact that an actor is playing a broker role in a high number of instances.

Burt also specifies his idea of a broker for a business context – he links this structural position to clear outcome variables based on notions of profit, higher salaries and good ideas within an organizational setting (Burt, 1976, 1992, 2001, 2004, 2005). He therefore takes the more general idea of *teritus gaudens* and gives it more precision within a particular research context.

Analysing for structural holes

Burt measures structural holes through a complicated set of equations he developed over the course of his research career (Burt, 1976, 1992, 1997, 2001, 2005). The mathematical equation(s) Burt develops for measuring structural holes is too complicated for the level and scope of this book. Thus, I will demonstrate a few measures already introduced in this book that you may use to investigate structural holes, and at the end of this chapter, I will point you towards additional material if you wish to pursue further the mathematics behind Burt's approach to structural holes.

As mentioned earlier, the idea behind betweenness centrality is very similar to that of structural holes. The big difference is that betweenness centrality focuses on complete networks and structural holes on ego networks. Thus the calculation of betweenness centrality involves looking at the length of geodesics, and this can be misinterpreted as an indicator for having a high number of structural holes. This concern for confusing length of geodesics for structural holes is largely removed, however, if you use betweenness centrality on ego network data (Marsden, 2002). By their very nature, ego network data can not hold long geodesic lengths, and thus, a high betweenness score for an ego would be a good indicator of the extent to which an ego's network contains structural holes.

In our present example (Figure 5.3), Jim has a betweenness centrality score of 0.67. Sophia's betweenness centrality score is 6.00. Sophia clearly has the higher betweenness centrality score, and thus we can say that her ego network is characterized by more structural holes than Jim's.

In addition to betweenness centrality, you can also use the ego network density measure I presented above. The logic is simple: an ego network that is very dense, by definition, is one that can not have many structural holes. Thus, a high density score for an ego would indicate that the ego's network does not have many structural holes. For Sophia, her ego network density score is 0.00, whereas Jim's density score is 66.67. Once again, this indicates that Sophia's ego network contains more structural holes than Jim's.

Research examples on structural holes

Structural holes, as a concept and analytical technique, have gained in popularity in the research community. Following Burt's research on structural holes (Burt, 1976, 1992, 1997, 2000, 2001, 2004, 2005), research on this topic has continued, with examples ranging from (i) the role of structural holes in a company's innovation capacity (Ahuja, 2000); (ii) how structural holes help an individual attain status (Lin, 1999); (iii) the relationship between structural holes and an ego's employee performance evaluations (Mehra et al., 2001); (iv) the role of structural holes in the performance and success of individuals and work teams (Burt, 1992, 2004); and (v) how structural holes relate to the capacity for generating good ideas (Burt, 1992, 2004).

There have been some criticisms of structural holes. These include, for example, the work of Xiao and Tsui (2007), who show the cultural contingency of structural holes. Their research on China demonstrated how actors who openly bridge structural holes for particular gains is perceived in negative terms, as such behaviour is seen as going against Chinese communal values. In addition, in a recent book on social networks, Bruggeman (2008) notes that higher status individuals benefit more from bridging structural holes than lower-status ones. Bruggeman (2008) notes previous research showing how lower-status individuals rely more on dense network structures for meeting their needs. The conclusion he draws from this analysis is that brokerage seems to be a class-dependent concept.

BROKERAGE: COMBINING ACTOR ATTRIBUTE DATA WITH EGO NETWORK DATA

Structural holes focus attention on the benefits an individual actor can gain from brokering between two disconnected alters. Analysis takes place on ego network data, and the focus is on looking at the number of instances an ego

brokers between two others, and how this broker role coincides with beneficial outcomes. Gould and Fernandez (1989) extended this concept of a broker
to include more information on the broker and his or her alters. In particular, Gould and Fernandez (1989, 1994) argue that the interactions between
actors can take on different meanings when one considers the key interests (or
activities) of these actors in relation to a particular venture. These different
interests result in different classifications or groups, that is, actors holding one
sort of interest are placed in one group, and actors with a different or competing interest get placed in a different group. All groupings should be discrete
and exclusive. In other words, an actor should belong to one group only, and
the divisions between groups must be clearly made. Once actors have been
assigned to groups, however, Gould and Fernandez (1989) demonstrated, in
precise terms, how the meaning of that broker role changes. These different
broker roles are summarized here.

Within-group broker roles

The first two broker roles assume that ego is brokering between two alters who
are within the same group. The first, the *coordinator broker,* is a situation where
all three actors – A, B and C – are part of the same group. Because they are all
part of the same group, the broker is seen as a 'local' broker, or rather, a coordinator of events between two members of the broker's group. For example, a
manager within a particular department in an organization who brokers transactions between two other employees within the same department can be seen
as a coordinator (see Figure 5.4)

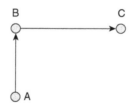

Figure 5.4   Coordinator broker

The second within-group role is referred to as the *consultant broker.* Here,
actors A and C belong to the same group, and broker B belongs to a different group. For example, a stockbroker tends to play the role of consultant,
as he/she is separate from the group of buyers and sellers. From the stockbroker's perspective, buyers and sellers are considered to be part of the same
group. Thus, the stockbroker is the consultant brokering between the two
(see Figure 5.5).

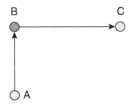

Figure 5.5   Consultant broker

Between-groups broker roles

The next three measures are based on the idea that the transactions between actor A and C occur with A and C belonging to different groups. The first between-groups broker role is referred to as a *representative broker*. In this scenario, actors A and B come from the same group. Actor B negotiates on behalf of actor A with actor C. In doing so, actor B is representing the interests of actor A. For example, political parties could send a member of their party to negotiate with someone from a different party. In this instance, the negotiator is representing his or her own party in interacting with the other party (see Figure 5.6).

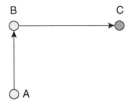

Figure 5.6   Representative broker

The next broker is referred to as the *gatekeeper broker*. Here, the transaction begins with actor A, who is not part of the group to which actors B and C belong. Actor A approaches actor B in order to reach actor C. Actor B, as the gatekeeper, can decide whether or not to grant actor A access to actor C. An example given by Gould and Fernandez (1989) for a gatekeeper is that of the Census Bureau, a government organization which gathers and processes information taken from the public and passes this information on to other government organizations (see Figure 5.7).

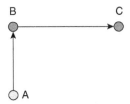

Figure 5.7   Gatekeeper broker

A *liaison broker* situation refers to an instance where all three actors are embedded in different groups. Here, broker B plays a more or less neutral role. An example could be the role of agents for film actors: these agents are not from the world of actors, nor are they part of the world of film producers. As agents not embedded in either world, they are able to negotiate agreements between these two worlds (see Figure 5.8).

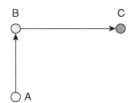

Figure 5.8   Liaison broker

These five measures thus break down the concept of a broker into five distinct roles. In addition, as you have noticed from the pictorial graphs above, the brokerage roles take into consideration the direction of ties.

Analysing for brokerage

To analyse data according to the five brokerage roles developed by Gould and Fernandez, you need directional network data as well as data regarding which group each actor belongs to. Your directional network data is inputted as a matrix, and the data for each actor's grouping is inputted as a column vector (please see UCINET helpfile for more details). The actual procedure in UCINET is *Networks > Ego networks > G&F brokerage roles*. The output shows you a simple count of the number of times an actor takes on each type of broker role, as described above.

Research examples using brokerage roles

The concept of brokerage devised by Gould and Fernandez has received empirical support within a number of different contexts, for example, (i) explaining the success and failure of actors trying to influence policies on environmental issues (Stevenson and Greenberg, 2000); (ii) understanding how actors experience role conflicts in labour negotiations (Friedman and Podolny, 1992); and (iii) understanding how technology firms can use brokerage for developing new technologies and solutions (Hargadon and Sutton, 1997).

Gould and Fernandez's brokerage measures rely on a combination of network data as well as data on actor attributes. Another SNA concept that incorporates information on both kinds of data is homophily, which is described in the next section.

HOMOPHILY: FORMING TIES BASED ON ACTOR SIMILARITY

Homophily refers to the social situation of actors preferring to have social relations with others who are similar to themselves. This is a relatively old concept in sociology, and as such, there has been a fair amount of research on this topic (Blau, 1977; McPherson et al., 2001). As such, I would like to spend a brief amount of time in discussing this concept, and how it is being measured on the actor level through ego networks.

There are two main arguments regarding how homophily takes place. The first argument states that organizational settings determine that ties will form among similar actors (Coleman et al., 1981; Feld, 1981, 1982). For example, a voluntary organization that has a particular focus will draw in members who share that focus, and this similarity among the actors will also (most likely) coincide with other similarities. Thus, the group composition produces homophily. Examples of this sort include bridge groups, churches, sports clubs and so forth.

The second argument states that actors are drawn to form ties with others who are similar to themselves (Skvoretz, 1985, 1990). This implies that the organizational setting does not matter; that individuals will seek out and find others who are similar to themselves and form ties with these others, regardless of the organizational setting. Thus, for example, friendship ties are seen as developing as a result of individuals being in a similar age group or coming from a similar educational background.

Homophily: chicken or egg?

As this discussion on homophily implies, it is difficult to measure (and thus account for) the causal direction of homophily; is it that people come together and become more similar over time or is it that they are attracted to similar others and form a social tie accordingly?

This issue of what comes first, the social tie or the similarity, is at the heart of the distinction between social influence theory (Friedkin, 1998) and social selection ideas (Lazarsfeld and Merton, 1954; McPherson and Smith-Lovin, 1987; McPherson et al., 2001; Robins et al., 2001). Social influence implies that people, through interaction, influence one another and thus become more similar over time. Social selection implies that people select their network partners based on their perceived similarity to oneself.

(Continued)

(Continued)

Many people liken homophily to social selection, and treat social influence as a separate theory. However, there is a body of literature that emphasizes this tension surrounding the causal nature of the similarity 'effect', and many note that it is difficult to disentangle the two (Ennett and Bauman, 1994; Kirke, 2004; Robins et al., 2001). Increasingly, there is a strong body of research on developing statistical models to help disentangle social selection from social influence effects (Huisman and Snijders, 2003; Snijders, 2005, 2008).

Analysing for homophily

For the present purposes, I shall discuss homophily within the context of ego networks, as the measure being used here and found in UCINET takes place on the ego level.[1] Thus, for ego networks, a simple means for calculating homophily is to calculate the portion of ties in the ego network that are homophilous. More specifically, you count all the ties where ego and alters all share the same attribute, and divide this number by all the ties found in the ego network. If the result is 1, then all the ties are homophilous ties. Any number below 1 can be seen as the portion of ties that are homophilous (see Figure 5.9).

The two graphs in Figure 5.9 show how actors are similar according to gender. Because all of Jim's ties to alters are homophilous, i.e. he is male and all his alters are male as well, he receives a score of 1. Sophia has one tie with a female alter, and one tie with a male alter. Thus, only half of Sophia's ties are homophilous, and so her score is 0.5.

In UCINET, you can measure the percentage of homophilous ties by going to *Networks –> Ego networks –> Ego network homophily*. You will see fields for inputting both the attribute data and the social network data. The help file in UCINET will give you more instruction on how to interpret the results.

---

[1] It is important to note, in the context of the previous discussion, that I am presenting the analysis for homophily under ego networks, yet understanding of the concept can also be situated under the category of dyad interactions, i.e. that two actors have a stronger likelihood of sharing a tie with one another, based on similarity. In fact, in the analysis of longitudinal data, homophily is broken down into the two competing hypotheses of social selection and social influence. Thus, for example, actors are attracted to form ties with others who are similar (social selection) or actors who share a tie with one another are more likely to become similar over time (social influence). This distinction between social influence and social selection is captured through the actor-based models developed by Snijder and his colleagues in Huisman and Snijders (2003) and Snijders (2005). See also Chapter 10 for more information on this topic.

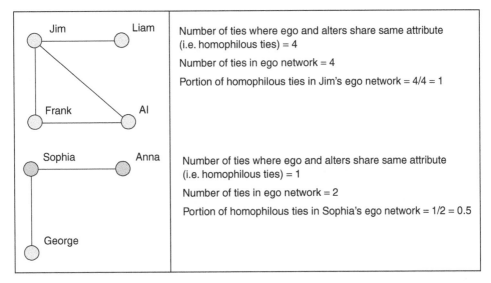

Figure 5.9   Homophily example

Research examples on homophily

Homophily has been studied within a wide range of research contexts. Support for the homophily effect has been found for attributes such as age, sex and/or race (Lazarsfeld and Merton, 1954; Moody, 2001); as well as acquired characteristics such as education and status (Coleman et al., 1981; Curtis, 1963; McPherson and Smith-Lovin, 1987); and acquired attitudes and behaviours (Billy et al., 1984; Byrne, 1971). Taken together, there has been a lot of support for the homophily argument.

CONCLUSIONS AND SUMMARY

In this chapter, we looked at actor-level concepts and measures for ego networks. These included ego network size and density, as well as some social networks concepts such as homophily, brokerage and structural holes. In looking at homophily and brokerage, we made use of data on actors' attributes to explore how social networks relate to similarity in actors' characteristics or behaviours.

REFERENCES

Ahuja, G. (2000) 'Collaboration networks, structural holes, and innovation: A longitudinal study', *Administrative Science Quarterly,* 45: 425–55.

Billy, J., Rodgers, J. L. and Udry, J. R. (1984) 'Adolescent sexual behavior and friendship choice', *Social Forces,* 62.

Blau, P. M. (1977) *Inequality and Heterogeneity: A Primitive Theory of Social Structure.* New York: Free Press.

Bott, E. (1955) 'Urban families: Conjugal roles and social networks', *Human Relations,* 8: 345–83.

Bott, E. (1957) *Family and Social Network: Roles, Norms, and External Relationships in Ordinary Urban Families.* London: Tavistock.

Bruggeman, J. (2008) *Social Networks: An Introduction.* London: Routledge.

Burt, R. (1976) 'Positions in networks', *Social Forces,* 55: 93–122.

Burt, R. S. (1992) *Structural Holes: The Social Structure of Competition.* Cambridge, MA: Harvard University Press.

Burt, R. (1997) 'The contingent value of social capital', *Administrative Science Quarterly,* 42: 339–65.

Burt, R. S. (2000) 'The network structure of social capital', in R. I. Sutton and B. M. Staw (eds), *Research in Organizational Behavior.* Greenwich, CT: JAI Press.

Burt, R. (2001) 'Structure holes versus network closure as social capital', in N. Lin, K. Cook and R. Burt (eds), *Social Capital: Theory and Research.* New York: Aldine de Gruyter.

Burt, R. S. (2004) 'Structural holes and good ideas', *American Journal of Sociology,* 110: 349–99.

Burt, R. (2005) *Brokerage and Closure: An Introduction to Social Capital.* Oxford: Oxford University Press.

Byrne, D. E. (1971) *The Attraction Paradigm.* New York: Academic Press.

Coleman, J. S., Johnstone, J. W. C. and Jonassohn, K. (1981) *The Adolescent Society: The Social Life of the Teenager and its Impact on Education.* Westport, CT: Greenwood Press.

Curtis, R. F. (1963) 'Differential association and the stratification of the urban community', *Social Forces,* 42: 68–77.

Ennett, S. T. and Bauman, K. E. (1994) 'The contribution of influence and selection to adolescent peer group homogeneity: The case of adolescent cigarette smoking', *Journal of Personality and Social Psychology,* 67: 653–63.

Feld, S. (1981) 'The focused organisation of social ties', *American Journal of Sociology,* 86: 1015–35.

Feld, S. (1982) 'Social structural determinants of similarity among associates', *American Sociological Review,* 47: 797–801.

Fischer, C. S. (1982) *To Dwell Among Friends: Personal Networks in Town and City.* Chicago: University of Chicago Press.

Fischer, C. S. and Shavit, Y. (1995) 'National differences in network density: Israel and the United States', *Social Networks,* 17: 129–45.

Friedkin, N. E. (1998) *A Structural Theory of Social Influence.* Cambridge and New York: Cambridge University Press.

Friedman, R. A. and Podolny, J. (1992) 'Differentiation of boundary spanning roles: Labor negotiations and implications for role conflict', *Administrative Science Quarterly,* 37: 28–47.

Gould, R. V. and Fernandez, R. M. (1989) 'Structures of mediation: A formal approach to brokerage in transaction networks', *Sociological Methodology,* 19: 89–126.

Gould, R. V. and Fernandez, R. M. (1994) 'A dilemma of state power: Brokerage and influence in the National Health Policy domain', *American Journal of Sociology,* 99: 1455–91.

Hargadon, A. and Sutton, R. I. (1997) 'Technology brokering and innovation in a product development firm', *Administrative Science Quarterly,* 42: 716–49.

Huisman, M. and Snijders, T. (2003) 'Statistical analysis of longitudinal network data with changing composition', *Sociological Methods and Research,* 32: 253–87.

Kirke, D. M. (2004) 'Chain reactions in adolescents' cigarette, alcohol and drug use: Similarity through peer influence or the patterning of ties in peer networks?', *Social Networks,* 26: 3–28.

Lazarsfeld, P. F. and Merton, R. K. (1954) 'Friendship as social process: A substantive and methodological analysis', in P. L. Kendall (ed.), *The Varied Sociology of Paul F. Lazarsfeld.* New York: Columbia University Press.

Lin, N. (1999) 'Social networks and status attainment', *Annual Review of Sociology,* 25: 467–87.

Marsden, P. V. (2002) 'Egocentric and sociocentric measures of network centrality', *Social Networks,* 24: 407–22.

Mcpherson, J. M. and Smith-Lovin, L. (1987) 'Homophily in voluntary organizations: status distance and the composition of face-to-face groups', *American Sociological Review,* 52: 370–9.

Mcpherson, M., Smith-Lovin, L. and Cook, J. M. (2001) 'Birds of a feather: Homophily in social networks', *Annual Review of Sociology,* 27: 415–44.

Mehra, A., Kilduff, M. and Brass, D. J. (2001) 'The social networks of high and low self-monitors: Implications for workplace performance', *Administrative Science Quarterly,* 46: 121–46.

Merton, R. K. (1957) 'The role-set: Problems in sociological theory', *British Journal of Sociology,* 8: 106–20.

Moody, J. (2001) 'Race, school integration, and friendship segregation in America', *American Journal of Sociology,* 107: 679–716.

Robins, G., Elliott, P. and Pattison, P. (2001) 'Network models for social selection processes', *Social Networks,* 23: 1–30.

Simmel, G. (1922/1955) *Conflict and the Web of Group Affiliations.* Translated by Wolff, Kurt H., Bendix, Reinhard. New York: Free Press.

Skvoretz, J. (1985) 'Random and biased networks: Simulations and approximations', *Social Networks,* 7: 225–61.

Skvoretz, J. (1990) 'Biased net theory: Approximations, simulations and observations', *Social Networks,* 12: 217–38.

Snijders, T. A. B. (2005) 'Models for longitudinal network data', in P. Carrington, J. Scott and S. Wasserman (eds), *Models and Methods in Social Network Analysis.* New York: Cambridge University Press.

Snijders, T. (2008) 'Longitudinal methods of network analysis'. in B. Meyers and J. Scott (eds), *Encyclopedia of Complexity and System Science.* Berlin: Springer Verlag.

Stevenson, W. B. and Greenberg, D. (2000) 'Agency and social networks: Strategies of action in a social structure of position, opposition, and opportunity', *Administrative Science Quarterly,* 45: 651–78.

Wellman, B. (1983) 'Network analysis: Some basic principles', *Sociological Theory,* 1: 155–200.

Wellman, B. and Berkowitz, S. (1988) *Social Structures: A Network Approach.* Cambridge: Cambridge University Press.

Xiao, Z. and Tsui, A. (2007) 'When brokers may not work: The cultural contingency of social capital in Chinese high-tech firms', *Administrative Science Quarterly,* 52: 1–31.

6

DYAD AND TRIAD LEVELS

The previous chapters focused on looking at the actor level of social networks, i.e. the centrality of the actor, an actor's ego network, and the various broker roles an actor can play in a network. The next level you will learn about will be dyads. A dyad consists of two actors and the ties linking these actors together. In focusing on dyads, you are studying pairs of actors and the link joining these two actors together.

Dyad studies tend to look at how ties are initiated and continued as well as terminated; what kind of resources get exchanged between pairs of actors; reciprocity; and the strength of tie. Examples of early research looking at dyads include the work of Homans on social exchange (Homans, 1950, 1961). Here, the exchange of valued items was researched on the dyad level, and as later research demonstrated (Cook et al., 1983; Emerson, 1972a, 1972b), such a focus on dyads could not account for issues of power and inequality in exchanges across an entire network.

Indeed, many researchers now see dyad analyses as another form of reductionism, as dyad analyses disregard the role that larger structures have on the development and continuance of these dyad ties (Wellman and Berkowitz, 1988). For example, larger structures such as workplaces, neighbourhoods, organizations and clubs, create an environment that encourages the formation and continuation of ties (Coleman, 1990; Feld, 1981). In addition, the structure of a network influences how much power an actor can have in negotiations with other actors (Cook et al., 1983). Dyads also influence how larger structures form: for example, if I have a close friendship with one person, and this person has a close friendship with a third, it is highly likely that I will at least become acquainted with this third individual. Finally, dyad analysis ignores how people make use of indirect ties to gain access to resources or other segments of the network.

In spite of these criticisms, the fact remains that much of the conceptualization and measurement of social networks takes place on the dyad level. By this I mean the way data are gathered and structured, which in turn influences how networks are perceived by the researcher and the analyses that are possible. For example, as Chapter 3 discusses in great detail, we gather data about social relations based on questions pertaining to two actors. 'With whom do you communicate?', a typical name-generator question in network analysis, gathers data on an entire network (be it ego network or complete network) on the dyadic level; each name generated from the above question results in one tie between two actors, and the accumulation of these answers and the structuring of these answers into a matrix gives us the resulting social network. In turn, whatever analyses take place, at whichever level, they are dealing with data that have this inherent, dyadic structure within it. That is, network data are inherently biased (or reduced), through conceptualization and measurement, to the dyad level.

Thus, although not too many analyses take place on the dyad level, it is worthwhile to introduce the notion of dyads, and at least address this fundamental structural quality of dyads, before moving on to other levels. Thus, in this section, I will discuss first discuss a dyad census, which in turn highlights issues pertaining to the nature of ties, and then move onto how dyads can be linked to the attributes of individuals through the concept of homophily.

DYAD CENSUS

Think about yourself and the sorts of relationships you have with others. Sometimes you think of an entire group of friends or associates, but many times you often think of one person at a time, and the kind of tie you have with that person. This might be a strong friendship tie, a person you rely heavily upon for giving you advice (e.g. a mentor or tutor), or a particular family member, for example your mother or father. Thus, you have different types of relations with individuals, and these relations also differ according to the strength of the tie and the direction of the tie. For example, you might have many people with whom you share a friendship tie, but you might only have one person whom you would deem your 'best' friend. In addition, you and your best friend most likely take turns giving each other emotional support, advice and different kinds of help. It is a very reciprocal, mutual tie. This is quite different from the tie you share with your mentor: here, advice tends to flow in just one direction, i.e. from your mentor to yourself. In addition, you might view your mentor as a very important person in your life, because of the advice and help they give you, yet your mentor may or may not share this same feeling. Finally, whereas you and your best friend might very well have some sort of strong tie for a substantially long period in your lives, you and your mentor might only share a tie for a short period of time, for example, for the duration of your studies, or for the time you work at a particular organization, or until you reach a certain stage in your career.

These examples I have given above are to illustrate the different sorts of ways to understand or characterize dyad relations. Dyads can be understood in terms of the kind of relational tie; the tie strength, the direction of the tie, and the duration of the tie. Many of these properties of dyads can be understood through the use of a dyad census. A dyad census categorizes all the dyads in a given network into three possible 'states'. These three states for dyads are Mutual, Asymmetric and Null. These three states (M, A, N) comprise a dyad census. Figure 6.1 illustrates these three states.

In Figure 6.1 the top pair of actors represents a null dyad, the next two pairs of actors are the two forms of asymmetric dyads, and the last pair of actors represents a mutual dyad. (Please note that in discussing these three states, one is basically assuming that the relational data under question are binary, i.e. that they are not valued relations.)

Figure 6.2 is an example of a digraph and that digraph's matrix. Examining this graph first for the number of mutual dyads, one looks for those instances when i sends a tie to j and j sends a tie to i. That is, one looks for the times when a tie is reciprocated. In this graph, the dyad formed by actors D and E is a

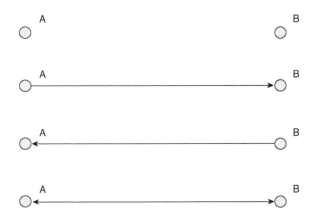

Figure 6.1   Dyad MAN census

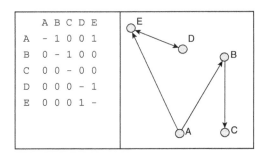

Figure 6.2   Digraph and matrix for Dyad census example

mutual dyad. In the matrix, both cell (D, E) and cell (E, D) = 1. This is the only mutual dyad in this digraph.

An asymmetric dyad is one where i sends a tie to j or j sends a tie to i, but not both. In the current example, actor B sends an arc to actor C, and this is reflected in the matrix, where cell (B, C) = 1, but cell (C, B) = 0. Similarly, A sends B and E an arc, but these ties are not reciprocated. Thus, in this digraph, there are three asymmetric dyads. Finally, a null dyad is reflected in a matrix when both the (i, j) and (j, i) cells are 0. In the matrix, you can see that cell (B, D) and (D, B) are both 0. Neither actor nominated the other for this relation. In this digraph, there are six null dyads.

What are the theoretical implications of these three different states for dyads? In social network analysis, mutual dyads are seen as more stable ties, and also ties that contain more trust and positive affection (Carley and Krackhardt, 1996; Molm et al., 2000; Wasserman and Faust, 1994). Mutual ties can be expected to be more frequent when the relation under question is friendship, although research has shown that friendship networks actually contain a high number of asymmetric dyads (Freeman, 1992; Hallinan, 1978). Some argue that such asymmetries in friendship networks are a sign that the dyad in question is really just a transition to becoming a reciprocal, mutual dyad. For example, that one person offers another a sign of wanting to be friends, and the receiver of this request has yet to reciprocate (Hallinan, 1978). Yet Carley and Krackhardt (1996) argue that histories and larger context can play more subtle roles in allowing asymmetric friendship dyads to persist.

Advice relations or relations based on exchange are more likely to contain higher instances of asymmetric dyads than friendship. This has to do with the intuitive idea that power, knowledge and expertise are distributed unevenly in a network, thus resulting in certain actors being more actively sought after than others, and certain actors deferring to the status of others (Knoke and Burt, 1983). Finally, a network that holds a large number of null dyads is largely an empty network.

Conducting a dyad census involves counting how many null, asymmetric and mutual dyads exist in a network. As this can be done in the context of analysing for triads, I shall save further discussion on the analysis of dyads for the discussion of a triad census.

A dyad census helps one to zoom-in on properties of ties between two actors, yet the census fails to account for all such properties. Two additional properties of interest for the network analysis include the strength of a tie and the idea of tie multiplexity. Tie strength is a relative concept and best understood in relation to other ties. For example, an actor can have a variety of ties to others, but some of those ties will exhibit more intimacy, mutual confiding, and frequency of contact than others. Indeed, this perception of tie strength as containing a variety of dimensions is what Granovetter (1973) promoted in his article,

'The strength of weak ties'. In particular, Granovetter argued that a tie's strength would be a combination of the amount of time two actors spent together; the emotional intensity of their relationship; the level of intimacy and/or mutual confiding between two actors; and the amount of reciprocal services or favours.

Granovetter posited that as two actors spend more time together, they will likewise form a more emotionally intense and intimate tie, and also engage in more acts of reciprocity with one another. Thus, tie strength would increase as frequency, emotional intensity and mutual confiding increased. One can think of family members as a classic example of such a strong tie: most of us spend or have spent a lot of time with our spouses, parents or children. These ties are also ones filled with a great deal of intimacy and also ones that tend to come to one's aid when in trouble or need.

This conceptualization of tie strength is closely related to that of multiplexity (Kapferer, 1969), which refers to actors sharing more than one kind of tie with one another. For example, your neighbour might also be your friend, or a colleague might also be a family member. Granovetter (1973) also notes that his conceptualization of tie strength is a type of multiplexity.

Analysing for tie strength and multiplexity

Tie strength is typically conveyed through the use of valued data; for example, at the time you gather your data, you may ask your respondents the frequency in which they interact with others, or how would they rate their level of intimacy with others. The answers to these questions results in values, which are inputted into the data matrix, as shown in Figure 6.3.

In Figure 6.3, higher values refer to higher frequencies in communication contact, and lower values refer to lower frequencies. With the next example, two separate graphs have been drawn on the same set of actors (see Figure 6.4). The graph to the left refers to friendship, and the one to the right to advice. In those instances where two actors sharing a friendship tie also share an advice tie,

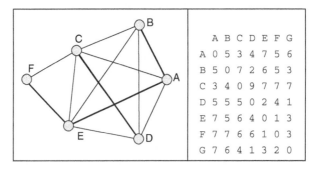

	A	B	C	D	E	F	G
A	0	5	3	4	7	5	6
B	5	0	7	2	6	5	3
C	3	4	0	9	7	7	7
D	5	5	5	0	2	4	1
E	7	5	6	4	0	1	3
F	7	7	6	6	1	0	3
G	7	6	4	1	3	2	0

Figure 6.3   Valued graph

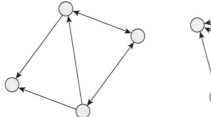

Figure 6.4   Multiplex digraph

these actors can be said to hold a multiplex tie. To achieve bringing these two networks together into one matrix, you can simply select *Transform –> Union* in UCINET, and input the two matrices. If the two matrices are binary matrices, the output will give you one matrix containing valued data.

Dyads are interesting in themselves for understanding a number of tie properties linking two actors together. On a theoretical level, a tie shared between two actors can also help to uncover how attributes or behaviours of those actors might alter as a result of that dyadic interaction, as shown in the example of Erickson (1983) in the accompanying textbox.

Exploring theory through dyads: Social comparison theory

Erickson (1988) looked at how social comparison theory could be studied from a social network perspective. Social comparison theory refers to the process whereby individuals exchange views with one another, comparing their own views with those of others to arrive at a sense for having, ultimately, the 'correct' perspective (Suls and Miller, 1977. For example, if someone is uncertain about a particular issue, they will turn to others in their social network to discuss the matter, comparing views and attitudes about the issue, and eventually arriving at the commonly held view of the issue at hand.

Erickson discusses how social comparison theory can be studied on the dyad level. She distinguished four dimensions of dyadic relationships that could potentially influence actors' attitudes. These are:

1 *Frequency of interaction* The more frequently two actors interact with each other, the more opportunities they have for influencing one another's attitudes. Thus, frequency of interaction should positively correlate with similarity in attitudes.

(Continued)

(Continued)

2   *Tie multiplexity* When actors share more than one kind of relational tie with one another, they exhibit a multiplex tie. Erickson argues the more multiplex the tie between two actors, the more widely the pair of actors will agree on various issues.

3   *Strength of tie* Erickson refers to strong ties as ones exhibiting strong feelings of liking, intimacy and friendship. The stronger the tie between two actors, she argues, the more likely actors will agree on issues.

4   *Asymmetry* Asymmetry could potentially affect attitudes in different ways. When the asymmetric relation is based on authority, this relation will most likely lead to a dissimilarity in opinions. However, if the asymmetric tie is based on esteem and status, i.e. one actor holds another actor in high esteem, then the subordinate actor most likely will adopt the views of the other, assuming this person's views and attitudes are the valid ones to have.

Simmel (1950) was especially interested in dyads in relation to triads (see Chapter 2). In particular, Simmel (1950) noted that two people involved in a dyad relation tended to share a stronger, more durable tie if that dyad were embedded within a triad. Empirical research has supported this argument that dyadic relations, when found within triad structures, are more stable over time (Krackhardt, 1998). Such ties have since come to be known as 'Simmelian ties' (Krackhardt, 1992, 1998, 1999; Krackhardt and Kilduff, 2002).

As such, the idea of studying dyad relations in the context of triad relations makes a lot of sociological sense; one can study dyads on their own or in the context of triads by looking at a variety of triad structures. Thus, in the next section, we shall continue the discussion of dyads in the context of triads.

TRIADS AND TRIAD CENSUS

A triad consists of three actors (or nodes) and all the arcs between them. As such, triads are basically seen as being composed of different kinds of dyad configurations among a set of three actors. As such, triads can be broken down into six different triples by counting the presence or non-presence of an arc between two actors in the triad. For example, in Figure 6.5, the six different triples found in this triad are listed.

Thus, each triad always contains six triples, as each triad contains three actors and all possible arcs between these actors.

In the historical outline of social network analysis, found in Chapter 2, I briefly discussed the work of Cartwright and Harary (1956), who had developed a

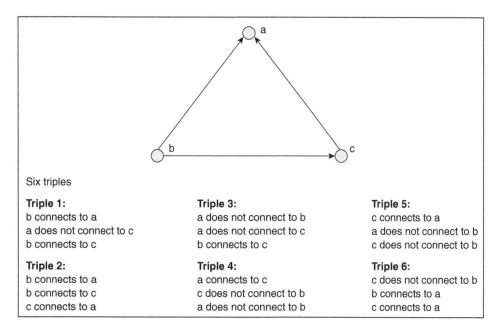

Figure 6.5   Example of a triad

graph-theoretic model of structural balance involving the use of signed (+ and −) triads. Their work launched a stream of research focusing on the use of triads for understanding local and more global network structures. Ultimately, this stream of research led to the development of the structural concept of *transitivity*, a concept explored through the use of a triad census (shown in Figure 6.6). Transitivity refers to the situation where actor i is tied to actor j; actor j is tied to actor k; and actor i is likewise tied to actor k. In social terms, a transitive triad is one where 'a friend of my friend is also my friend'. As will be seen below, this idea of transitivity has come to be seen as a main structural characteristic of networks, to the extent that many network analysts have questioned what remains to be discovered about network structure, once an analyst has accounted for transitivity (Wasserman and Faust, 1994). Holland and Leinhardt (1970, 1971, 1972) developed a triad census, and they used this census to investigate the extent to which a graph can be characterized by transitivity. Figure 6.6 is an illustration of the triad census these two developed.

In Figure 6.6 the various triad configurations are organized in a systematic way to show all the possible types of triads that could be found in a given network. This triad census is, in many respects, an extension of the dyad census I discussed in the previous section. Like a dyad census, a triad census looks at the number of mutual, asymmetric and null dyads. In doing so, a triad census codes the different triads according to how many of each kind of dyad exists in

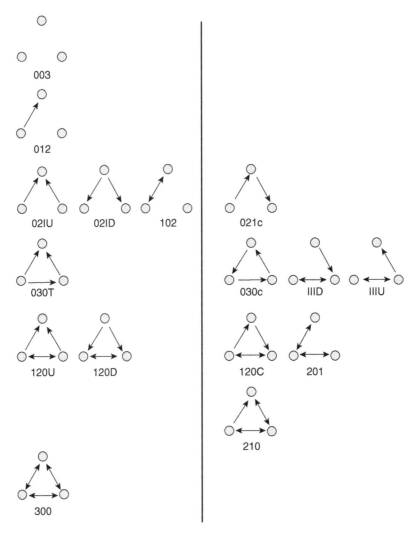

Figure 6.6   Triad census (adapted from Holland and Leinhardt, 1970)

that particular triad. The coding reflects both the number and kind of each dyad in the census. For example, the very first triad in the above census, 003, consists of zero mutual dyads, zero asymmetric dyads and three null dyads. Triad 012 holds zero mutual dyads, one asymmetric dyad and two null dyads. Thus, the first number refers to the number of mutuals, the second to the number of asymmetric dyads and third to the number of null dyads. Finally, there are some triads that have the exact same number of dyads, but the direction of the ties making up these dyads is different. In this situation, the census uses letters to indicate the direction of the ties in the dyads. For example, triads 021U, 021D and 021C all have the same number of dyads, these being zero mutual, two asymmetric and one null. However, if you look closely, the direction of the ties in these dyads are different. Thus, the 'U' refers to ties directed upwards, whereas 'D' refers to ties directed downwards, and 'C' refers to ties structured in a cyclic formation.

Holland and Leinhardt then discussed how all triads can be classified as transitive intransitive or vacuously transitive. A transitive triad is one where all the triples within that triad are transitive. Thus, triads 030T, 120U, 120D and 300 are all transitive triads. A vacuous transitive triad is one where either i is not tied to actor j and/or actor j is not tied to actor k. Vacuous transitive triads are neither transitive nor intransitive, as there are not enough arcs in the triad to meet the conditions of transitivity. Thus, Holland and Leinhardt found that a digraph can contain vacuous transitive triads and still hold the structural property of transitivity. Vacuous triads are 003, 012, 021U, 021D and 102.

The remaining triads on the right hand side of the figure are considered intransitive. An intransitive triad is one where actor i is tied to actor j; actor j is tied to actor k; yet actor i is not tied to actor k. In social terms, this would translate as saying that 'a friend of my friend is *not* my friend'. For the triad census found above, a triad can be considered intransitive if just one of the triples is intransitive. Triad 210 is such a triad: this triad has six triples, and where two are vacuously transitive, three are transitive and one is intransitive. Because of this one intransitive triple, the entire triad is considered intransitive.

Transitivity is seen as a key unifying concept that brings together ideas of structural balance and clustering (see the review of this literature in Chapter 2). Holland and Leinhardt (1971) argued that transitivity can explain much of the structure found in a graph, i.e. once you have accounted for the extent to which a network is transitive, you have already accounted for much of the structure in the network. The empirical work that has resulted over the years supports this claim (Wasserman and Faust, 1994; Wellman and Berkowitz, 1988).

THEORETICAL CONCEPTS AND TRIAD STRUCTURES

Transitivity is a unifying concept that links earlier structural concepts and theories pertaining to triads and larger network structures. In Chapter 2, I discussed the Cartwright and Harary (1956) breakthrough work on structural balance. As you may recall from that chapter, structural balance refers to graphs that share the following characteristics; all the ties within the graph can be grouped into two clusters whereby the ties within the clusters are positive and the ties between the clusters are negative. Positive ties can refer to positive feelings of affection or liking, but they can also refer to relations where actors receive power when connected to others who have higher status than themselves, or others who are likewise well-connected. Examples of positive relations include communication, advice or friendship.

In balance theory, the negative ties between the two clusters can refer to those described above, but they could also refer to the *absence* of ties. In fact, in a review of the empirical research done up until that point, Davis and Leinhardt (1972) discovered that negative ties – in the form of feelings of dislike or distrust – are unusual to find in social networks. Either a tie is present, and it is positive, or it simply does not exist. Since this time, social network analysis has largely focused on the study of positive ties of affection, where negative ties of affection are treated largely as absent ties (Wasserman and Faust, 1994).

Popularizing transitivity: Forbidden triangles and biased nets

Although transitivity has a relatively long history in social network analysis, the concept gained a great deal of popularity with the work of Granovetter (1973). Granovetter (1973, 1982) came up with the notion of a 'forbidden triangle' to convey the idea that strong ties have a tendency to form transitive triads. To illustrate, it might be helpful to look at the figure below:

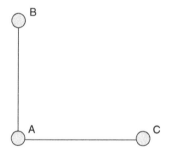

Granovetter would characterize this triad as composed of 'weak' ties, i.e. one in which little intimacy or mutual confiding occurs. People linked by weak ties are rarely ones we would consider 'close friends'. Because these ties are weak, the triad is 'permitted' to remain open. However, if B and C were both friends with A, i.e. they shared a strong tie with A, then the likelihood that B and C would form a tie to one another dramatically increases.

Granovetter based his argument on the idea that strong ties create a kind of structural force, one that pressures actors to acknowledge one another's presence and form some kind of social tie with each other. Thus, when a triad consists of strong ties, an open triad (or triangle) is 'forbidden'.

Relating these ideas to our discussion on transitivity and triad census, one could say that intransitive triads are instances of Granovetter's forbidden triangle.

(Continued)

(Continued)

The popularity and importance of transitivity can also be traced in the literature pertaining to Biased Net Theory (Rapoport, 1957; Skvoretz, 1985, 1990; Skvoretz et al., 2004). This theory states that social networks have structural biases that make them different from random networks. These biases include the tendency for reciprocity between dyads (i.e. reciprocity bias), and the tendency for a network to exhibit transitivity (i.e. triad closure bias). For the most part, the general effect of the biases is to reduce the tendency of actors to establish new links with others in the network, and instead to turn 'inwards' and direct their links to the pool of others to whom contacts have already been made.

Thus, in conceptualizing negative ties as absent ties, one can look at the above triad census and locate triads that reflect the idea of structural balance; in particular, triads 102 and 300. Both 102 and 300 contain mutual, positive ties linking actors together. Further, if the entire network is balanced, then all actors in the network should fall into either a 102 triad or a 300 triad.

Why is this the case? If two actors belong to the same cluster (and in a balanced network, there are only two clusters), then those two actors must share a positive tie between them, where positive tie would mean a reciprocal tie. Positive ties are represented in this instance as reciprocal ties because an asymmetric tie would indicate that the two actors do not share the same (balanced) feelings for one another. Thus, we first need to just consider those that are only composed of reciprocal and/or no ties. These are triads 003, 102, 201, and 300. Yet not all of these can be considered in our definition of balance; Triad 003 can be eliminated right away, as this triad represents an instance where three actors are embedded in three different clusters, which is not allowed under the definition of balance. In addition, triad 201 can be eliminated, as this triad represents two actors having dissimilar views regarding a third actor; one has a positive tie with the third actor, and the second a negative (i.e. absent tie).

In fact, triad 201 is not only an unbalanced triad; it is a special kind of unbalanced triad referred to in the literature as a Forbidden Triangle (see textbox). Thus, we need to look at triads that represent the two actors either sharing positive ties with a third actor, or sharing no tie with a third actor. The two triads that represent these two scenarios are triads 102 and 300.

Thus, just as Chapter 2 discussed, balance can be thought of as one kind (a more restricted kind) of transitivity; both 300 and 102 are categorized as transitive triads in the above census, but not all transitive triads are considered to be balanced! Two other theoretical concepts that relate to this discussion on transitivity and triads include clustering and ranked clustering. Recall from Chapter 2 the discussion pertaining to Davis' (1967) work on clustering; here, Davis built upon the findings of Cartwright and Harary (1956) by asking under what conditions can a network be split into more than two subgroups. Here, balance is still the main criterion, yet in addition, the graph is permitted to be broken down into more than two clusters. Davis argued that a signed graph, consisting of two or more subgroups, can be called a *clusterable* graph if it contained no cycle holding a negative tie. Davis' (1967) theorems thus showed that all balanced graphs, as defined by Cartwright and Harary (1956), were in essence clusterable ones, but this did not imply that the reverse was also true, i.e. that clusterable graphs were balanced. Thus, in the above triad census, triads 300 and 102 are balanced and clusterable, and in addition, actors falling within triad 003 can be considered clusterable, as this triad shows three actors each embedded in a different cluster.

Finally, Davis and Leinhardt (1972) in their review of empirical data, noted that not only were negative ties a relatively infrequent occurrence in network data, but directional ties were plentiful. Thus, dyads in which the tie shared between the two actors was asymmetrical were a common occurrence, and the idea of balance and clustering therefore needed to accommodate for this. Their first attempt was to consider the role asymmetric ties play in a network (Davis and Leinhardt, 1972), which led to the notion of ranked clustering. Here, actors that hold mutually positive ties are not simply in the same cluster, but they are also in the same rank. Differences in rank get communicated through a negative or asymmetric tie; an asymmetric tie between one actor and another implies that one actor is in a different rank than the other. Typically, it is viewed that the receiver of ties is in a higher position than the sender, as the receiver can afford to not reciprocate. Thus, asymmetric and/or negative ties are seen as separating actors in ranked clusters and positive, mutual ties are seen as linking actors together in the same cluster. Finally, in keeping with notions of balance and clustering, the absence of ties was seen as instances of actors existing in different clusters of equal rank. Thus 120D, 120U, 021U and 030T contain actors who are embedded in clusters, but who also contain an asymmetric tie to another actor embedded in a differently ranked cluster.

To summarize, different kinds of triads can be linked to different structural concepts (Nooy et al., 2005). The below table summarizes which triads from the above triad census (shown in Figure 6.6) can be linked to these theoretical concepts:

Concept	Triad
Structural balance	300, 102
Clustering	300, 102, 003
Ranked Clustering	300, 102, 003 120D, 120U, 021U and 030T
Transitivity (where (v) means vacuous transitive)	300, 102(v), 003(v), 120D, 120U, 021U(v), 021D(v) and 030T 012(v)

The importance of transitivity in particular and triad census more generally is the idea that, in locating which triads actors are found, one can uncover some important structural tendencies of the entire network. Thus, to understand the structural features of the entire network, one need only consider the sorts of triads that exist, and the frequency in which such triads occur. A digraph that contains an abundance of 300 and 102 triads can be said to be a balanced graph, which in turn implies that the graph can be broken down into two clusters whereby actors within the clusters are mutually linked, and no ties exist between the two clusters. Thus, by focusing on a lower level feature, i.e. triads, you can describe and explain something about the entire network.

It is extremely rare for a graph or digraph to exhibit, entirely, one of the properties above, for example, it is rare for a graph to be perfectly balanced or a digraph to be perfectly transitive. Nonetheless, through analysing a graph or digraph for the kinds of triads found in the above triad census, you can develop a heuristic feel for the tendency to which a network exhibits, for example, balance of transitivity.

To conduct a triad census in UCINET, go to *Network > Triad* census. Input your network data, which should ideally be directed, binary data. The procedure uses the triad census introduced here. Thus, the output gives you the codes for the range of triads, and then offers a simple count of how many times each kind of triad appears in your data.

From UCINET, you can also export social network data in Pajek, a visualization tool associated with UCINET that also conducts a number of analyses on network data. Once you have exported your data to Pajek (in UCINET go to *Data > Export > Pajek > network*), Pajek will automatically open for you. Within Pajek, go to *Info > Network > Triadic census*. The resulting output gives you a triadic count, and in addition, a listing of the structural models associated with each triad, for example, transitivity, structural balance, clustering and the forbidden triangle.

EXTENSIONS AND CONCLUDING REMARKS

Research on dyads and triads continues. Theoretically, the notion of Simmelian ties has gained ground as a means for explaining the stability of ties (Krackhardt, 1998), as well as the cultural understandings of workers (Krackhardt, 1999). In one study, dyadic relationships embedded in closed triad structures have been linked to similarity in perception amongst respondents regarding the wider network structure. In particular, the work of Krackhardt and Kilduff (2002) considered whether those actors involved in a dyadic relationship that was embedded in a closed triad tended to share similar views regarding who was friends with whom in the wider organization. Their findings showed that the tendency to share common views of the wider network structure increased among those actors whose dyadic relationship was embedded in a closed triad.

In addition, the work of de Nooy (1999) has extended triadic analyses based on transitivity, for example, to consider incomplete, signed directional networks. Noting that affective relations are often signed ones, displaying liking or disliking, yet are seldom complete, de Nooy (1999) outlines a procedure to account for these sorts of empirical data.

Researchers have also made use of Holland and Leinhardt's triad census to investigate other social structural concepts and ideas besides those discussed by the authors. These include Bearma's (1997) research on intransitive triads called 'cycles'. Triad 120C in Figure 6.6 is an example of an intransitive cycle. Here, actor i nominates actor j and actor j nominates actor k. Bearman (1997) argues that cyclic triads illustrate the notion of 'generalized exchange', where favours are done for others with the hope that they will be, indirectly, returned one day. Prell and Skvoretz (2008) also made use of a triad census to investigate notions of brokerage and closure, as discussed in the social capital literature. Here, the direction of ties were ignored, and attention was focused on triads that were either open or closed to assess the extent to which brokerage or closure tendencies were present in a given network. Taken together, the research on triads is not likely to end anytime soon.

SUMMARY AND CONCLUSION

In this chapter you learned about dyads, which are configurations consisting of two actors, and the MAN dyad census, which breaks down the different dyad configurations according to mutual, asymmetric and null dyads. Dyads were then discussed as building blocks for triads; triads are local configurations consisting of three actors, and similar to the MAN dyad census, a MAN labelling scheme is used in relation to a triad census, as developed by Holland and Leinhardt (1971). This triad census consists of 16 triads, which are then categorized as transitive, vacuously transitive or intransitive. A transitive triad is one in which all triples in the triad contain the following structure: i connects to j; j connects to k; and i connects to k. Intransitive triads are ones where at least one triple breaks this structural rule. Vacuously transitive triads are ones where not enough ties are present to determine whether the triad is transitive or intransitive. The chapter finished by showing how a triad census can be used to explore notions of structural balance, clustering and ranked clustering, and transitivity.

REFERENCES

Bearman, P. S. (1997) 'Generalized exchange', *American Journal of Sociology,* 102: 1383–415.

Carley, K. and Krackhardt, D. (1996) 'Cognitive inconsistencies and non-symmetric friendships', *Social Networks,* 18: 1–29.

Cartwright, D. and Harary, F. (1956) 'Structural balance: A generalization of Heider's theory', *Psychological Review,* 63: 277–92.

Coleman, J. S. (1990) *Foundations of Social Theory.* Cambridge: Belknap Press of Harvard University.

Cook, K. S., Emerson, R.M., Gilmore, M.R. and Yamagishi, T. (1983) 'The distribution of power in exchange networks: Theory and experimental results', *American Journal of Sociology,* 89: 275–305.

Davis, J. A. (1967) 'Clustering and structural balance in graphs', *Human Relations,* 20: 181–7.

Davis, J. A. and Leinhardt, S. (1972) 'The structure of positive interpersonal relations in small groups', in M. Berger, J. Zelditch and B. Anderson (eds), *Sociological Theories in Progress.* New York: Houghton-Mifflin.

De Nooy, W. (1999) 'The sign of affection: Balance-theoretic models and incomplete signed digraphs', *Social Networks,* 21: 269–86.

Emerson, R. M. (1972a) 'Exchange theory, part I: A psychological basis for social exchange', in J. Berger, J. Morris Zelditch and B. Anderson (eds), *Sociological Theories in Progress, Vol. 2.* Boston: Houghton-Mifflin.

Emerson, R. (1972b) 'Exchange theory, part II: Exchange relations and networks', in J. Berger, J. Morris Zelditch and B. Anderson (eds), *Sociological Theories in Progress, Vol. 2.* Boston: Houghton-Mifflin.

Erickson, B. (1988) 'The relational basis of attitudes', in B. Wellman and S. D. Berkowitz (eds), *Social Structures: A Network Approach.* Cambridge: Cambridge University Press.

Feld, S. (1981) 'The focused organisation of social ties', *American Journal of Sociology,* 86: 1015–35.

Freeman, L. C. (1992) 'Filling the blanks: A theory of cognitive categories and the structure of social affiliation', *Social Psychology Quarterly,* 55: 118–27.

Granovetter, M. (1973) 'The strength of weak ties', *American Journal of Sociology,* 78: 1360–80.

Granovetter, M. (1982) 'The strength of weak ties: A network theory revisited', in P. Marsden and N. Lin (eds), *Social Structure and Network Analysis.* Beverly Hills: Sage.

Hallinan, M. T. (1978) 'The process of friendship formation', *Social Networks,* 1: 193–210.

Holland, P. and Leinhardt, S. (1970) 'A method for detecting structure in sociometric data', *American Journal of Sociology,* 76: 492–513.

Holland, P. W. and Leinhardt, S. (1971) 'Transitivity in structural models of small groups', *Small Group Research,* 2: 107–24.

Holland, P. W. and Leinhardt, S. (1972) 'Some evidence on the transitivity of positive interpersonal sentiment', *American Journal of Sociology,* 72: 1205–9.

Homans, G. C. (1950) *The Human Group.* New York: Harcourt.

Homans, G. C. (1961) *Social Behavior: Its Elementary Forms.* New York: Harcourt.

Kapferer, B. (1969) 'Norms and manipulation of relationships in a work context', in J. C. Mitchell (ed.), *Social Networks in Urban Situations*. Manchester: Manchester University Press.

Knoke, D. and Burt, R. S. (1983) 'Prominence', in R. S. Burt and M. J. Minor (eds), *Applied Network Analysis: A Methodological Introduction*. Beverly Hills: Sage.

Krackhardt, D. (1992) 'The strength of strong ties: The importance of philos in organisations', in N. Nohria and R.C. Eccles (eds), *Networks and Organisations: Structure, Form, and Action*. Boston: Harvard Business School Press.

Krackhardt, D. (1998) 'Simmelian ties: Super, strong and sticky', in R. Kramer and M. Neale (eds), *Power and Influence in Organizations*. Thousand Oaks, CA: Sage.

Krackhardt, D. (1999) 'The ties that torture: Simmelian tie analysis in organizations', in S. B. Bacharach, S. B. Andrews and D. Knoke (eds), *Research in the Sociology of Organizations*. Stanford, CT: JAI.

Krackhardt, D. and Kilduff, M. (2002) 'Structure, culture and Simmelian ties in entrepreneurial firms', *Social Networks*, 24: 279–90.

Molm, L. D., Takahashi, N. and Peterson, G. (2000) 'Risk and trust in social exchange: An experimental test of a classical proposition', *The American Journal of Sociology*, 105: 1396–427.

Nooy, W. D., Mrvar, A. and Batagelj, V. (2005) *Exploratory Social Network Analysis with Pajek*. New York: Cambridge University Press.

Prell, C. and Skvoretz, J. (2008) 'Looking at social capital through triad structures', *Connections*, 28: 4–16.

Rapoport, A. (1957) 'Contribution to the theory of random and biased nets', *Bulletin of Mathematical Biology*, 19: 257–77.

Simmel, G. (1950) 'Individual and society', in K. H. Wolff (ed.), *The Sociology of Georg Simmel*. New York: Free Press.

Skvoretz, J. (1985) 'Random and biased networks: Simulations and approximations', *Social Networks*, 7: 225–61.

Skvoretz, J. (1990) 'Biased net theory: Approximations, simulations and observations', *Social Networks*, 12: 217–38.

Skvoretz, J., Fararo, T. J. and Agneessens, F. (2004) 'Advances in biased net theory: Definitions, derivations, and estimations', *Social Networks*, 26: 113–39.

Suls, J. M. and Miller, R. L. (1977) *Social Comparison Processes: Theoretical and Empirical Perspectives*. Washington: Hemisphere.

Wasserman, S. and Faust, F. (1994) *Social Network Analysis: Methods and Applications*. Cambridge: Cambridge University Press.

Wellman, B. and Berkowitz, S. (1988) *Social Structures: A Network Approach*. Cambridge: Cambridge University Press.

7

SUBGROUPS LEVEL

In the previous chapter on dyads and triads, I gave an overview of small, network configurations consisting of relations between two nodes (dyads) or relations between three nodes (triads). These dyads and triads are perceived as building blocks for larger network structures. A subgroup in a network refers to an area of a network larger than a dyad or triad yet smaller than an entire network. A cohesive subgroup is a subgroup in which a high proportion of the actors within the subgroup share strong, direct, mutual, frequent or positive ties (Wasserman and Faust, 1994). Although the notion of a cohesive subgroup is intuitively easy to understand, measuring cohesive subgroups is not always so straightforward. Furthermore, the idea of cohesion in general (Freeman, 1984; Moody and White, 2003) is not as straightforward as it appears, and tends to apply to more than just subgroups. As such, before starting a discussion on how to measure cohesive subgroups, I think it wise to start this chapter with a brief background discussion on the meaning of cohesion in the social sciences, and in network analysis in particular.

THINKING ABOUT COHESION: A MULTILEVEL VIEW

The idea of cohesion has interested sociologists, political scientists and psychologists for decades. For example, ideas referring to cohesion can be found in Tönnies' (1887) discussion of Gemeinschaft, and Simmel's (Simmel and Wolff, 1950) distinction between dyads and triads, where the relations between two actors, when embedded in a triad, were seen as stronger and more durable than those not embedded in triads. Finally, Kurt Lewin (1951), a social psychologist discussed in Chapter 2, perceived cohesion as a field of forces that keep people in a group (or network) together.

Definitions of cohesion range from a more psychological oriented view that emphasizes people's feelings of belonging or identification with a group to a relational view that emphasizes the ties linking actors together (Moody and

White, 2003). Usually, feelings of belonging are seen as going hand in hand with relational belonging (Friedkin, 1984; Moody and White, 2003), and groups that are tied together relationally are also seen as composed of individuals who share similar beliefs and values (Collins, 1988; Friedkin, 1984).

Thus, cohesion, when conceptualized as a form of network structure, is seen as influencing the behaviour and/or values of individuals and the collective. Some of these aspects of network structure, as they relate to ideas of cohesion, have already been discussed in this book, although I have not drawn attention to them as such. For example, in Chapter 6, you were introduced to the notion of closed triads and Simmelian ties. Simmelian ties are dyad relations embedded in triads, and such ties are shown to be (i) more stable over time (Krackhardt, 1998); (ii) exert more pressure on the individuals to conform to group norms (Krackhardt, 1999); and (iii) induce similar perceptions about the larger network structure (Krackhardt and Kilduff, 2002). Thus, the closed triad, as a cohesive structure, has been shown to have effects on the behaviours and attitudes of the individuals embedded in such a triad. Likewise, Granovetter's (1973, 1982) strength of weak ties and the role of Forbidden Triangles (see Chapter 6) also pertained to cohesion; here, Granovetter argued that society is dense clusters composed of individuals linked together through strong ties. In addition to such clusters, individuals also hold a number of weak ties to others, and such weak ties form the bridges across clusters, thus helping to bring cohesion on the societal level. Finally, you have also come across in this book the idea of bonding social capital; here network structures in which the majority of individuals are linked together through strong ties are seen as benefiting individuals and groups through increased access to emotional and social support (Agneessens et al., 2006; Coromina and Coenders, 2006; Stoloff et al., 1999; Wellman and Wortley, 1990; Wellman et al., 1997).

Taken together, cohesion is a fundamental concept found in many theories and measures pertaining to social networks. In addition, when thinking about and attempting to analyse for subgroups in networks, cohesion becomes the primary guiding concept. As such, a great deal of attention has been given towards conceptualization and measurement of a 'cohesive subgroup'. This chapter will illustrate this range through introducing measures for components, cliques, n-cliques and k-cores.

Some different aspects of cohesion are listed below, and how these aspects relate to particular measures in this chapter is also given:

- The number of direct (or indirect) ties linking individuals in the group together (Alba, 1973). See clique and n-clique below.

- The relative isolation of groups to outsiders (Collins, 1988). See LS sets below.

- The extent to which individuals can reach one another (Alba and Moore, 1978; Mokken, 1979). See components and n-clique below.

- The extent to which the group is vulnerable to fragmentation (Markovsky, 1998; Seidman and Foster, 1978). See k-core below.

As this list suggests, cohesion is inherently a multilevel concept, involving the mutuality of ties in dyads, how dyads are embedded in larger structures, and the role individuals play in linking the overall network together.

COMPONENTS

A **component** is generally considered the most minimum requirement for a cohesive subgroup (Moody and White, 2003). A component consists of a subgroup of individuals, whereby all the individuals are connected to one another by at least one path.

A weak component refers to actors who are connected to one another, regardless of the direction of the ties, whereas a strong component refers to actors being connected to one another via direct or indirect ties. Thus, with a weak component, you ignore the direction of the ties, and with a strong component you pay attention to the directionality of ties. Finally, isolates, i.e. an actor not having any ties to anyone else, is also considered a component. Figure 7.1 shows three different components within one network.

In Figure 7.1, the first component, a weak component, shows four actors (E, F, G and H) who are connected to one another, if one were to *ignore* the direction of the ties. For example, actor F can reach actor G via actor E, only if one were to ignore the direction of the arc connecting G to E. A path linking an actor to

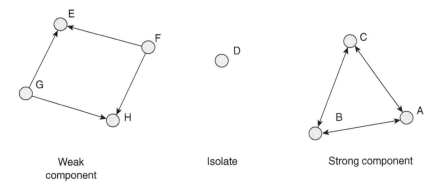

Figure 7.1   Three components in a network

all other actors, when the direction of the arcs is ignored, is called a *weak path*. Thus weak components are ones were the actors are connected through a weak path.

However, if we paid attention to the direction of the arcs, then F could only reach E and H. Actor G could only reach E and H, but neither G nor F could reach one another, nor could E or H reach one another.

In comparison, the strong component on the right of Figure 7.1 shows all actors A, B and C being able to access one another through the directional arcs shown. Here, paying attention to the direction of arcs enables any actor to reach any other actor. A path linking an actor to all other actors, when the direction of the arc is recognized, is called a *strong path*. Thus, this strong component is connected via its strong paths.

The final component, in the middle is an isolate. Isolates can be considered their own components in a graph/digraph.

Identifying the components of a network is important, as some network analyses require the network being fully connected, or strongly connected, for the particular analysis. You saw this in relation to closeness centrality in Chapter 4; closeness centrality is best computed on strongly connected networks.

In relation to ideas of cohesion, a network consisting of just one component is seen as a connected graph, and a connected graph where all actors can reach all others via the direction of arcs is a strongly connected graph. A network that is connected, but only when one ignores the direction of the arcs, is considered a weakly connected graph. A network that is broken into several components is seen as a disconnected graph. Such a disconnected graph might best be treated as several separate networks for conducting certain analysis, such as closeness centrality.

The number of components in a network is one means of thinking about cohesive subgroups. However, this approach is only meaningful if your network breaks down into several different components, such as the one in Figure 7.1. Otherwise, if the network is fully connected, you need to make use of alternative techniques to uncover subgroups within the network.

Analysing for components

To analyse for components, you need to consider the direction of ties, as the distinction between strong and weak components depends on the direction of ties connecting actors. In UCINET, go to *Network > Regions > Components > Simple Graphs*. Your network data must be dichotomous (only 1s and 0s), but it may be either symmetric or asymmetric network data (keep in mind that asymmetric data holds information on the direction of ties). If using asymmetric data, the program will ask you to specify whether you are analysing for strong or weak components. Based on your choice, the program will then count the number of strong or weak components your network data contains. Symmetric data will result in an analysis that does not distinguish between strong or weak components. Please note that if your data have several components, and if you wish to perform an additional analysis such as closeness centrality, which demands that you use a strongly connected network or subgraph (see Chapter 4 for further discussion), you are advised to first extract the main component of the network and perform the analysis on the main component. To do this in UCINET, go to *Data >Extract > Main component.*

CLIQUE AND N-CLIQUES

As noted in Chapter 2, the notion of a clique has an interesting historical development in social network analysis. One of the earliest uses of the term came from Warner and Lunt (1941) who defined cliques as informal groupings of people in which feelings of intimacy exist, and where the presence of particular group norms and sub-culture exist. The important distinction of a clique from the larger network structure was this sense for strong cohesiveness in the subgroup, which went hand in hand with that subgroup developing its own set of norms, rules and culture different from the larger network or social system in which it is embedded. Such cliques were important also as reference points for individuals and an individual's identity (Scott: 100).

In addition, Festinger (1949), Luce (1950) and Luce and Perry (1949) also offer early definitions of cliques, which formalize the definition according to graph-theoretic properties. Here, cliques refer to subgroups of people consisting of mutual ties. More specifically, a clique consists of a complete subgraph, i.e. one consisting of three or more actors, who are directly connected to one another through mutual ties. Such a definition offers a clear, precise articulation of how to define a clique based solely on network structural features, and does not depend on notions of culture, norms or intimacy (Wasserman and Faust, 1994).

An example of a clique, as defined above, can be found in Figure 7.2. In the network in Figure 7.2, there are two cliques: {A, B, C} and {H, G, E}. Actor F is only connected to actor E, and not to any of E's neighbours. Thus, actor F is not part of a clique. The same is true for actor D. Actor D is connected to actors B and E, but these two actors are not connected to one another.

Cliques are usually analysed on graphs, as opposed to digraphs, and indeed the UCINET procedure recommends symmetrizing your data prior to conducting a clique analysis. However, if you were to look for cliques in a digraph, it would be important to pay attention to the direction of the lines, i.e. cliques

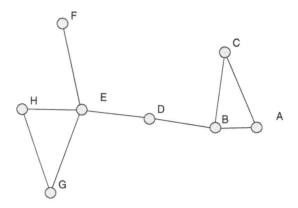

Figure 7.2 Two cliques in a network

would only include those ties that were reciprocal ones, and as such, a digraph can be expected to hold fewer cliques than a graph.

Problems/criticism with cliques and clique analysis

One potential problem in conducting clique analysis is that of clique overlap (Everett and Borgatti, 1998). A clique overlap occurs whenever one (or more) actor(s) from one clique can simultaneously be included as a member(s) of another clique. This co-membership in cliques is reflective of the notion of 'social circles' in sociology, where actors belonging to multiple groups are seen as playing important bridging roles that link social groups together and build cohesion on the societal level (Granovetter, 1973; Simmel, 1950).

Yet such co-membership, or overlap, can also cause confusion in interpreting the results of a clique analysis, as they can actually work to hide the underlying subgroup/clique structure. Recognizing this, Everett and Borgatti (1998) developed for UCINET a relatively simple way of handling these overlaps to reduce their complexity, and offer analysts a relatively straightforward means of seeing clique overlap. To illustrate, we will summarize the example offered by Everett and Borgatti (1998), making use of the Games relation from the Bank wiring dataset (one of the datasets found in UCINET).

Analysing for clique overlaps

Look at the Games relation (see Figure 7.3) of the Wiring dataset which is found in UCINET's example datafiles. Here, you can see 14 actors who appear to be grouped together in two cohesive subgroups, which are in turn connected together through actors W5 and W7.

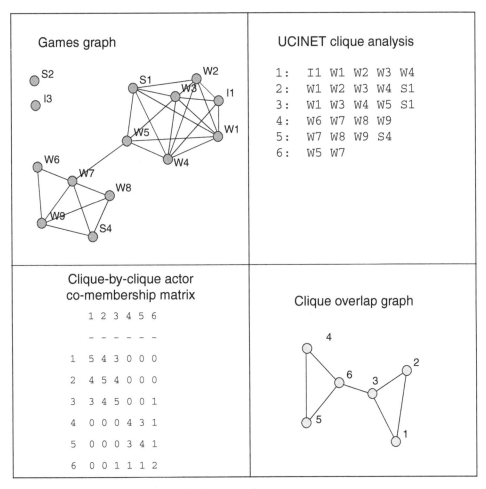

Figure 7.3   Games relation and clique analysis

However, conducting a clique analysis in UCINET where you specify the minimum number of nodes allowed in a clique to be two, results in a different kind of picture (see Figure 7.3): six cliques have been identified, and upon looking closely at the list, you can see multiple actors appearing in two to three different cliques. To reduce this complexity, UCINET next uses these results to first construct a two-mode matrix (i.e. which actors belong to which cliques), and from this two-mode matrix, UCINET then constructs a clique-by-clique matrix, the values in the cells representing the number of actors in each clique. Looking at this matrix, you can see that cliques 1, 2 and 3 are highly overlapped, sharing a high number of actors in common. Similarly, cliques 4 and 5 share a high number of actors in common. Clique 6, the last remaning one, shares only a few actors with the other cliques, but this is the only clique that bridges across the two larger groupings. In the final cell of the Table above, you can see a 'Clique overlap graph' of this clique-by-clique matrix. As you can see, the structure of the two graphs (Games graph and Clique overlap graph) appear quite similar, with the exception of the isolates not being included in the latter graph. Thus, the intuitive feeling of 'subgroup', captured by the visual graph of the Games relation, is again recaptured by analysing for the clique overlaps. In this way, cliques that overlap via a number of shared actors are brought together into larger groups, thus allowing the cliques with less overlaps to emerge to the surface.

Another criticism aimed at cliques and clique anlaysis, is that the definition of a clique is often seen as being overly strict in their criteria for which actors to include and exclude from a subgrouping. For example, the absence of one single tie (or arc) from a network would prevent a subgroup from being labelled a clique. As such, subgroups that reflect the intuitive notion for what constitutes a 'clique' would potentially be missed from the analysis.

In order to widen the possibilities for identifying cliques, early researchers on clique analysis developed another method, called *n-cliques* (Luce, 1950; Luce and Perry, 1949). An n-clique is a subgroup in which every pair of actors is connected by a path of length *n* or less. Thus, the '*n*' in the term n-clique, stands for the length of the path connecting one actor to another. For example, a traditional clique analysis would say that 'everyone in this clique are friends'. With a two-clique, however, one would expand this definition to say, 'Everyone in this clique is at least a friend of a friend'. Thus, the 'rules' by which one allows an actor to 'join' a clique have been relaxed. With the graph in Figure 7.2, a two-clique analysis reveals three two-cliques. These include the following:

{D, E, F, G and H}; {B, D and E}; {A, B, C and D }

Identifying subgroups through the n-clique method is a good strategy for times when you wish to understand how information can flow through intermediaries. This is because of n-clique's reliance on path lengths as a criterion for defining who is and is not part of a subgroup. Thus, if you wish to understand how information diffuses, or how information circulates within a cohesive subgroup, both through direct and indirect ties, the n-clique method is a good approach (Erickson, 1988; Wasserman and Faust, 1994).

Analysing for cliques and n-cliques

To analyse for cliques and n-cliques, your data should be dichotomised (1s and 0s) and symmetrical (i.e. undirected). In UCINET, go to *Network > Subgroups > Cliques* for analysing cliques and *Network > Subgroups > N-cliques* for n-cliques. For the n-cliques procedure, you will see an option for specifying the value of n. Please refer to the UCINET help files for further information on specifying the procedures and interpreting the output files.

Potential problems with using n-cliques

Keep in mind that an n-clique higher than three is not very meaningful. For example, with a three-clique, you are already essentially saying that 'a friend of a friend of a friend' is allowed to be part of a clique. Once *n* becomes higher than three, you are starting to move away from the sociological understanding of what a clique means.

In addition, using the n-clique approach is not advised when you believe that direct contact between individuals is most important for determining the level of cohesion in the subgroup. For such a consideration, an approach is needed that identifies subgroups based on direct ties between actors. The k-core approach, described below, is one such method.

K-CORES

A k-core is another way to conceptualize and measure cohesive subgroups. K-cores are not cohesive per se, but rather, k-cores contain cohesive subgroups. They build on the concept of degree centrality (see Chapter 4 for discussion of degree centrality); an actor is part of a k-core if they have (at least) a degree centrality of *k* within that group. Another way to define a k-core is to say that an actor is part of a k-core if they are part of *k* members of that subgroup. As the value of *k* becomes lower, subgroup sizes will increase, that is, it becomes easier to draw a boundary around the subgroup. As *k* becomes higher, it becomes harder for an actor to join a group. The lower and higher values for *k* translate into a hierarchy of subgroups, i.e. the k-cores are seen as 'nested' in one another. This is what I mean when I said earlier that k-cores 'contain' cohesive subgroups.

For example, if you are a member of a four-core, then you are also a member of a three-core and a two-core. This nesting implies that actors involved in higher level k-cores are seen as the more important actors for holding the network together. In addition, this nesting can be quite helpful for identifying the levels of cohesion in a wider network in that lower k-cores tend to connect higher (i.e. more dense) k-cores together. Thus, analyse for k-cores and then remove the lower k-cores until you see the network breaking apart. Such a strategy is particularly helpful when your network is very large.

Analysing for k-cores

To analyse a network for k-cores, your network data must be dichotomized and symmetric. In UCINET, go to *Networks > Regions > K-cores*. Here, you input your network dataset. The output shows you the nesting of k-cores, where 'degree' refers to the value of *k* for each k-core.

LAMBDA SETS

Finally, cohesive subgroups can be defined by contrasting the ties within the group to the ties outside the group. More importantly, if a subgroup is cohesive, then it should be difficult to break apart by the removal of one or more of its ties. If two actors are well-connected to one another, then ideally there is more than one path connecting them together. Thus, if you remove one of these paths, the two actors would still remain connected to each other.

Lambda sets build on this idea of connectivity between two actors, and it also takes into consideration how connectivity within a group compares to connectivity outside the group. More specifically, two actors – e.g. i and j – are considered to be part of the same lambda set if the number of paths connecting i and j together is larger than the number of paths connecting i to an outside actor (e.g. k) or j to k. As the lambda λ values increase, this restricts how many actors can join the set, as high values of λ imply a need for high numbers of independent paths linking two actors together. Thus, a lambda set with a high value for identifies the vulnerable bridges in a network; deleting or eliminating the ties in this particular set would disrupt and fragment the network.

Lambda sets are not based on ideas of nodal degree or path connectivity, and so they look different from the other cohesive subgroups defined by the other measures listed here.

In UCINET, to analyse for Lambda sets, go to *Network > Subgroups > Lambda sets*. Here, you input symmetrized, binary network data.

GIRVAN-NEWMAN ALGORITHM

This algorithm was developed by Girvan and Newman (2002) as a means to break down a complex network into clusters or 'communities'. The procedure works by a process of removing edges; more particularly, one first identifies which edges rest between cohesive segments of a network, and then one removes those edges. This results in a fragmentation process whereby the edges that remain are those contained with a cohesive subgroup. The process is repeated until the desired number of cohesive subgroups is attained.

As indicated above, the Girvan-Newman algorithm is based on the identification and removal of 'between' edges. Edge betweenness is similar to node betweeness, or what I have earlier discussed as 'betweenness centrality'. Here, the betweenness score for an edge is the number of times that edge lies on a geodesic path between a pair of disconnected actors.

Once the edge with the highest betweenness score is identified, then we remove that edge. This results in an increase in the number of components in the network, i.e. it will increase the network's fragmentation. The process of identifying between edges, removing them, and increasing the number of components gets repeated iteratively until all that remains are isolates. Thus, it is advisable to first identify how many components we would like to have remaining, in order to halt the algorithm before the network results in a group of isolates.

Through the NetDraw program in UCINET, you can make use of this Girvan-Newman algorithm. Proceed as follows:

1 In NetDraw go to *Analysis > Subgroups > Girvan-Newman*

2 In the window that appears, set the minimum and maximum range of cohesive subgroups you would like to attain.

3 Press OK. NetDraw will then proceed in calculating edge betweenness of the network; finding the edges with the highest score; and deleting these edges. If deleting the edge(s) results in the desired number of components, the algorithm will stop, otherwise, it will start the process again.

4 NetDraw displays which nodes belong to which partition through a colouring scheme. In the algorithm window, NetDraw also gives you Q values for the partitions. The Q value is a numerical score that reflects how good each partition is through comparing the number of internal links in the subgroups with how many one would expect if these links were distributed at random. Higher values of Q mean that the algorithm has found more significant groupings, whereas negative values are possibly showing that the groups are worse than one would expect from a random process.

RESEARCH EXAMPLES AND EXTENSIONS

Not surprisingly, much empirical research on adolescence and teenage relationships has made use of social network data and clique analyses. For example, research on the influence of cliques on teenager's drug use habits has been examined (Oetting and Beauvais, 1986), as well as on teenagers' smoking habits (Ennett et al., 1994). In general, this research shows that teenagers' behaviour is strongly linked to membership in a clique, whereby individual teenagers' behaviours mirror those of other clique members.

In addition to empirical work on cliques, extensions to the idea of cohesive subgroups, as presented in this chapter include (i) the use of affiliation networks as a basis for grouping individuals together (see Chapter 1 for discussion on affiliation networks); and (ii) clique analysis on valued data.

Affiliation networks

An affiliation network is an example of a two-mode network, where actors are shown in relation to events or organizations, resulting in an actor × event matrix and/or a bipartite graph. In using affiliation networks for uncovering subgroups, actors are organized into subgroups by virtue of their affiliation to different organizations or events (Kadushin, 1966; Simmel and Wolff, 1950). Thus, when two actors participate in the same event or belong to the same club, for example, these two can be conceptualized and portrayed as sharing a link between them.

A common method for analysing affiliation networks for subgroups is to transform the affiliation network into two, one-mode networks. These would consist of an actor × actor matrix, where cells contain the number of events shared by two actors, and an event × event matrix, which shows the number of actors two events share. Analysis would then take place, typically, on one of these one-mode networks, using the sorts of procedures used above. However, one needs to use some caution in interpreting the results; much of the structural information is lost in the transformation of two-mode networks to one-mode networks. For example, in the actor by actor matrix, although you have the number of events shared by two actors, you do not know which events these were, and similarly, in the event by event matrix, you lose the identity of the actors. Thus, some care is needed in interpreting the results.

Clique analysis on valued data

You can also perform clique analyses on valued social network data. Here, you first dichotomize the data according to a particular cut-off value c, and then search for cohesive subgroups within each dichotomized matrix. For example, if your social network data consists of valued data ranging from 1 (little contact) to 5 (frequent contact), then you can create five separate matrices, with each matrix representing data at level c or higher. Thus, matrix one would consist of all ties at level 1 or higher; matrix 2 would hold all ties at level 2 or higher and so forth. Typically, one expects for fewer and fewer subgroups to appear, the higher the cut-off value being used.

Extensions on algorithmic procedures

In a recent article, Davis and Carley (2008) developed a stochastic model and algorithm for detecting more 'fuzzy', overlapping groups, i.e. groups where the membership is not always so clear, and the boundaries between cliques/subgroups not so exclusive. Thus, the algorithm identifies the relative strength of membership to different groups, and in doing so, allows for a distinction between 'exclusive' categories of clique membership, and other more 'fuzzy' ones.

COMPARING THE DIFFERENT MEASURES

Here is a summary of the considerations you should keep in mind in choosing a particular measure:

- With components, you are mainly seeing whether actors are all linked together through some path (strong or weak). Weak components are considered the weakest form of cohesion, followed by strong components. You might wish to begin an analysis of cohesion with an analysis for components, to get an initial feel for the network's level of cohesion.

- With cliques, you are mainly interested in the mutuality of ties, and perceive membership to a subgroup as based on all actors having ties to all other actors in the clique. This analysis can be extended, as noted in this chapter, to an analysis of clique overlap, affiliation networks and valued data.

- If you perceive having direct ties to others an important consideration in your idea of a cohesive subgroup, but find the requirements of a clique analysis too strict, then looking for k-cores is preferable; here, you define subgroup membership as dependent on an actor being directly tied to a specified proportion of other subgroup members versus all subgroup members. Such an analysis is preferred if you believe, for instance, that multiple, redundant paths between group members is an important subgroup property (Erickson, 1988).

- N-cliques are a more relaxed version of a clique, and is preferable if you are interested in looking at how information can quickly reach others in the subgroup, and the role intermediaries might play in how information travels through the group (Erickson, 1988).

- If you feel defining subgroups in your study would be strengthened by a comparison between ties within the subgroup to ties outside the subgroup, then Lambda sets is the preferred measure.

- Girvan-Newman is helpful for very large networks, and it can also be a good alternative to clique analysis, especially if one can not identify a few, clear subgroups through clique analysis.

Finally, I find it both interesting and helpful to compare the results of the different analyses with one another. Such a comparison can highlight persistent patterns in the data, i.e. patterns that are repetitively captured by the different measures.

CONCLUSIONS AND SUMMARY

In this chapter, I introduced a variety of measures for uncovering cohesive subgroups. I began with a general discussion on the nature of cohesion, and proceeded with outlining a variety of different measures pertaining to subgroups. An important point in this discussion has been the difficulty in pinpointing one exact definition of cohesion that can be conceptualized and measured easily. Thus, different measures have developed to emphasize different dimensions of the discussion, such as the reachability of actors, mutuality of ties, and the extent to which a group's structure is resistant to fragmentation. In general, before attempting to measure for cohesive subgroups, it is a good idea to be clear on the theoretical implications of the different measures to use.

REFERENCES

Agneessens, F., Waege, H. and Lievens, J. (2006) 'Diversity in social support by role relations: A typology', *Social Networks*, 28: 427–41.

Alba, R. D. (1973) 'A graph-theoretic definition of a sociometric clique', *The Journal of Mathematical Sociology*, 3: 113–36.

Alba, R. D. and Moore, G. (1978) 'Elite social circles', *Sociological Methods Research*, November 7(2): 167–88.

Collins, R. (1988) *Theoretical Sociology*. San Diego: Harcourt Brace Jovanovich.

Coromina, L. and Coenders, G. (2006) 'Reliability and validity of egocentered network data collected via web: A meta-analysis of multilevel multitrait multimethod studies', *Social Networks*, 28: 209–31.

Davis, G. B. and Carley, K. M. (2008) 'Clearing the FOG: Fuzzy, overlapping groups for social networks', *Social Networks*, 30: 201–12.

Ennett, S. T., Bauman, K. E. and Koch, G. G. (1994) 'Variability in cigarette smoking within and between adolescent friendship cliques', *Addictive Behaviors*, 19: 295–305.

Erickson, B. (1988) 'The relational basis of attitudes', in B. Wellman and S. D. Berkowitz (eds), *Social Structures: A Network Approach*. Cambridge: Cambridge University Press.

Everett, M. G. and Borgatti, S. P. (1998) 'Analyzing clique overlap', *Connections*, 21: 49–61.

Festinger, L. (1949) 'The analysis of sociograms using matrix algebra', *Human Relations*, 2: 153–8.

Freeman, L. C. (1984) 'The impact of computer based communication on the social structure of an emerging scientific specialty', *Social Networks*, 6: 201–21.

Friedkin, N. E. (1984) 'Structural cohesion and equivalence explanations of social homogeneity', *Sociological Methods and Research*, 12.

Girvan, M. and Newman, M. E. J. (2002) 'Community structure in social and biological networks', *Proceedings of the National Academy of Sciences (PNAS)*, 99: 7821–6.

Granovetter, M. (1973) 'The strength of weak ties', *American Journal of Sociology*, 78: 1360–80.

Granovetter, M. (1982) 'The strength of weak ties: A network theory revisited', in P. Marsden and N. Lin (eds), *Social Structure and Network Analysis*. Beverly Hills: Sage.

Kadushin, C. (1966) 'The friends and supporters of psychotherapy: On social circles and urban life', *American Sociological Review*, 31: 786–802.

Krackhardt, D. (1998) 'Simmelian ties: super, strong and sticky', in R. Kramer and M. Neale (eds), *Power and Influence in Organizations*. Thousand Oaks, CA: Sage.

Krackhardt, D. (1999) 'The ties that torture: Simmelian tie analysis in organizations', in S. B. Bacharach, S. B. Andrews and D. Knoke (eds), *Research in the Sociology of Organizations*. Stanford, CT: JAI.

Krackhardt, D. and Kilduff, M. (2002) 'Structure, culture and Simmelian ties in entrepreneurial firms', *Social Networks*, 24: 279–90.

Lewin, K. (1951) *Field Theory in Social Science: Selected Theoretical Papers*. New York: Harper.

Luce, R. (1950) 'Connectivity and generalized n-cliques in sociometric group structure', *Psychometrika*, 15: 169–90.

Luce, R. and Perry, A. D. (1949) 'A method of matrix analysis of group structure', *Psychometrika*, 14.

Markovsky, B. N. (1998) 'Social network conceptions of group solidarity'. *The Problem of Solidarity: Theories and Models*. London: Routledge. Pp. 343–72.

Mokken, R. J. (1979) 'Cliques, clubs and clans', *Quality and Quantity*, 13: 161–73.

Moody, J. and White, D. R. (2003) 'Structural cohesion and embeddedness: A hierarchical concept of social groups', *American Sociological Review*, 68: 103–27.

Oetting, E. R. and Beauvais, F. (1986) 'Peer cluster theory: Drugs and the adolescent', *Journal of Counseling and Development*, 65: 17–31.

Scott, J. (2000) *Social Network Analysis: A Handbook*: Newbury Park, CA: Sage Publications.

Seidman, S. B. and Foster B. L. (1978) 'A graph theoretic generalization of the clique concept', *Journal of Mathematical Sociology*, 6: 139–54.

Simmel, G. (1950) 'Individual and society', in K. H. Wolff (ed.), *The Sociology of Georg Simmel*. New York: Free Press.

Simmel, G. and Wolff, K. H. (1950) *The Sociology of Georg Simmel*. Glencoe, II: Free Press.

Stoloff, J. A., Glanville, J. L. and Bienenstock, E. J. (1999) 'Women's participation in the labor force: The role of social networks', *Social Networks*, 21: 91–108.

Tönnies, F. (1887) *Gemeinschaft and Gesellschaft; Abhandlung des Communismus and des Socialismus als empirischer Culturformen*. Leipzig: Fues.

Warner, W. L., and Lunt, P. S. (1941) *The Social Life of a Modern Community*. New Haven: Yale University Press.

Wasserman, S. and Faust, F. (1994) *Social Network Analysis: Methods and Applications*. Cambridge: Cambridge University Press.

Wellman, B. and Wortley, S. (1990) 'Different strokes from different folks: Community ties and social support', *American Journal of Sociology*, 96: 558–88.

Wellman, B., Wong, R. Y.-L., Tindall, D. and Nazer, N. (1997) 'A decade of network change: Turnover, persistence and stability in personal communities', *Social Networks*, 19: 27–50.

8

NETWORK LEVEL

We began this section of the book looking at structural concepts and analyses pertaining to individual actors, and then we moved on to dyads and triads, and subgroups. We are now looking at the level of the network as a whole.

When you analyse the entire network, you are hoping to uncover some features of the network that characterize the network as a whole. In certain ways, I have already shown you how you can do this through analysing for 'lower' level properties such as triads; as discussed earlier, much of the research occurring in the 1960s and 1970s was interested in seeing the extent to which networks contained tendencies for transitive triads, as doing so enabled an analyst to characterize a network as being 'transitive' or not. Characterizing a network as 'transitive' through the presence of transitive triads automatically implied other global structural features, for example clustering. Thus, conducting a triad census has often been seen as linking micro-level structures to global ones, i.e. through uncovering lower-level structural tendencies, one can say something about the network as a whole.

Here, in this chapter, we will focus just on those structural measures that take into consideration the global network in two important respects: the extent to which a network 'stays together' versus the extent to which a network breaks apart. When we are discussing the extent to which a network *does not* break into these sub-structures, we are looking at issues of cohesion (Moody and White, 2003; White and Harary, 2001).

As we have already discussed strong ties and subgroups earlier in this book, let me start off here with a discussion on the network-level measures of cohesion with that of density.

DENSITY

Density refers to the proportion of ties in a network that are actually present. In essence, it looks at the extent to which all the individual actors in a network are linked together. For example, suppose you enter a classroom at University; you look around at the other students in the classroom, and you notice that there are roughly seven other students in the room. Further, you also notice that roughly five of these students seem to already know each other; they sit off to one side and seem to be engaged in a casual group discussion with one another. The other two students, like yourself, do not appear to know any of the other students in the room. In this sort of situation, potentially, all eight of the students (including yourself) could have known each other previously. In fact, however, only five of the eight students seem to have some sort of social tie. Thus, roughly 60 per cent of the students in the room know one another. This network of classroom students then has a density of 60 per cent.

Network density (d) is calculated as follows:

$$d = \frac{L}{n(n-1)/2};$$

where L refers to the actual number of lines present in the network and n to the number of nodes present in the network. In calculating density, you need to calculate the number of maximum possible ties in the network. This is done by counting how many nodes a network contains; each node can be connected to all other nodes, potentially, except to oneself, and so an undirected graph with n nodes could contain a maximum number of $n(n-1)/2$ lines.

Calculating density on a digraph is similar. As you are interested in the direction of the lines, then you count all lines, which is reflected in the denominator of the equation:

$$d = \frac{L}{n(n-1)}$$

If your data are valued, then the density score represents the total of all values divided by the number of possible ties in the network. Thus, the density score is the average value found in the network.

The above example encapsulates the idea of density; in general, density counts how many actual ties exist in a network, and expresses this number as a proportion of the potential ties that could exist in the network. The higher the density score, the denser your network, and thus, one might say, the more cohesive is your network.

In the network shown in Figure 8.1, the density is 0.38, which means that 38 per cent of the potential ties this network *could* have are *actually* present. The mathematical formula for calculating density is found to the right in the textbox.

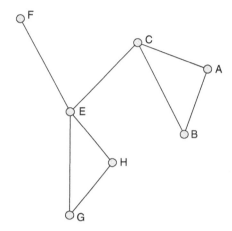

Figure 8.1 Graph showing two cliques

Another point to be made regarding the density of the graph shown in Figure 8.1, is that this graph holds two cliques, which are highly dense structures themselves (see Chapter 6). This issue of the role subgroups play in density scores, and how this relates to notions about cohesion, is something I shall discuss later in this chapter.

Issues in using density: Thinking about centralization and size

Although density is a popular means for conceptualizing and measuring cohesion, there are a number of issues one needs to be wary of in its use. Establishing the link between a density score and the conclusion that a network is or is not cohesive is not so straightforward. Three of the biggest concerns are summarized below.

Increasing density through one person: Centralization

What if the density score for a particular network is relatively high (for example 50 per cent or more), but this high score results mainly from the ties occurring through a single person? Does this mean the network is cohesive? Because density is based on how many ties are present in the network, one or two individuals having a disproportionately high number of ties to others in the network might raise the density score. Figure 8.2 illustrates this situation.

In Figure 8.2, Graph A and Graph B have the same number of nodes (g = 6), yet the structures are very different: Graph B has most of its ties passing through a single

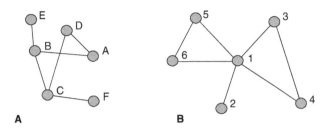

Figure 8.2   Two graphs with the same level of density

node (node 1), whereas Graph A has a more even distribution of ties amongst the nodes. Does this difference in structure affect the density score? No it does not: both Graph A and Graph B have a density score of 0.40, although one would hesitate in saying the two are equally cohesive. Because Graph A has ties more evenly distributed amongst all the nodes, this graph appears more *interconnected* than Graph B, and this interconnectedness is more in keeping with the idea of cohesion, i.e. that all the actors in a network are (more or less) tied to one another.

A good way to see the extent to which your graph's density score depends on the ties of one individual node is to make use of the degree centralization score. Degree centralization looks at the extent to which one actor in a network is holding all of the ties in that network. Like density, centralization is measured as a proportion, where a network with a centralization score of 1 indicates all ties centring around one actor. This is demonstrated in Figure 8.3, which has a centralization score of 1.

Degree centralization is based on degree centrality. Thus, the variation in the degree centrality of the actors is divided by the maximum possible degree

---

The centralization score, based on degree centralization is expressed as follows:

$$C = \frac{\Sigma C_D \text{max} - C_D(n_i)}{\text{max}\Sigma C_D \text{max} - C_D(n_i)} \quad \text{Where,}$$

C_D max = the largest degree centrality score across the set of actors $C_D(n_i)$ = degree centrality of actor n_i

max ΣC_D max–CD (n_i) = the theoretical maximum possible sum of differences in actor centrality.

Centralization scores can be computed for each measure of centrality, as discussed by Freeman (1979). Please visit this article if you are curious about any of these other centralization measures.

Figure 8.3   Star graph

centrality variation, and this variation also takes into consideration the network's size. The formula for degree centralization is given in the Text box. As with degree centrality, degree centralization should be computed on simple graphs, i.e. undirected, binary network data.

Using degree centralization alongside density is somewhat similar to what statisticians do when they make use of a mean and standard deviation. The mean is a measure of central tendency and the standard deviation is a measure of spread or variance. Similarly, centralization measures the extent to which ties hover around one actor, and density measures the extent to which all the ties are actually present.

In Figure 8.2, Graph A has a centralization score of 0.30 versus graph B, which has a network centralization score of 0.80. Thus, the high centralization score for B alerts you to the fact that this network's density is highly dependent on small (in this case one) actor(s).

Network centralization can also be used as an indicator for a core–periphery structure. If a network is characterized by a high centralization score, then it has a clear delineation between core and periphery. That is, a centralization score tends to be higher when it contains both very central and very peripheral actors. If there is more variation in centrality scores among actors, then this implies that the centralization score will be higher, as centralization is based on variation. The core is composed of only a small number of nodes, which makes the diffusion of information relatively efficient: once the core has news of the innovation, the rest of the network quickly hears.

Decreasing density through increasing network size

Another issue to consider when calculating density is the size of your network; as the formula for density shows, calculating density depends on the size of your network, as the amount of ties that exist in a network depends on how many actors are in that network. Larger networks (that is, networks with higher numbers of actors) can have a larger number of ties within them than smaller networks. For example, in the scenario I gave you earlier, the classroom holding just eight students had a higher 'chance' of having a large portion of the students knowing one another. If the situation had been different, that is, if the classroom I described had contained 100 students, the small group of five students would not have translated into such a high density score. It's hard to know a lot of people (unless, perhaps, you have been on Facebook for a long time!).

Thus, because larger networks have a greater potential for more ties, this very fact makes it difficult for large networks to have high density values; it is much easier for smaller networks to reach their full potential density score. Therefore, in interpreting your density score, you need to consider your network's size.

There exists a second issue regarding network size and density, and that pertains to comparing the density scores of different networks. If you wish to compare the density of one network to another, to see which network is 'more' cohesive, you need to make sure that the two (or more) networks you are comparing are the same size! For example, it would not be very fair to compare the classroom network of eight students with the one of 100 students! Density scores are calculated based on the size of networks, which results in some networks having a higher likelihood to have high density than others.

Thus, when calculating and presenting your density score, you need to consider both centralization and network size, and I would advise you to present both these scores alongside your density score.

An easy way to see the size of a network is to go to *Data > Display* in UCINET. This procedure shows you the matrix of your network, where rows and columns are numbered. At the bottom of the matrix, UCINET tells you how many rows and columns are in your network. Thus, for example, a 21×21 matrix indicates that there are 21 nodes/actors in your network.

Increasing density through number of cohesive subgroups

Friedkin's (Friedkin, 1981) study on density as a measure of network cohesion highlighted another problematic issue pertaining to the use of density. As he notes, density is a misleading indicator of cohesion in cases where the network in question has many cohesive subgroups; similar to the issue of having high network density resulting from a high centralization score, a high network density score can easily result from many subgroups. Friedkin's findings show that low densities in large networks may reflect more structural cohesion than higher densities in smaller networks, as such large networks have fewer cohesive subgroups, and hence, less amount of 'fragmentation'. Thus, in looking at density scores alongside network size, one need not jump to the conclusion that a low-density score in a large network indicates a network is *not* cohesive, just as a network with high density and a high number of subgroups need not imply the network *is* cohesive. This is precisely the issue with the graph shown in Figure 8.1.

DIAMETER AND AVERAGE PATH LENGTH

Given that density seems somewhat problematic, an alternative means for exploring network-level cohesion is through the network's diameter and/or average path length. Diameter refers to the longest geodesic in a network, where a geodesic refers to the shortest path between two actors. If the diameter of a network is relatively small, then everyone in the network is fairly 'close' to one another, and thus, the network can be seen as cohesive. Similar to this idea of network diameter is that of average path length. Here, you average the geodesics in the network as an indicator for how close together actors are to one another.

To find the geodesics linking actors together, go to *Network > Cohesion > Distance* in UCINET. Here, specify the network file you wish to analyse. The output gives you a matrix showing you the geodesic distance between any two actors in the network. The diameter of the network would be the longest geodesic distance in this matrix. The average path length would be the average geodesic in this matrix. You can then bring the output of this file into a different procedure so that UCINET can isolate the diameter and average path length for you: go to *Tools > Univariate Stats*. Here, the file you input is the matrix created by the previous procedure (i.e. the distance procedure). Be sure to specify 'matrix' as the dimension you wish to analyse. The output of this procedure gives you univariate statistics on your distance matrix. The mean value is the average path length, and the maximum value is the matrix diameter.

COMPARING MEASURES OF COHESION

To understand how diameter, average path length, density and centralization compare to one another, let's return to our earlier example of the two graphs found in Figure 8.2. Below, in Table 8.1, you will see that I have inserted the various cohesion measures in order to compare them.

Table 8.1 is useful for comparing the various measures of cohesion, which in turn can aid you in interpreting how, and in what ways, your network is cohesive. As you may have realized already, trying to determine at which point your network is or is not 'cohesive' is a tricky business; there is no absolute cut-off point where you can say, for example, that below a certain density value the network is lacking in cohesion and above another value the network is cohesive. Thus, all these measures and their subsequent values are relative ones, and are best understood in those terms; is a network or actors appearing, over time, to become more cohesive? Are two networks (of the same size!) different in terms of their level of cohesion? Such questions can be answered through use of these measures, as well as any other theoretical justifications you may have developed for determining that a particular value reflects a level of cohesion.

The important thing to remember in comparing two or more networks' levels of cohesion is that the networks are of the same size. As with many measures discussed in this book, the size of the network (that is, how many

Table 8.1 Cohesion measures for Graph A (n = 6) and Graph B (n = 6)

	Graph A	Graph B
Density	0.40	0.40
Centralization	0.30	0.80
Diameter	3	2
Average path length	1.8	1.53

actors are in the network) affects the scores of density, for example, as well as centralization, diameter and so forth.

EXTENSIONS: MEASURING THE GLOBAL NETWORK PROPERTIES OF SMALL WORLDS AND LARGE-SCALE NETWORKS

As noted in Chapter 2, with the rise in computational power, alongside the increased interest in topics such as the Internet, the worldwide web, small worlds and scale-free networks, recent social network research has focused on large-scale networks (e.g. Fenner et al., 2007; Gonzalez-Bailon, 2009; Goodreau, 2007; Latapy et al., 2008; Moody, 2001). Of key interest here are such topics as how such large networks form and evolve (Doreian, 2006; Goyal et al., 2006; Hummon, 2000; Jackson and Wolinsky, 1996; Robins et al., 2005), and some of the issues pertaining to the analysis of such large networks (Fenner et al., 2007; Latapy et al., 2008; Moody, 2001).

In relation to network-level measures, one popular topic is that of small worlds (Robins et al., 2005; Watts, 1999, 2003, 2004). Here, a particular kind of large network is of interest, that is, one which has the following characteristics: low density, high average clustering and short average path length. Such networks are characterized as 'small worlds' in that, while they contain a large number of actors, all actors can reach all other actors through a small number of intermediary links in a chain of acquaintance. This sort of paradox is one of the main interests in small worlds, but in addition, scholars are intrigued by the idea that one could hypothetically figure out, on the local, individual level, the optimum short path linking oneself to any other target individual in the network (see Schnettler, 2009 for a review).

In this chapter, you learnt about density and average path length, and such network-level measures are used in identifying small worlds. In addition, measuring for average clustering, another important characteristic of small worlds, is quite similar to taking the average of all the ego network density scores found in a given network (see Chapter 4 on actor-level measures). In fact, such a means for calculating average clustering is used by Watts (1999), but you can see Newman's (2003) suggestions for alternatives.

SUMMARY AND CONCLUSION

This chapter focused on the network level, with a particular emphasis on cohesion measures such as density, centralization, diameter and average path length. In discussing the topic of small worlds, these measures, as well as average clustering, were shown to be quite important for identifying which large-scale networks could be characterized as being 'small worlds.'

Also, discussion was given in this chapter regarding some of the issues or concerns in measuring for cohesion, and Table 8.1 illustrates how using multiple measures for cohesion, alongside a visual display of your graph, are a good way forward for coming to grips with notions of cohesion with your given network.

REFERENCES

Doreian, P. (2006) 'Actor network utilities and network evolution', *Social Networks*, 28: 137–64.

Fenner, TO, Levene, M. and Loizou, G. (2007) 'A model for collaboration networks giving rise to a power-law distribution with an exponential cutoff', *Social Networks*, 29: 70–80.

Freeman, L. C. (1979) 'Centrality in social networks', *Social Networks*, 1: 215–39.

Friedkin, N. E. (1981) 'The development of structure in random networks: An analysis of the effects of increasing network density on five measures of structure', *Social Networks*, 3: 41–52.

Gonzalez-Bailon, S. (2009) 'Opening the black box of link formation: Social factors underlying the structure of the web', *Social Networks*, 31: 271–80.

Goodreau, S. M. (2007) 'Advances in exponential random graph (p*) models applied to a large social network', *Social Networks*, 29: 231–48.

Goyal, S., Van der Leij, M. J. and Moraga-Gonzalez, J. L. (2006) 'Economics: An emerging small world', *Journal of Political Economy*, 114: 403–12.

Hummon, N. P. (2000) 'Utility and dynamic social networks', *Social Networks*, 22: 221–49.

Jackson, M. O. and Wolinsky, A. (1996) 'A strategic model of social and economic networks', *Journal of Economic Theory*, 71: 44–74.

Latapy, M., Magnien, C. and Del Vecchio, N. (2008) 'Basic notions for the analysis of large two-mode networks', *Social Networks*, 30: 31–48.

Moody, J. (2001) 'Peer influence groups: Identifying dense clusters in large networks', *Social Networks*, 23: 261–83.

Moody, J. and White, D. R. (2003) 'Structural cohesion and embeddedness: A hierarchical concept of social groups', *American Sociological Review*, 68(1): 103–27.

Newman, M. E. J. (2003) 'The structure and function of complex networks', *SIAM Review*, 45: 167–256.

Robins, G., Pattison, P. and Woolcock, J. (2005) 'Small and other worlds: Global network structures from local processes', *American Journal of Sociology*, 110: 894–936.

Schnettler, S. (2009) 'A structured overview of 50 years of small-world research', *Social Networks*, 31: 165–78.

Watts, D. J. (1999) 'Networks, dynamics and the small world phenomenon', *American Journal of Sociology*, 105: 493–527.

Watts, D. J. (2003) *Six Degrees: The Science of a Connected Age*. New York: Norton.

Watts, D. J. (2004) 'The "new" science of networks', *Annual Review of Sociology*, 30: 243–70.

White, D. R. and Harary, F. (2001) 'The cohesiveness of blocks in social networks: Node connectivity and conditional density', *Sociological Methodology*, 31: 305–59.

9

POSITIONS AND ROLES ANALYSIS

We have discussed all the different levels of networks thus far: ego networks and actor centrality; dyads and triads; cohesive subgroups; and the network as a whole. I have left this discussion on position and role analysis as the last chapter in the discussion of levels, as this analysis starts bringing together the different levels of networks for understanding the network structure as a whole.

Positions and roles are important concepts in sociology and in network analysis in particular, and the two concepts are intrinsically linked. In general, one begins with a positional analysis, and from this, one derives the role analysis (although Wasserman and Faust, 1994 discuss ways for reversing this order). The position of an actor is defined by the group or 'block' to which an actor is assigned. In contrast, roles are defined by the relations between blocks. For example, if one block seems to be more active in connecting with the other blocks, then the actors in this block are seen as, in general, taking on the 'role' of active communicators.

Because the process of conducting a positional and roles analysis is a bit complicated, I would like to first start this chapter off with some intuitive examples to help you develop a mind-frame for the importance (and distinctions between) positions and roles.

EXAMPLE OF POSITIONS AND ROLES

The example of primary school

Let's start with the example of a primary school. In such a setting, the group of actors we would like to analyse include all the teachers and students in this particular school. In this setting, the 'teachers' tend to have similar ties to the 'students' and vice versa. In other words, the teachers 'teach' the students and the students 'are taught' by the teachers. Not all the teachers in this school teach exactly the same students in the school, but the patterning of relations from one group of actors (teachers) to another (students) is strong enough to assign the label of 'teachers' to one subset of actors and 'students' to the other.

What I have described above essentially reflects positional and role analysis; subsets of actors are grouped together into what we call positional 'blocks' or 'classes', and these subsets are derived from how actors within the subset share similar ties to others in a different subset. Thus, unlike cohesive subgroups, which are essentially defined by how closely knit actors are to one another in the subgroup, subsets based on positions are derived from how actors within the subset connect to others outside the subset as well as within the subset. All the teachers in the school tend to have similar sorts of relations with students and vice versa.

Roles are defined by how these positional blocks relate to one another. In the above example, actors in the teacher's block relate to actors in the student's block in the same way, that is, they all 'teach' these students, but again, not all teachers teach all the same students.

Conducting a positional/role analysis is typically done on multiple relations; more particularly, looking at the multiple relations that link positions together give an analyst an overall picture of the role structure in a given network. In the above example, teachers relate to students through teaching, but teachers might also 'advise' students and 'mentor' students. Teachers, however, would not tend to be 'friends' with students, but they would probably be friends with one another. Thus, multiple relations across the same set of actors and their positions give a richer portrayal of what it means for an individual to fulfil the 'role' of a teacher.

The above example illustrates how *roles* derive from looking at the *multiple relations* linking *positions* together. This process may seem a bit complicated, but keep in mind that we already perform such analyses, on some level, in our day-to-day life. For example, the term 'sister-in-law' refers to a particular role in our society, one that is derived from two different kinds of relations, i.e. descent and marriage, and the position a particular female holds in the network.

In what follows, I shall walk you through the steps of positional and roles analysis. Because the process is a bit detailed, and can be slightly complicated, I would like to offer you a quick overview before getting started. The process involves a clear set of steps, but each step in itself can be somewhat complicated.

THE STEPS IN POSITIONAL AND ROLE ANALYSIS: A QUICK OVERVIEW

1 *Defining equivalence* First, in assigning actors to positions, you need to choose a definition of equivalence that meets your requirements, and then you must choose a suitable means for measuring for equivalence. Here, I focus upon the

'classic' definition of equivalence, that being structural equivalence (Lorraine and White, 1971) as well as regular equivalence White and Reitz (1983).

2 *Measure for equivalence* There are a variety of ways to measure for equivalence, and only some are covered in this text. I spend most of the time introducing the use of Pearson r as a measure for equivalence, but interested readers can explore other measures, one popular alternative being Euclidean distance (Burt, 1976). I also give a brief discussion to the REGE algorithm in this chapter, under the discussion of regular equivalence.

3 *Assign actors to positions* Next, you need to assign actors to positions, based on the definition of equivalence you have chosen. Here, you use multirelational data for assigning actors to positions, or 'blocks'. Once again, there are different options for how you assign actors to positions. In this chapter, I focus on the 'classic' technique for assigning actors to positions, i.e. the CONCOR procedure (Boorman and Harrison, 1976; Brieger et al., 1975; White et al., 1976), and in doing so, I measure equivalence through Pearson correlation coefficient similarity matrix. However, there are other ways to measure equivalence, and I shall offer some suggestions for this in this chapter.

In assigning actors to positions, one typically makes use of either block matrices or hierarchical clustering to more clearly see the similarity of actors, and how similarity groups actors together. Here, I focus on block matrices, again, to reflect the more classic way of conducting a positional analysis, but readers can also make use of other procedures, e.g. hierarchical clustering or multidimensional scaling.

4 *Formulate a simplified statement of the relations between positions, i.e. role anlaysis*: The classic means of simplifying positions and showing how they relate is through image matrices and reduced graphs. In simplifying the positions and showing how positions relate to one another, one is now able to analyse the roles in the network.

5 *Interpret* From the image matrix and/or the reduced graph one gains an overall view of the role structure of the network. To help interpret these roles better, one either makes use of aggregated attribute data for individual actors, such as average age and/or gender, or one compares these matrices to 'ideal' types that offer a theoretical picture of the role structure of the network.

In what follows, you will see a step-by-step description for conducting block modelling, which is the 'classic' approach to conducting a positional/role analysis, and which makes use of the theoretical concept of 'structural equivalence'. I then offer readers a more general description of an alternative approach to structural equivalence, that being regular equivalence and the use of the REGE algorithm.

CLASSIC POSITIONAL AND ROLE ANALYSIS: BLOCK MODELLING AND CONCOR

As Chapter 2 discussed, Lorraine and White (1971) formalized a means of looking at positions through use of matrix algebra. They defined actors as sharing the same position if they were structurally equivalent, and in White et al. (1976) they expanded on this earlier work to demonstrate how structural equivalence as a form of positional analysis could be used to analyse for network roles. Their positional and role analysis was an example of *block modelling*, and in deriving block models, they made use of the CONCOR procedure. Thus, in this section, I will demonstrate this version of positional and role analysis proposed by Harrison White and his colleagues, i.e. I will describe and demonstrate the block modelling approach for positional and role analysis, making use of structural equivalence as the definition of equivalence, and making use of the CONCOR procedure as a means for measuring the extent to which actors are equivalent.

Block modelling groups actors together into blocks, according to how similar these actors are to one another in their relations to others. The goal of block modelling is to reduce a large network to a smaller and simpler representation so that positions and roles can be more easily interpreted. A block model consists of two main components: (i) a partitioning of actors in a network into blocks based on multirelational data, where each block represents a unique position in the network; and (ii) a representation of the ties within and between positions. Taken together, block models are seen as formal *models or hypotheses* about multirelational networks.

White et al. (1976) made use of the CONCOR procedure when they conducted their block models, and we shall be using that same procedure in this chapter. CONCOR stands for 'the convergence of iterated correlations', and as the name implies, it makes use of the Pearson correlation coefficient as a means for measuring for structural equivalence between actors (although in UCINET, you can also use other similarity matrices as input. See the Help files in UCINET for discussion).

Step 1: Assembling a multirelational network data file

A full positional and role analysis is typically conducted on multirelational data. In UCINET, all positional and role procedures allow you to input multirelational datasets. For example, you can input the dataset SAMPSON, a multirelational dataset found within the UCINET application, and all ten relations will be automatically included in the positional analysis procedure you choose. You can also create your own multirelational file in UCINET. This can be done through the *Data > Join* command (see textbox).

In what follows, I shall walk you through the steps of building a block model for a given network. We will be using Krackhardt's High-Tech data, found in UCINET. These data consist of three relations on a group of managers in a high-tech firm. The relations are FRIENDSHIP, ADVICE and REPORTS_TO. All the relations are directional and dichotomous. In addition, the High-Tech dataset includes actor attribute data, such as age, length of tenure, level in the corporate hierarchy, and each actor's department. These data are excellent for positional and role analysis; they are multirelational and the attribute data will allow us to see how positions and roles derived from the networking data compare with formal roles such as level in the hierarchy and actors' department. Please note that you can make use of directional or symmetric data in conducting a positional/role analysis.

Creating a multirelational data file in UCINET

For this example, I am only using two of the three network files found in the Krackhardt High-Tech data. This is because I wish to focus on the informal, personal ties linking actors together versus the formal hierarchy which is reflected in the 'who reports to whom' dataset. Thus, I shall focus on the social network data files ADVICE and FRIENDSHIP, versus the formal hierarchy that is reflected in the REPORTS_TO network datafile.

To create a multirelational network datafile with only these two files, I must first unpack the entire dataset of three relations (*Data > Unpack*), and then combine the two relations of interest into a separate, new datafile through the *Data > Join* command. The resulting network datafile is called 'Joined'. This is the datafile I shall use in my positional and role analysis.

Step 2: Choose a definition of equivalence

Now that you have your network data, you need to assign actors to positions based on a definition of how equivalent these actors are to one another. There are a few different ways to conceptualize and measure 'equivalence', but for this chapter, we will mainly focus upon one of the earliest definitions of equivalence, that being *structural equivalence* as defined by Lorraine and White (1971). Structural equivalence defines two actors as equivalent if they share the exact same ties to the exact same others. Figure 9.1 offers a visual interpretation of this definition.

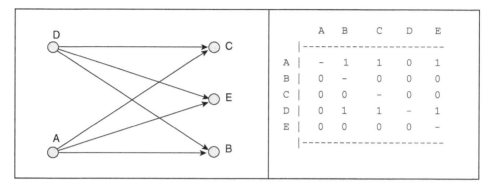

Figure 9.1   Digraph showing structurally equivalent actors

Figure 9.1 shows a digraph and matrix for a network of structurally equivalent actors. In the above digraph, actors A and D are structurally equivalent as are actors B, C and E. Looking at the matrix of this network, you will notice that the cell entries for actors A and D are the same, and at the cell entries for actors B, C and E, one can see that these cell entries are also the same. Thus, structurally equivalent actors have the exact same cell entries for their rows and columns in an adjacency matrix.

Note that the arcs of structurally equivalent actors also share the same direction. If, for example, the tie linking actor D to actor B were to reverse directions, so that B is choosing D and not the reverse, then only C and E would be structurally equivalent for this network. Actors A and D would no longer be structurally equivalent, nor would actors B, D and E. Similarly, if we were to start playing with the ties' strengths, i.e. if we were to start looking at valued network data, then actors could only be structurally equivalent if all ties to all others also had the same value. *Thus, we say that actors are structurally equivalent if they share the same ties with the same others, and in addition, the same values, type of relation(s), and direction of ties.*

Because structural equivalence demands that actors have the exact same ties to others, it is rare, if not impossible, to find structurally equivalent actors in real life networks. Thus, structural equivalence can be seen as a type of ideal, and the analyst is mainly interested in seeing to what extent actors approach this ideal. Thus, analysing data for structural equivalence is an exercise in seeing the extent to which actors *approximate* structural equivalence (Burt, 1976; Wasserman and Faust, 1994). Measuring for structural equivalence (found in the next step) can thus be used for uncovering *the extent to which* two actors share the same ties to the same others in a given network.

There are a number of ways to measure the extent to which actors are structurally equivalent, and a careful look at the UCINET program and Help File will show you many of the options. For this chapter, however, I have opted to describe the CONCOR procedure, as this was the procedure used in White et al.'s (1976) classic article on block modelling, the basis of this chapter.

Step 3: Measuring for equivalence through CONCOR

Using CONCOR in UCINET to measure for equivalence is a relatively simple procedure, yet there are some initial choices and options you need to be aware of before running the procedure. Thus, in this section, I will quickly demonstrate how to run CONCOR in UCINET, explaining the different options to you along the way.

In UCINET, you select CONCOR by going to *Network > Roles and Positions > Structural > Concor > Standard*. The CONCOR window that appears in UCINET, as shown in Figure 9.2, offers you a number of initial options for running the CONCOR procedure.

- *Including the transpose* The transpose of a network matrix refers to a new matrix, whereby the columns of the original matrix become the rows in the new matrix, and the rows in the original matrix become the columns in the new one. For directional network data, it is advised that you include the transpose of the matrix.

- *Self ties* Another initial option for running CONCOR is choosing whether to ignore the matrix diagonal. The diagonal of matrix, you may recall, looks at an actors' ties to him/herself (and thus referred to as 'self ties'). With most social networks, we are not interested in self ties, and so the default option to ignore the diagonal would be accurate for most situations.

- *Interactive* Finally, you can select whether you want the procedure to be interactive or not. Choosing the 'interactive' option will give you some flexibility in deciding how many 'blocks' or 'positions' you want to create in your data matrix, and I would advise you to select this option.

Once you have inputted your dataset and made selections for the various options, you can run the CONCOR procedure by clicking the 'OK' button. CONCOR now goes through a process of assigning actors to positions, based on how similar they are to one another. Along the way, UCINET asks you whether you want to further break-down blocks or not. In general, if the block has a large number of nodes in it, then you might wish to consider breaking the block down into smaller ones.

The process of assigning actors to blocks involves the use of a correlation matrix; you may have come across a correlation matrix in other texts or courses in the context of discussing the Pearson correlation coefficient (also commonly known as Pearson r). Here, the correlation matrix shows the similarity between two actors through using the standard Pearson product–moment correlation

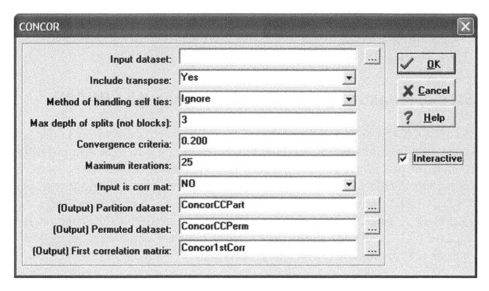

Figure 9.2   CONCOR Window

coefficient for each cell in the matrix. Each coefficient between each pair of actors is found in a separate cell, where the value of 1 indicates perfect correlation, and a 0 the opposite (no correlation). CONCOR uses these correlation coefficients as measures for structural equivalence between actors, so that a 1 would mean two actors are perfectly, structurally equivalent; a 0 would indicate no equivalence/similarity between actors, and the values between 0 and 1 the extent to which a pair of actors are structurally equivalent.[1]

[1]Measuring for the extent to which actors are equivalent involves using a similarity matrix, and besides Pearson r, another common way to form a similarity matrix, is through *Euclidean distance* (Burt, 1976). Here, the distances between rows and columns for the two actors are calculated, and if the distance between two actors is zero, these two actors have the exact same ties to others in the network, i.e. a value of zero means the two actors are structurally equivalent. Larger values for Euclidean distance indicate the extent to which two actors are not structurally equivalent.

The difference between Euclidean distance and Pearson correlation is not great, and conceptually, the two measures are nearly the same. However, research has shown that Pearson correlation is better at picking up general patterns of ties between two actors. In contrast, Euclidean distance seems to be more sensitive to valued data; if two actors differ in the values of their ties, for example, where one offers higher ratings to others than the second actor, but otherwise the two actors nominate the same others as contact, then Euclidean distance would show less structural equivalence than would Pearson correlation (Burt, 1986; Faust and Romney, 1985, 1986). Thus, Euclidean distance retains the differences in valued data when calculating for the equivalence of actors. On a more technical point, keep in mind that Pearson's r always ranges between −1 and +1. In contrast, Euclidean distance can range from 0 (meaning perfect structural equivalence) to infinity.

The CONCOR procedure calculates a correlation matrix for you, and shows this matrix as part of its output. Figure 9.3 shows you the correlation matrix calculated on the Krackhardt multirelational datafile, using the CONCOR procedure and including the transpose matrices for the multirelational datafile. This correlation matrix is part of the output UCINET gives you when you use the CONCOR procedure.

The matrix in Figure 9.3 shows higher values indicating more similarity between actors. For example, actors 5 and 3 seem to be more structurally equivalent than actors 3 and 1. Once again, this correlation matrix is automatically created as part of the UCINET output file.

Although a careful study of the above matrix enables us to see which pairs of actors are more equivalent than others, it is still difficult to make any assignment of actors, as the matrix itself holds a lot of numbers that are in no way arranged into any sort of visible patterns. Thus, a procedure is needed that will make use of this information to assign actors to positions, and display these assigned positions in a visually intuitive representation.

Step 3: Assigning actors to blocks

To assign actors to positions, the CONCOR procedure takes the initial correlation matrix and runs successive correlations on this matrix until a final matrix is reached containing only +1s and −1s. In other words, CONCOR forces actors into positions through iterative rounds of analyses. When this is completed, the correlation matrix is seen as having 'converged', and all cell entries are now either 1 or −1. This converged matrix is then used to split the network into two 'blocks', where all actors within the same block are positively correlated, and all actors within different blocks are negatively correlated. With CONCOR, after initially separating actors into two blocks, each of these two blocks then undergo

	1	2	3	4	5	6	7	8	9	10	11	12
1	–	0.4	0.1	0.4	0.1	0.2	0.1	0.4	0.2	0.3	0.3	0.2
2	0.4	–	0.0	0.1	−0.1	0.3	0.3	0.4	0.1	−0.2	0.2	0.5
3	0.1	0.0	–	0.4	0.6	−0.1	0.3	0.4	0.6	0.2	0.1	0.1
4	0.4	0.1	0.4	–	0.3	0.1	0.2	0.5	0.4	0.3	0.1	0.2
5	0.1	−0.1	0.6	0.3	–	0.0	0.1	0.2	0.6	0.2	0.2	0.0
6	0.2	0.3	−0.1	0.1	0.0	–	0.3	0.2	0.0	0.1	0.4	0.4
7	0.1	0.3	0.3	0.2	0.1	0.3	–	0.3	0.4	0.1	0.0	0.1
8	0.4	0.4	0.4	0.5	0.2	0.2	0.3	–	0.4	0.2	0.2	0.5
9	0.2	0.1	0.6	0.4	0.6	0.0	0.4	0.4	–	0.2	0.0	0.2
10	0.3	−0.2	0.2	0.3	0.2	0.1	0.1	0.2	0.2	–	0.2	−0.2
11	0.3	0.2	0.1	0.1	0.2	0.4	0.0	0.2	0.0	0.2	–	0.2
12	0.2	0.5	0.1	0.2	0.0	0.4	0.1	0.5	0.2	−0.2	0.2	–

Figure 9.3   Pearson correlation matrix for multirelational Krackhardt file (Advice and Friendship) (only first 12 actors shown)

additional splits, and UCINET will continue splitting actors into blocks as small as two actors/blocks unless you specify otherwise. In UCINET, the CONCOR procedure creates a block matrix for you as part of the overall procedure.

> A 'block' in a matrix is a subdivision in the matrix that represents a mutually exclusive class of actors.

As said earlier, the CONCOR input window in UCINET offers you an 'inter-active' option that can be selected by ticking (or un-ticking) a box. Ticking the box for this selection allows you, as CONCOR proceeds, to make decisions on how many blocks you want the final block matrix to contain, and thus, the number of positions you want your network to hold.

Figure 9.4 shows how CONCOR has taken an initial Pearson correlation matrix found in Figure 9.3, and from these data performed iterative correlations to assign actors into blocks.

The matrices in Figure 9.4 contain 3 × 3 blocks, each block representing a sub-division in the network, and therefore a position within the network. These blocks, designated by β1, β2 and β3 contain the following actors:

β1 = actors 3, 4, 5, 9, 10, 13, 15, 18, 19 and 20.
β2 = actors 1, 8, 11, 12, 16 and 17.
β3 = actors 2, 6, 7, 14 and 21.

You further see that some of these blocks appear denser than others; by this I mean that some of the blocks have more 1s in them than others. Further, you may notice that these relative densities are different for the two relations. For example, β1 has many more 1s in the ADVICE relation than the FRIENDSHIP relation.

Under each matrix, you can see some additional output given to you by UCINET. This is the density matrix for each relation. A density matrix takes the *density* score of each block, and the matrix displays that score in the corresponding cell. Thus, for the ADVICE relation, the density for β1 is 0.578, whereas for FRIENDSHIP, the density value for β1 is 0.189. Thus, those actors in the β1 position are more densely tied together according to advice as opposed to friendship. In contrast, those actors in position β2 are more tightly bond together according to friendship as opposed to advice.

These density matrices become quite important for the next step in the process, i.e. defining how positions relate to one another.

Relation ADVICE

```
            1  11112     1111        1  2
       3 4 5 8 9 0 3 9 5 0   1 2 7 6 1 8   7 2 4 6 1
      ------------------------------------------------
 3 |    1   1 1 1        1 | 1 1 1    1 1 | 1 1 1 1 1 |
 4 |        1   1        1 | 1 1 1 1 1 1 |    1    1 1 |
 5 |        1   1 1 1    1 | 1    1 1 1 1 | 1 1 1 1 1 |
18 | 1 1 1   1 1 1 1 1   1 | 1      1 1 1 | 1 1 1    1 |
 9 |        1   1        | 1 1 1 1 1 1 | 1 1 1 1 1 |
10 | 1 1 1 1     1 1 1 1 | 1    1 1 1 1 |    1      |
13 |    1 1 1           | 1           |    1 1    |
19 | 1   1 1   1     1 1 | 1      1    | 1 1 1    |
15 | 1 1 1 1 1 1 1 1   1 | 1 1 1 1 1 1 | 1 1 1 1 1 |
20 |        1         1 | 1 1 1 1 1 1 |   1 1 1 1 |
      ------------------------------------------------
 1 |    1   1           |    1   1 | 1    1    1 |
12 |                   |         | 1          1 |
17 |    1               | 1       | 1 1       1 |
16 |        1   1       | 1       |    1        |
11 |                   | 1       | 1 1        |
 8 |    1   1   1       |       1 | 1 1    1 1 |
      ------------------------------------------------
 7 |        1           |    1 1   1 | 1 1 1 1 |
 2 |                   |         | 1      1 1 |
14 |        1           |         | 1 1     1 |
 6 |                   |         |          1 |
21 | 1 1   1         1 |    1 1    1 | 1 1 1 1    |
      ------------------------------------------------
```

Relation FRIENDSHIP

```
            1  11112     1111        1  2
       3 4 5 8 9 0 3 9 5 0   1 2 7 6 1 8   7 2 4 6 1
      ------------------------------------------------
 3 |                1   |         |      1    |
 4 |                   | 1 1 1 1    1 |    1        |
 5 |        1       1   |        1 1 | 1 1    1 |
18 |                   |         |    1        |
 9 |                   |         |            |
10 | 1   1   1       1 |    1   1    1 |            |
13 |    1               |       1 |            |
19 | 1   1         1 1 | 1 1    1 | 1 1        |
15 | 1   1   1       1 | 1       1 |      1 1 |
20 |        1           |         |    1        |
      ------------------------------------------------
 1 |    1               |    1   1    1 | 1          |
12 |    1               | 1 1       |          1 |
17 | 1 1 1   1 1   1 1 1 | 1 1    1 1 1 | 1 1 1 1 1 |
16 |                   | 1       |    1        |
11 | 1 1 1 1 1   1 1 1 | 1 1 1    1 | 1          |
 8 |    1               |         |            |
      ------------------------------------------------
 7 |                   |         |            |
 2 |        1           | 1       |          1 |
14 |            1       |         | 1          |
 6 |        1           |    1 1   | 1 1    1 |
21 |        1           |    1 1   | 1          |
      ------------------------------------------------
```

Density Matrix

	1	2	3
1	0.578	0.767	0.740
2	0.133	0.200	0.467
3	0.120	0.200	0.750

Density Matrix

	1	2	3
1	0.189	0.283	0.200
2	0.317	0.500	0.300
3	0.080	0.167	0.300

Figure 9.4   Blocked matrices for Advice and Friendship relations

Step 4: Role analysis, i.e. analysing the relations between blocks

In Step 3, I discussed how CONCOR created a block matrix across the two different relations, and this assignment of actors to blocks is the assignment of actors to a particular network 'position'. Thus, actors within a block all share an equivalent position in the network. In this next step, we will use the output generated by the CONCOR procedure to create simplified views of how these blocks relate to one another.

To some extent, we have already begun this process of simplification in Step 3, with the density matrices. The density matrices have reduced the larger matrices in size by summarizing the number of actors/block through use of the density scores. However, one can simplify these blocks even further by creating an image matrix, based on the density matrix. In Figure 9.5, you can see examples of image matrices and their corresponding graphs, which are referred to as reduced graphs.

In Figure 9.5, information from the density matrices in Figure 9.4 has been transformed into a 'coarser' or simpler form. The first transformation occurs through an image matrix, which is a matrix that gives blocks with high density a score of 1 (referred to in the literature as 'one blocks' or 'bonds',) and blocks with low density a 0 (referred to as 'zero blocks'). The trick in transforming a density matrix into an image matrix is in deciding at which density value a cell becomes a one block as opposed to a zero block. This is discussed below.

Advice density matrix ($\Delta = 0.45$)	Advice image matrix	Reduced digraph
``` 1 2 3 ----- ----- ----- 1 0.578 0.767 0.740 2 0.133 0.200 0.467 3 0.120 0.200 0.750```	``` B1 B2 B3 B1 1 1 1 B2 0 0 1 B3 0 0 1```	
Friendship density matrix ($\Delta = 0.24$)	Friendship image matrix	Reduced digraph
``` 1 2 3 ----- ----- ----- 1 0.189 0.283 0.200 2 0.317 0.500 0.300 3 0.080 0.167 0.300```	``` B1 B2 B3 B1 0 1 0 B2 1 1 1 B3 0 0 1```	

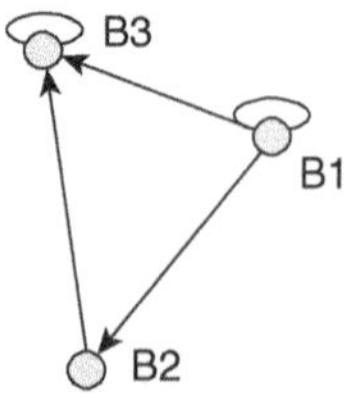

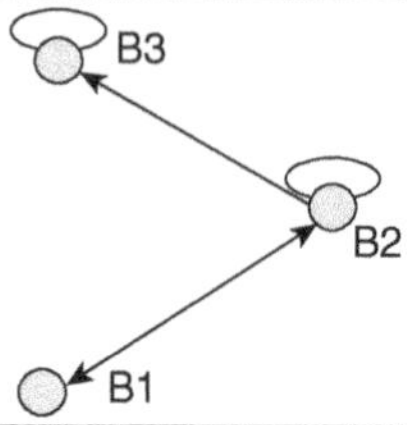

Figure 9.5 Image matrices and reduced graphs

The most straightforward way to decide whether a cell should be assigned a '1' or '0' is through the density criterion rule (Arabie et al., 1978). Here, you calculate the density (Δ) for each relation in your network (*Network > Cohesion > Density*), which in the present example is the relation ADVICE and the relation FRIENDSHIP, and this density score (Δ) becomes the criterion for deciding which blocks become 1s and which ones 0s. As you can see, the density for ADVICE is 0.45, making the Advice Δ = 0.45. Similarly, the Friendship Δ = 0.24, which is again based on the density score for FRIENDSHIP. Thus, for each relation, those blocks in the density matrix below Δ become 0s and those equal to or above Δ become 1s. You can see how this was done by looking at Figure 9.5 above.

Also in Figure 9.5 you see that I have drawn digraphs of the image matrices. These digraphs are referred to as reduced graphs, and like image matrices, they are meant as simplified views of the relationships between positions. Through looking at these reduced graphs and image matrices in Figure 9.5, you can start discussing the way blocks relate to each other within and across the two relations, and in doing so, you begin to assess the roles within the network.

With the ADVICE relation, $\beta 1$ and $\beta 3$ are both quite dense, and as such, can be thought of as cohesive subgroups, as described in Chapter 6. Furthermore, whereas $\beta 1$ has many within ties, it also has many ties to the two other blocks. This is not the case with $\beta 3$; it only has within ties, implying that people within this block only turn to one another for advice and do not seek out the advice of actors in other positions in the network.

A similar statement can be made of $\beta 3$ in the friendship relation: once again, the actors in this block appear to only be friends with one another. In contrast, actors in $\beta 2$ hold many friendship ties both within its own block and with the other blocks.

Taken together, it appears that actors in $\beta 3$, across both relations, are the most insular actors, and actors in $\beta 2$ are the most active, i.e. they form ties with many other actors in different positions. Actors in $\beta 3$ tend to be active when it comes to advice, and they also tend to only choose actors as friends in $\beta 2$. Furthermore, when it comes to advice, $\beta 3$ seems to be the most popular, i.e. both $\beta 1$ and $\beta 2$ choose to form ties with $\beta 3$.

Step 5: Further interpretation and role analysis

In Step 4, we reduced our block matrices to image matrices and reduced graphs in order to see how positions relate to one another. In doing so, we began seeing that different blocks appear to be behaving differently than other blocks. For example, our discussion shows how $\beta 3$ emerges as a very interesting sort of block in this network, one that appears to be playing a unique sort of *role*. Thus, when we start to think and discuss a network in terms of roles, we are no longer looking at individual actors and how they are positioned; rather, we are looking at the network on a more abstract level to see what kinds of roles emerge from the way positional blocks relate to one another.

In addition to looking at relations between positions, however, our role analysis can include looking at actor attribute data.

Actor attribute data

This particular dataset has a number of different attributes to choose from, yet for now, I shall just focus on the two attributes of Level and Department. For Level, there were three categories: 1 = the CEO, 2 = Vice presidents and 3 = managers. For departments, there were four listed (coded 1,2,3, 4) with the CEO having no department (0). To compare these attribute data for actors within the three blocks, I calculated the mean and standard deviation for each attribute for each block. You can see the results of these calculations as they compare to the three blocks in Table 9.1.

Bringing this attribute data alongside the three blocks, it appears that managers (Level = 3) tend to occupy $\beta 1$ and $\beta 2$; that $\beta 1$ tends to consist of more members from the same department, and further, that these members have been with the organization a shorter period of time (tenure). In contrast, $\beta 3$ is the most diverse in terms of actors from different levels and from different departments. In addition, $\beta 3$ also contains the older actors in this network (Age) who have also been with the firm the longest (tenure).

Comparing these attribute data to the image matrices and reduced graphs in Figure 9.5, it seems that the managers in $\beta 1$ tend to be the most 'needy' when it comes to seeking out advice, as they turn to both $\beta 2$ and $\beta 3$. In addition, it appears that $\beta 3$'s main role seems to be giving advice, which seems in keeping with these actors having more years in the firm and being, in general, more senior (i.e. older) than the others. Actors in $\beta 2$ play an interesting go-between (or broker) role in this network, forming links with both other blocks when it comes to friendship, and also offering advice to actors in $\beta 1$. Finally, $\beta 1$ seems the most dependent on the others, and this dependency seems to go hand in hand with the homogeneity of the actors in this block.

Table 9.1   Attribute scores for the three blocks

Block β	Age Mean (st. dev.)	Tenure Mean (st. dev.)	LEVEL Mean (st. dev.)	DEPT Mean (st. dev.)
1	39.5 (9.34)	7.25 (3.83)	3 (0.0)	2.4 (0.69)
2	34 (6.5)	12.28 (7.69)	3 (0.0)	2.3 (1.51)
3	47 (9.61)	20.1 (8.83)	2 (0.71)	1.6 (1.52)

Image matrices and ideal structures: A core-periphery network

In addition to comparing image matrices with attribute data as part of your role analysis, you can also compare image matrices to 'ideal' image matrix types, i.e. image matrices that show, in an extreme form, a theoretical, ideal structure. The most common example of such an ideal structure is a core-periphery structure, shown below as both an image matrix and reduced graph. In this structure, the core contains actors who relate to others in the core and periphery, and a periphery contains actors who only relate to those in the core, and no one in the periphery. Thus, a core-periphery structure tends to indicate which subset of actors, i.e. those occupying the core, have more power than others.

With our example, there does not appear to be a core-periphery structure at work, and so one thing we can conclude is that there are no 'core' or 'peripheral' roles in this network.

SUMMARY ON BLOCK MODELLING AND STRUCTURAL EQUIVALENCE

This concludes the discussion on block modelling, making use of the definition of structural equivalence and the CONCOR procedure for measuring structural equivalence. Although a bit complicated, block modelling can be broken down into a series of specific steps involving the full richness of network data to reveal structural features on different levels and the network as a whole. Through the Krackhardt dataset, I showed you how different relations, actors and their attributes, positions, and the network as a whole can be brought together

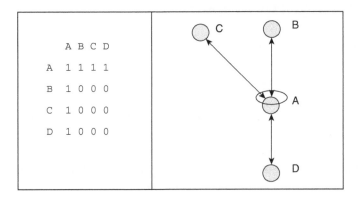

Figure 9.6   Core periphery structure

through block modelling to tell a story of the ways actors play particular roles in this network, and thus, the role structure of this network.

Problems with structural equivalence

Structural equivalence as a means for assigning actors to positions, and thus, deriving a role structure for a network can be a good, accurate reflection of many social phenomena: a mother and father, for example, are structurally equivalent and play the same role of 'parent' to their children. Structural equivalence's reliance on exact ties to exact others, however, is a bit strict, and often does not reflect the many ways social positions and roles operate in everyday life. For example, a nurse taking care of patients in a hospital can perform a very similar role as another nurse in the same hospital, yet the two nurses need not have ties to the exact same set of patients. The fact that both have patients and interact with patients in a similar way is enough to perceive the two as fulfilling the same role in a hospital.

Structural equivalence would say the two nurses in our above example do not share the same position (and hence the same role) because they are not 'nursing' the exact same 'patients'. Clearly, our intuitive notion of the role of a nurse in society would object to this statement!

Thus, in what follows, I describe an alternative definition to structural equivalence, that being regular equivalence, and I offer a brief description of how a reader can start exploring ways of measuring regular equivalence in UCINET. Please note, though, that this description of regular equivalence will not be as thorough as that on structural equivalence: constraints on space and concerns for reader-fatigue prevent me from launching into another full description. However, interested readers can refer to a number of references I offer at the end of the chapter for further reading.

REGULAR EQUIVALENCE

Regular equivalence derived partly as a critique of structural equivalence; this form of equivalence takes a more relaxed view of what defines actors as being 'equivalent'. Here, actors are seen as equivalent if they share *similar* ties to *similar* others (White and Reitz, 1983). Thus, actors do not need to have the exact same kinds of ties to the exact same others, as they would under the definition of structural equivalence. Figure 9.7 illustrates how actors can be classified into subsets according to structural and regular equivalence.

From the example shown in Figure 9.7, you can see how regular equivalence is a more flexible form of equivalence; more actors are 'allowed' to share the same position with this form of equivalence. Further, you can see that structurally

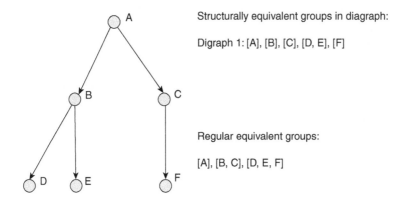

Structurally equivalent groups in diagraph:

Digraph 1: [A], [B], [C], [D, E], [F]

Regular equivalent groups:

[A], [B, C], [D, E, F]

Figure 9.7   Structural versus regular equivalence

equivalent actors can become regularly equivalent ones, but not the reverse. In addition to being a more relaxed, or abstract form of equivalence, there are some other theoretical differences between regular and structural equivalence that a reader should be aware of, which are summarized below (see also Borgatti and Everett, 1992):

1 *Local structure versus wider structure* Structural equivalence is a local concept, meaning that the ego networks of actors are compared in deciding whether or not two actors are structurally equivalent. This local quality of structural equivalence has a number of implications:

   • Structural equivalence does not take into consideration the wider network structure.

   • Structurally equivalent actors tend to be located within the same components of a graph, meaning that actors in disconnected components of a graph can never be considered structurally equivalent.

   • Being located within the same component, structural equivalence is closely tied to ideas of cohesion, and in fact, sets of structurally equivalent actors can be seen as a form of a cohesive subgroup (Friedkin, 1984).

In contrast, regular equivalence is not dependent on proximity, i.e. it is not a local concept. Regular equivalent nodes may be directly or indirectly tied to one another and may even be completely unreachable, e.g. be located in disconnected components.

2 *Surface versus 'deeper' structure* With structural equivalence, emphasis is placed on who the actor is, and where the actor is located. With regular equivalence,

emphasis is placed on the position of the actor, and how that position relates to other positions. As such, regular equivalence takes into consideration a deeper structure in considering whether actors are equivalent.

3 *Exactness versus abstractness* This has already been touched on above. Whereas structural equivalence would require two doctors to share the same ties to the same patients in order to both be called 'doctors', regular equivalence only requires that two doctors share the same kind of ties (i.e. doctor–patient ties) with their own patients. Further, the quantity of ties from one doctor to the next may differ with regular equivalence; with structural equivalence the quantity of ties must be the same.

Based on these distinctions, regular equivalence is sometimes argued as being more reflective of the original 'spirit' of role theory, as described by early social network scholars such as Nadel (1957). This is not to say that one should not make use of structural equivalence; indeed, as I have tried to illustrate above, some situations imply that local structure or direct ties are important for uncovering similarity in positions, and hence, structural equivalence would be the correct measure to employ. Further, this emphasis on direct ties is an important consideration when thinking about issues of redundancy, i.e. how actors sharing the same position may be considered redundant (Burt, 1976). Indeed, in my own research (Prell et al., 2008, 2009), this aspect of communication redundancy was an important factor for making use of structural equivalence.

To measure for regular equivalence, a common procedure to use is that of the REGE algorithm (White and Reitz, 1983). This algorithm measures the extent to which an actor's ties match another actor's ties to similar (but not the same!) others (see Borgatti and Everett, 1993). The results of a REGE analysis are displayed in matrix form in much the same way as one made use of a correlation matrix for measuring structural equivalence. Here, however, the values in the cells represent percentages, with 0 meaning no equivalence and 100 meaning perfect (100 per cent) regular equivalence. In UCINET you can make use of the REGE algorithm by going to *Network > Roles and Positions > Maximal regular > REGE*. For information on how to interpret the output files of the REGE algorithm, please refer to the UCINET Helpfile. You might also find the Borgatti and Everett (1993) helpful.

EXTENSIONS, SUMMARY AND CONCLUDING REMARKS

In this chapter I showed you the classic method for conducting a positional and role analysis. I also introduced you to an alternative definition and measure of equivalence. In doing so, this chapter focused on a number of points:

- Roles are derived from the relations among positions in a network, are make use of multirelational data.

- There are different definitions of equivalence, and this chapter offered two: structural equivalence and regular equivalence.

- Structural equivalence can be seen as the more traditional definition of equivalence. It looks at the extent to which actors share the exact same ties to the exact same others.

- Regular equivalence can be seen as a more general or abstract form of equivalence. It looks at the extent to which two actors share similar ties to similar others in the network.

- In this chapter, I showed how you can measure for structural equivalence through the CONCOR procedure, and I made use of Pearson correlation as a measure of positional similarity. Alternatively, one can make use of Euclidean distance as a measure of similarity, or multidimensional scaling.

- For regular equivalence, the REGE algorithm is commonly used.

- Block modelling is the classic, social network approach to positional and role analysis. The approach consists of a definition of equivalence, the use of CONCOR procedure (typically) on multirelational data, the use of block models, image matrices and reduced graphs.

The major differences between a structural equivalence approach, as compared to a regular equivalence approach, lies in how particular actors are assigned to blocks, and as discussed above, the REGE algorithm, in focusing on the similarity (as opposed to the exactness) of relational patterns between pairs of actors, incorporates a view of the network structure that takes into consideration how actors are already sub-divided into similar classes. In this way, REGE seems to incorporate within it a sensitivity to the underlying structure of the network in a way that a procedure based on structural equivalence does not (Borgatti and Everett, 1992).

One lesson to learn from this chapter is that it is probably a good idea to perform a comparative role analysis using different procedures to help develop a better understanding of the positions and roles in the network. Indeed, Michaelson and Contractor (1992) did such a comparative analysis in their paper focusing on the perception of interpersonal similarity. Here, social network data were gathered in a class of 18 college students. Positional similarities in the network were measured according to structural equivalence, automorphic equivalence and regular equivalence, and these were compared with respondents' ratings of perceived similarity. Their results indicate that perception of similarity is related more closely to general equivalences than to specific positions based on structural equivalence.

Another interesting application of role analysis has been Johnson et al.'s (2001) paper on role analysis and food webs. Here, the authors examined the research to date on ecological network analysis, noting that academics in this field had uncovered a role-analysis procedure quite similar to the idea of structural equivalence. Using structural equivalence as common ground between social network analysis and ecological network analysis, the authors then went on to apply additional role-analytic procedures from social network analysis to food webs in an attempt to bring greater clarity to the idea of 'role' in food systems.

One means of assigning actors to positions that was *not* covered in this chapter is through multidimensional scaling (MDS). This approach is not germane to social network analysis, yet it is often seen as a worthy alternative when one wishes to take a spatial orientation to assigning actors to positions. MDS is also used for cluster analysis. You can read more about the use of MDS in Wasserman and Faust (1994) as well as Borg and Groenen (2005).

Finally, while the concept of role has a long history in the social sciences, and in sociology in particular (Linton, 1936), theoretical work on role concepts began to stagnate around the 1960s (Connell, 1979), as many scholars began to see the whole idea of role theory as reinforcing the status quo, and ignoring issues of power and coercion (Connell, 1979; Coulson, 1972). The empirical work related to role analysis, especially from a social network perspective, has flourished, and currently the field is seeing a resurgence of interest with regards to how roles emerge from local processes within a variety of different environments (Johnson et al., 2003).

REFERENCES

Arabie, P., Boorman, S. A. and Levitt, P. R. (1978) 'Constructing blockmodels: How and why', *Journal of Mathematical Psychology,* 17: 21–63.

Boorman, S. A. and Harrison, C. W. (1976) 'Social structure from multiple networks. II. Role structures', *The American Journal of Sociology,* 81: 1384–446.

Borg, I. and Groenen, P. J. F. (2005) '*Modern Multidimensional Scaling: Theory and Applications.* New York: Springer.

Borgatti, S. P. and Everett, M. G. (1992) 'Notions of position in network analysis', *Sociological Methodology,* 22: 1–35.

Borgatti, S. P. and Everett, M. G. (1993) 'Two algorithms for computing regular equivalence', *Social Networks,* 15: 361–76.

Brieger, R. L., Boorman, S. A. and Arabie, P. (1975) 'An algorithm for clustering relational data with applications to social network analysis and comparison to multidimensional scaling', *Journal of Mathematical Psychology,* 12: 328–83.

Burt, R. (1976) 'Positions in networks', *Social Forces,* 55: 93–122.

Burt, R. S. (1986) 'A cautionary note', *Social Networks,* 8(2): 205–11.

Connell, R. W. (1979) 'The concept of role and what to do with it', *Journal of Sociology,* 15: 7–17.

Coulson, M. A. (1972) 'Role: A redundant concept in sociology?', in J. Jackson (ed.), *Role*. Cambridge: Cambridge University Press.

Faust, K. and Romney, A. K. (1985) 'Does STRUCTURE find structure?: A critique of Burt's use of distance as a measure of structural equivalence', *Social Networks* 7: 77–103.

Faust, K. and Romney, A. K. (1986) 'Comment on "A cautionary note"', *Social Networks* 8 (2): 213.

Friedkin, N. E. (1984) 'Structural cohesion and equivalence explanations of social homogeneity', *Sociological Methods and Research,* 12.

Johnson, J. C., Borgatti, S. P., Luczkovich, J. J. and Everett, M. G. (2001) 'Network role analysis in the study of food webs: An application of regular role coloration', *Journal of Social Structure,* 2.

Johnson, J. C., Boster, J. and Palinkas, L. (2003) 'Social roles and the evolution of networks in isolated and extreme environments', *Journal of Mathematical Sociology,* 27: 89–122.

Linton, R. (1936) *The Study of Man: An Introduction*. New York: Appleton-Century.

Lorraine, F. and White, H. C. (1971) 'Structural equivalence of individuals in social networks', *Journal of Mathematical Sociology,* 1: 49–80.

Michaelson, A. and Contractor, N. S. (1992) 'Structural position and perceived similarity', *Social Psychology Quarterly,* 55: 300–10.

Nadal, S. F. (1957) *The Theory of Social Structure*. Glencoe, IL: Free Press.

Prell, C., Hubacek, K., Quinn, C. and Reed, M. (2008) '"Who's in the network?" When stakeholders influence data analysis', *Systemic Practice and Action Research,* 21: 443–58.

Prell, C., Hubacek, K. and Reed, M. (2009) 'Stakeholder analysis and social network analysis in natural resource management', *Society and Natural Resources,* 22: 501–18.

Wasserman, S. and Faust, F. (1994) *Social Network Analysis: Methods and Applications*. Cambridge: Cambridge University Press.

White, D. R. and K. P. Reitz. (1983) 'Graph and semigroup homomorphisms on networks of relations', *Social Networks* 5: 193–235.

White, H. C., Boorman, S. A. and Breiger, R. L. (1976) 'Social structure from multiple networks. I. Blockmodels of roles and positions', *The American Journal of Sociology,* 81: 730–80.

PART III

ADVANCES, EXTENSIONS AND CONCLUSIONS

10

STATISTICAL MODELS FOR SOCIAL NETWORKS

Up until this point, I have not written much about statistical significance in relation to social network analysis. This chapter addresses that issue, and introduces some of the statistical procedures used in relation to social network analysis. As Chapter 2 indicated, statistical modelling of social networks has really taken off in the direction of ERGMs (e.g. the p* model) and longitudinal network analysis (e.g. actor-based models). This chapter offers a brief explanation of the p* model as well as other statistical procedures such as Quadratic Assignment Procedure, i.e. QAP (Krackhardt, 1987), but more importantly, this chapter offers an overview of the issues pertaining to network data when one wishes to test for statistical significance.

Please note that one can easily calculate some simple descriptive statistics on the columns, rows and matrices of network data. Such descriptive statistics include the mean, standard deviation, min, max and sum. One can calculate these in UCINET by simply going to *Tools* > *Univariate Stats*. The options for these descriptive statistics can be found in the UCINET help file. In this chapter, however, I would like to move the discussion beyond descriptive statistics to one pertaining to tests of significance and stochastic models of network structure. Thus, before getting started with describing different procedures, I would like to begin with a brief discussion of statistical significance, more generally, and how statistical significance relates to network analysis.

When we analyse data and we achieve a result that is called statistically significant, this means that we have used some kind of procedure that shows that the result we gained from our analysis is rare, so rare that it is highly unlikely to be due to chance alone. In more 'classical' statistics, deciding whether a result is or is not statistically significant is often made through use of a statistical test, for example a T-test, to obtain a probability value, or 'p-value'. Comparing the p-value to a given cut-off point, i.e. the 'significance level', enables you to say that values below this level are significant, and values above this level are not. Thus, the smaller the p-value, generally, the more significant your result. Probability values (p-values) are typically used alongside the value of your calculated result, and you therefore have two pieces of information: the result itself, and the p-value telling you whether or not your result is significant.

The most common cut-off point used for comparison to a p-value is that of 0.05, or rather, 5 per cent. When using this significance level, you say that all results having a p-value of 5 per cent or less are considered significant results, and all results above this value are not. In the next section, I will discuss one means by which p-values are derived for social network analyses. This procedure is permutation testing (also sometimes referred to as bootstrap testing).

PERMUTATION TESTS FOR DERIVING SIGNIFICANCE

With more commonly used statistical tests, such a the T-test or chi-squared test, determining whether or not a result is significant depends on the use of a theoretical probability distribution, for example a 'normal' distribution, and comparing what would be observed for this distribution to the data of your random sample. Further, with these more common tests, one assumes that each of your cases (for example, each individual person you collect data on) is considered separate and independent from one another.

With social network data, many of these assumptions and procedures are the exact opposite. Social network data are rarely (if ever) derived from a random sample and all the individuals we gather data on are assumed to be interdependent. We want to understand, further, the patterns of these interdependencies and how these patterns translate into certain structures and network properties. For these reasons, we can not use the same sort of procedures in testing for significance. We can not, in other words, proceed in the 'typical' statistical way.

Network analysts thus can make use of a form of non-parametric testing called permutation tests (although there are other statistical approaches analysts can use, and we shall explore some of those shortly). In mathematics, a permutation is a reordering of numbers. For example, the below shows you ordering, or 'permutations' of the numbers one to five:

(1, 2, 3, 4, 5)
(1, 3, 2, 4, 5)
(4, 5, 2, 1, 3)
(3, 2, 1, 4, 5)

Here, each permutation contains all numbers, yet in a different order. Please note that I have not given you all the permutations possible. With permutations, there are n factorial (n!) permutations of the n numbers. Thus, the factorial for the above grouping of numbers is $1 \times 2 \times 3 \times 4 \times 5 = 120$ possible permutations for the numbers one to five through.

This idea of permutation is very helpful for statistics in deriving tests of significance. As you will note in the above example, all the numbers remain the same, i.e. all the information is present in each permutation. The only thing that alters is the ordering or structure of the numbers.

In statistics, the term permutation refers to rearrangements of data. And with social networks, the data that are permutated are matrices. Figure 10.1 illustrates how a network matrix, and its associated graph, looks once it has become permuted:

In Figure 10.1, the original 'observed' network graph appears on the left. In permuting the graph, the structure remains the same, but the assignment of rows and columns change, thus different actors are assigned different positions within the same network.

These permutations are used for testing levels of significance. First, one analyses the original matrix with your statistic of interest, for example the number of cross-gender ties, and then permutes the original dataset multiple times. With each permutation, one calculates the given statistic and compares the new result to the original result derived from the original matrix.

This process of permutation, analysis and comparison of results occurs many times, and the more often your results from your permutations are the same as the results from your originally observed dataset, the more likely that your original result was due to chance. However, if the result from your original observed dataset rarely appears so extreme in subsequent permutation tests, then you are in a stronger position for stating that your original result is a rare one, and thus a statistically significant one.

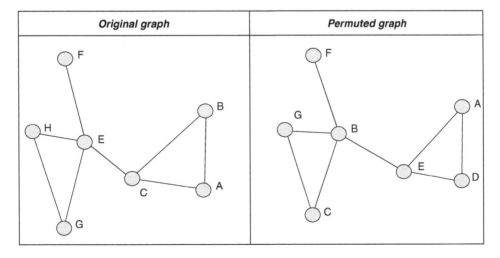

Figure 10.1   Example of a permuted graph

In the next section, I shall show you how permutation tests have been used for two common statistical tests; the first being the correlation of two matrices, and the second being the correlation of a matrix with actor attribute data. One note of warning: there are a couple of disadvantages to using permutation tests that you should be aware of. These include the fact that permutations can be very demanding on your computer's computational capabilities. If your data require many permutations, then it might take your computer software (in this case UCINET) a long time to compute a test statistic. In addition, although permutation tests typically are used for deriving p-values, they do not work so well for deriving confidence intervals.

QAP correlation: Network correlations

Quadratic assignment procedure (Krackhardt, 1987) is a popular method for testing the association between two networks (Hubert and Golledge, 1981; Krackhardt, 1987), and it makes use of permutation testing. The procedure relies upon permuting matrices to derive significance values, as described above, and UCINET has incorporated this procedure into its package.

As a first step, UCINET computes a Pearson's correlation coefficient (or Pearson's r) between two matrices. You are probably aware of the Pearson's correlation coefficient test; it is a pretty standard form of testing the correlation between two variables (see for example Wilcox, 2005 for an easy introduction to Pearson's r). With Pearson's r, you are correlating two continuous variables with each other, to see whether there is a significant relationship. In this case, the two variables are two networks.

In making use of Pearson's r, UCINET first computes a Pearson r on the two matrices, looking to see whether the presence of a tie in one cell in matrix 1 corresponds to the presence of a tie in the same, corresponding cell in matrix 2. Then, UCINET takes one of the two matrices and randomly permutes this matrix. Once this permutation is completed, Pearson's r is again computed on the two matrices, and the result of this test is compared to the original result. This process of permuting the matrix and re-computing the correlation coefficient happens thousands of times.

In making network permutations and recalculating Pearson r in this way, UCINET computes the proportion of times the results from these analyses on the permutated matrices are larger, smaller or equivalent to the result from the analysis on the two observed matrices. Computing this proportion, in essence, results in a p-value, where a low proportion, i.e. one less than 5 per cent, means that the relationship originally observed between the two matrices is a rare one, thus suggesting that this relationship between the two matrices is unlikely due to chance.

In addition to performing a QAP correlation, you can also perform a QAP regression. The procedure is basically the same as correlation, and the output of the regression procedure is basically the same kind of output one would expect in conducting a regression analysis in more 'traditional' software packages such as SPSS. Again, in UCINET, you will find these options for performing a regression analysis in *Tools > Testing Hypotheses*.

Autocorrelation: Attributes with networks

The next test is quite similar to the first. Here, instead of correlating two matrices, you correlate network data with actor attribute data. For example, if you have attribute data on the age of actors (interval attribute data), and network data on friendship ties, you can use permutation tests for uncovering the extent to which actors are friends with others who are a similar age. Similarly, you can test the relationship between friendship and gender, to see if girls tend to be friends with girls and boys with boys, for example. All of these tests make use of the permutation procedures explained above.

In UCINET, there are a number of tests you can use to explore how attributes of actors coincide with social relations. Go to *Tools > Testing Hypotheses > Mixed Dyadic/Nodal* and you will see you can test the relationship between networks and categorical data (such as gender) or between networks and continuous data (such as age). Read the help files carefully and you should be able to make the best test for your purposes.

p* MODEL: TESTING THE MULTIPLE LEVELS OF A GIVEN NETWORK

The two procedures described above are preferred when you wish to analyse the extent to which (i) two networks are significantly correlated with one another or (ii) a network and an actor attribute are significantly correlated. These are therefore useful procedures when one is not interested in network structure per se, but rather the relationship between two variables, either two networks as variables or a network variable and an actor variable. Permutation tests control for the structure of a network, versus attempting to explain that structure. The next set of models (p* and actor-based models) attempt to explain the structure of networks.

The p* model (also referred to in the literature as Exponential Random Graph Models or ERGMs) while making use of both network and attribute data, is a quite different tool than the ones described above. The history of the p* model has been discussed elsewhere (see Chapter 2). The intention behind developing p* was to develop a statistical model that could help analysts draw inferences about the underlying structural nature of networks. Thus, whereas QAP *controls* for network structure, p* attempts to *explain* it, and it looks to lower-level network configurations for clues.

What is a network configuration? A network configuration refers to a small set of nodes with a subset of ties amongst the nodes (Robins et al., 2007b). Examples include an edge, where two nodes are connected by one mutual tie; a 2-star, which consists of three nodes where one node is connected by a tie to each of the other two; and a triangle, where three nodes are connected together through three mutual ties. These are shown in Figure 10.2.

The network configurations in Figure 10.2 are based on non-directed graphs, but network configurations can also be derived for digraphs, and the p* model can be specified to analyse either directed or undirected network data.

The p* model looks at the extent to which such configurations explain more global network properties such as density and/or centralization. In addition, these configurations are seen as interdependent. For example, compare two friendship digraphs (network A and network B), each one consisting of five actors. In digraph A, there exists 15 arcs and in digraph B, there exists only 9 arcs. The simple fact that digraph A has a higher number of arcs than digraph B suggests a higher likelihood for ties to be reciprocal in digraph A than in digraph B (see Skvoretz and Agneessens, 2007). The p* model takes such dependencies into account, and indeed, such dependencies lie at the heart of the p* model.

The p* model uses network configurations to 'explain' a network's structure, but how exactly does p* do this? To answer this question, I need to walk you through a number of assumptions and concepts pertaining to the p* model. Thus, answering this question will involve discussion on the following topics: (i) the probability distribution used in p*; (ii) the dependency assumptions of p*; (iii) the estimation process; and (iv) the actual steps necessary in specifying and using the p* model.

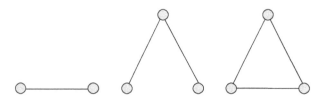

Figure 10.2   Network configurations

Before launching this discussion, however, I would like to start out with some notation and terminology that will be used throughout this discussion.

- A network is considered to have a size of n. That is, a network where n = 0 is a network consisting of 10 actors or nodes.

- A random network is denoted by **Y** and an observed network is **y**.

- actor i represents a sender and actor j represents a receiver.

- A network configuration refers to a subset of actors and ties. Examples of network configurations include edges, 2-stars and triangles.

- A network statistic refers to the number of observed counts of a network configuration in an observed network; for example, the number of reciprocal ties in an observed network.

- A parameter value corresponds to a network statistic, and it indicates the 'force' of a particular configuration occurring. Thus, if the reciprocity statistic for an observed network **y** is 15 (which indicates that 15 reciprocal ties exist in **y**), the parameter value associated with that statistic would indicate the likelihood of that amount of reciprocity occurring. A zero parameter means that the frequency of occurrence of this configuration depends on chance together with the value of all the other parameters. A positive value means that the configuration tends to occur more often than could be expected from the values of all other parameters.

Probability distributions and p*

When I discussed statistical significance at the beginning of this chapter, I discussed the difficulty of finding a suitable probability distribution for network data, given the interdependencies of actors and ties. With QAP models, the interdependencies are controlled for through permutations; with exponential random graph models such as p*, these interdependencies actually shape the probability distribution, and so they are very much taken into account. Before discussing how this happens, however, I would like to back-up slightly and re-visit what is happening when we are discussing probability distributions.

Statistically speaking, an observed network (i.e. the network **y**) is only one possible realization of a network. In statistics, one essentially wishes to see where this 'observed' realization falls on a distribution of 'all possible' realizations to gain a sense for whether the observed network is likely due to chance. This distribution of all possible realizations is considered the probability distribution for your observed network.

In p*, the probability distribution gets defined, partly, by the number of actors in the network. If there are 11 actors in a network, i.e. $n = 11$, then each actor can potentially have a tie to the 10 other actors, thus there exists the potential number of 11*10 ties in this network, where each tie has the opportunity to be present or absent. Thus, the total number of possible different directed networks is given by 2^{11*10}. At one end of this large range of possibilities lies an empty graph, i.e. a network of 11 actors with no ties present. At the other end of this range lies a complete graph, i.e. a network of 11 actors containing all 11*10 ties. Within this large distribution of probabilities, p* makes adjustments to the distribution through taking a look at the structural tendencies in the observed network. How p* adjusts the probability distribution according to underlying structures is through a look at the network configurations present in the observed network.

The role of network configurations in shaping the probability distribution

The p* model looks at the kinds of local, network configurations found within the observed network, and makes 'adjustments' to the probability distribution based on the number and kinds of configurations found in the observed network. Which kinds of network configurations get considered relies on assumptions that are made about the interdependencies of the network data. With p* there are two important kinds of dependency assumptions, one which is more restrictive than the other. I shall describe both here.

Markov graphs and Markov dependencies

As I discussed in Chapter 2, Frank and Strauss (1986) defined a probability distribution for networks based on an exponential function that included certain kinds of network statistics. The network statistics they included in their model were based on the idea of Markov dependence. Markov dependence refers to an assumption regarding the way in which ties are dependent on one another. Here, a possible tie between two actors (i, j) is seen as contingent on any and all other possible ties involving i or j. More specifically, if i and j have another actor k in common, their relationship is considered to be *conditionally dependent* on the relationship each shares with k.

For example, if an actor named Allan is friends with an actor named Peter, and if Peter is friends with Will, then Allan and Will's potential relationship is very much dependent on the sort of relationship each share with Peter. If Will has a dispute with Peter, and thus terminates the friendship, then this termination of the tie between Will and Peter might affect the sort of tie Peter shares with Allan. Thus, Peter and Allan are conditionally dependent, and a network that reflects such dependencies is considered a Markov graph.

These dependence assumptions can be extended to actor attributes. For example, whether actor i forms a tie with actor j may be conditionally dependent on both actors' age, where two actors similar in age are more likely to share a tie than two actors widely different in age. Thus, the attributes of actor i are seen as influencing the possible ties involving i. This is referred to as a *Markov attribute* assumption (Robins et al., 2007a).

These assumptions regarding the dependency of ties result in focusing attention on different kinds of network configurations in an observed network. In other words, the dependence assumption one adopts, in this case Markov dependence, constrains the frequencies of different kinds of configurations in a network (Robins et al., 2007a). Frank and Strauss (1986) noted that for Markov graphs, the number of edges, k-stars (where k >= 2), and triangles are important configurations. For digraphs, this list extends to outdegree and indegree, reciprocity, cyclic triads and transitive triads. For attribute or nodal effects, the list can include a homophily effect (e.g. two actors choosing one another based on similarity) or an ego-covariate effect (e.g. that in a given network, females attract more ties than males). Some examples of these configurations for Markov graphs are shown in Figure 10.3.

Please note that the figures in Figure 10.3 are not meant as an exhaustive list of the configurations important for Markov graphs, but rather illustrative of the sorts of configurations that are appropriate under this set of assumptions. Frank and Strauss (1986) used such configurations to define a probability distribution for an observed graph, stating that a Markov graph is one whose probability distribution can be defined according to the kinds of network configurations shown above. An example of the sort of equation that could be used to describe the probability distribution for a Markov graph can be found in Figure 10.4.

In Figure 10.4 you can see how examples of the network configurations shown in Figure 10.3 come together to define a probability distribution for a given, observed network (y), according to Markov dependency assumptions. The parameter values θ_κ and τ help define the actual probabilities of a given network to occur. The configurations of edges, k-stars and triangles are represented by network statistics, $S_1(y)$, $S_k(y)$ and $T(y)$. For example, if τ becomes higher, the probability of networks y with a high value of $T(y)$, i.e., with many triangles, will become relatively higher. Thus, these configurations, their corresponding statistics and parameters come together to define the probability distribution for a given, observed network.

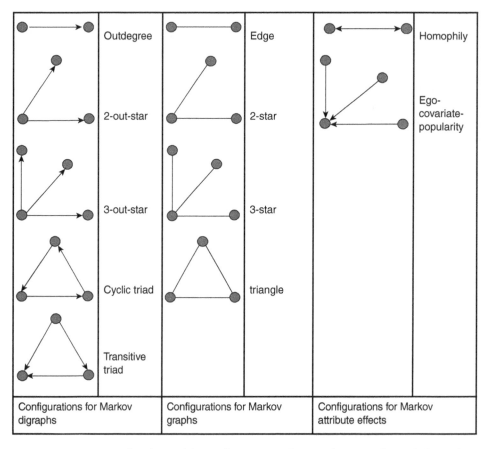

Figure 10.3   A sample of possible configurations for Markov graphs and digraphs

Prob (Y = y) =

$$\exp\left(\sum_{k-1}^{n-1} \theta_k S_k + \tau T(y) - \Psi(\theta, \tau) \right)$$

Where,

   Y = a random network, where each possible tie is considered a random variable;

   y = the observed network, where each tie is the observed tie; and where the statistics s_k and T are defined by:

   $S_1(y)$ = network statistic representing the number of edges

   $S_k(y)$ = network statistic representing the number of k-stars ($k \geq 2$)

   $T(y)$ = network statistic representing number of triangles

   $y(q,t)$ = a normalizing constant, which ensures that the probabilities sum to 1; and

   q_k and t = parameters of the distribution, corresponding with the above network statistics.

Figure 10. 4   Markov graph model of Frank and Strauss (notation adapted from Snijders et al., 2006).

Extending Markov graphs: The p* model

Wasserman and Pattison (1996) extended this Markov graph model, making a more general formula that could allow for a wider array of network statistics in the equation than those specified by Frank and Strauss. This more general equation was called the p* model (Wasserman and Pattison, 1996) and is shown in Figure 10.5

Figure 10.5 shows the general equation for a p* model, and as shown here, the $g_A(y)$ statistic can refer to any network statistic, not just edges, k-stars and triads. Thus, the p* model can be specified to include only those network statistics reflective of Markov graphs, or it can include other network statistics not reliant upon Markov dependence assumptions.

Over time, empirical and simulation research showed that the configurations offered by Frank and Strauss (1986) were too restrictive, resulting in models that had poor 'fit' to the actual data and thus did not 'explain' certain structural tendencies very well (Robins et al., 2007b). As a result, a wider array of network statistics were developed, which in turn reflected a slightly different dependency assumption than Markov dependence. Given the 'restrictive' nature of Markov graphs, a less restrictive dependency assumption was made, which was called *partial conditional independence* (Pattison and Robins, 2002)(Snijders et al., 2006). This new form extended Markov dependence to include the following: two potential ties (y_{il} and y_{kj}) are considered to be partial conditionally dependent if they (i) shared a common actor (this is Markov dependence), or (ii) if the two ties existed, they would be part of a four-cycle see Figure 10.1.

Thus, this new dependency assumption was seen as an extension, rather than a replacement of Markov dependency, and as such, opened up the possibility for a larger set of 'higher order' configurations, some of which can be seen in

---

$$\text{Prob}\,(Y = y)\left(\frac{1}{k}\right)\exp\sum_{A} \eta_A g_A\,(y)$$

Where,

Y = a random network, where each possible tie is considered a random variable;

y = the observed network, where each tie is the observed tie;

A = any configuration (and thus, the summation is for all configurations A);

h_A = the parameter that corresponds to a given configuration A.

$g_A(y)$ = the network statistic that corresponds to configuration A, for example, the number of reciprocal ties.

k = a normalizing quantity that ensures the equation reflects a proper probability distribution.

Figure 10.5 The p* model (notation adapted from Robins et al., 2007)

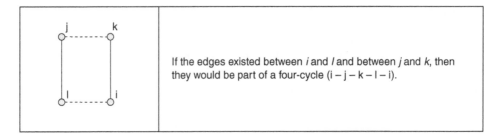

If the edges existed between *i* and *l* and between *j* and *k*, then they would be part of a four-cycle (i – j – k – l – i).

Figure 10.6   Example of partial conditional independence

Figure 10.7. These higher order configurations were seen as capturing more of the structure of a network, in particular, capturing a more granulated description of transitivity (Snijders et al., 2006).

Taken together, the p* model can be specified to reflect either Markov dependency or partial conditional independence, according to which network configurations are included in the model. For small networks (e.g. ones where $n < 20$) and/or very sparse networks (e.g. average degree < 2), Markov models still can have a good fit (Robins et al., 2007a). Finally, one should keep in mind that Markov models are suspect if they are fitted by maximum pseudo-likelihood.

Parameters and parameter estimation

The last section described network configurations based on assumptions regarding the conditional dependences of ties, and showed how these are brought together

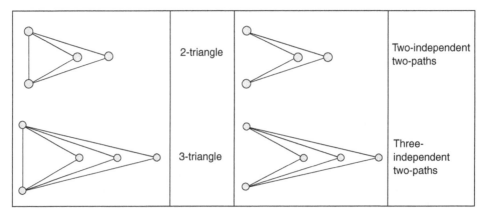

Figure 10.7   Higher order configurations

in the p* model to describe a probability distribution for an observed network. One aspect of the p* model I have not yet covered in any great detail is the role of the parameter values. As stated above, the value of a parameter indicates the strength of a particular network effect. For example, in friendship networks, it is common to find a relatively high amount of reciprocity, i.e. that there is a strong reciprocity effect. As such, when one analyses a directed friendship network using p*, the results are likely to show that the parameter value associated with reciprocity is rather high, thus indicating that networks with high levels of reciprocity – such as the friendship network observed – are more *probable* than networks without such a high level of reciprocity.

Yet how do the actual values get assigned to the parameters? The process is slightly complicated, but in essence, it involves 'trying out' different values for a given parameter, using the observed network as a starting point. Consider the following question: 'given the observed number of instances of reciprocity in this particular graph, what parameter value would give the highest likelihood of observing reciprocity in this particular graph?' To answer this question, p* makes use of a process called *Markov Chain Monte Carlo maximum likelihood* to choose parameter values that result in giving the observed effect (e.g. reciprocity) in the observed network the highest probability. This process involves computer simulation to create a distribution of graphs; where graphs are simulated based on a starting set of parameter values, and subsequent refinements (adjustments) to these values are made through comparing this distribution of graphs with the original, observed graph.

Once parameter values are estimated, if the parameter value for a given network statistic is zero, then the observed frequency of the corresponding configuration is assumed to be determined by chance – given the other, non-zero, parameters in the model. In the example of a friendship network, where the number of reciprocal ties in the observed network is high, a high positive parameter for reciprocity would indicate that the observed network contains more reciprocity than one would expect from chance.

To help gain clarity on p*, and how to use p* to analyse your own data, I shall attempt to walk you through the steps of using p*. These steps have been adapted and expanded from Robins et al., 2007a. They consist not only of the practical steps one takes in specifying a p* model for analysing data, they also include the assumptions an analyst is essentially making in applying the p* model. As such, the steps below summarize the above discussion and relate this discussion to a more practical application of the model to data. For this reason, a reader will probably find the steps below helpful in reinforcing and further clarifying many of the points made earlier.

Steps in making use of the p* model

For simplicity sake, the steps I outline below, and the example I offer readers, is focused on undirected networks. Actors are referred to as i and j, where i generally refers to the sender of ties and j as the receiver.

Step 1: Assumptions made about the network and the network ties

With p*, one works with a fixed set of nodes or actors, i.e. the size of the network is kept constant. In addition, whether there exists between any given pair of nodes a network tie is considered its own variable, and this variable is assumed to be random. This assumption pertaining to randomness is important, given the probabilistic nature of the model; one assumes that the presence or absence of a tie, for example, can only be explained in probabilistic (as opposed to deterministic) terms. For this reason, ties in the distribution are assumed to be 'random', where a random tie is represented as Y_{ij}, and $y_{ij} = 1$ when the tie is present and $y_{ij} = 0$ if the tie is absent. The observed tie is y_{ij}, it is the observed value of Y_{ij}. Y is therefore the matrix of all random variables and y is the matrix of all observed variables.

Step 2: Assumptions made regarding the contingencies among network variables

As discussed earlier, for a Markov graph model, one assumes that two ties are conditionally dependent on one another, according to the presence or absence of a shared node. For a graph model assumed to be partial conditionally dependent, two ties either share a node in common (Markov dependence) or if the two ties were present, they would be part of a four-cycle. Given these options in dependency assumptions, different configurations, their corresponding network statistics and parameters are included in the model, and the model is thus seen as representing a probability distribution of graphs based on certain dependency assumptions.

Step 3: Assumptions made about the homogeneity of parameters

I have not yet discussed this assumption. The *homogeneity of network configurations assumption* (Frank and Strauss, 1986) assumes all actors in the observed network share the same tendencies for a given effect, unless these tendencies are differentiated by nodal variables included in the model. For example, in a friendship network, all actors are assumed to have the same tendency towards reciprocity, and this is implied by the use of just one parameter for the network statistic for reciprocity. Thus, just one parameter value is used for each network statistic for each configuration.

Step 4: Specify your model

Snijders et al. (2006) have written guidelines on how to specify a p* model to include higher-order configurations for directed and undirected networks. For purposes of this introductory chapter, however, I suggest initially keeping to more 'traditional' network statistics such as k-stars and triangles, i.e. ones reflective of Markov graphs, keeping in mind that such statistics only work well for small networks. After becoming familiar with these 'lower-order' network statistics, I recommend reading about the new specifications, as it is usually necessary to generalize the Markov model and include higher-order configurations to get a good model fit.

Specifying a model, estimation and interpretation can be done through software applications such as Siena, StatNet, or Pnet. You can find these software packages on the Internet. Here, I demonstrate through the use of Siena, which is part of the larger StocNet application, and which can be downloaded at http://stat.gamma.rug.nl/stocnet. (You can also go to Appendix 2 for a description on how to get started in Siena.)

A helpful way to start thinking about specifying your model is in a forward step-wise fashion, building increasing levels of complexity. In general, you begin with including only a small number of configurations, and only increase the number of configurations if the model does not converge. (Please note that for larger networks using Markov specifications, the model will probably not converge, i.e. one needs the newer network statistics. Thus, this advice really applies more to smaller networks.) An example of a set of statistics that can be included in a p* model to test for structure includes the statistics foredges, 2-stars, 3-stars and triangle (Robins et al., 2007b). In Siena, you will see options for selecting these statistics to include in your model (again, please go to Appendix 2 for a practical step-by-step example).

Step 5: Estimate parameter values

I have discussed earlier the MCMC process for estimating parameter values from the data. The estimation algorithms available include the so-called Robbins-Monro algorithm or Geyer-Thompson algorithm. For simulating random draws from an ERGM distribution with the given parameters, one can make use of the Gibbs or Metropolis-Hastings algorithms.

Step 6: Interpret your model

Interpreting your model involves a look at the parameter values and their standard errors for the different network statistics. In general, if the ratio of parameter value/standard error exceeds 1.96, then you can safely assume that there is a significant effect.

A practical example

In what follows, I will offer a simple example of using the p* model for analysing the Florentine families dataset (Padgett and Ansell, 1993), found in UCINET. These data are non-directional.

For these data, I made use of the Markov random graph model, and thus the configurations used in this model include edges, 2-star, 3-star and closed triads. The Siena software package was used for fitting this model. In Siena, I selected the Metropolis-Hastings algorithm for estimating the parameters. The parameter values, along with their standard errors are presented below in Table 10.1. By dividing these values by their standard errors, one arrives at a score similar to a t-score, which may then be used for determining levels of significance using a table of the standard normal distribution.

In Table 10.1, the marriage relation shows no significant results, while for the business relation, the findings show two significant results: the density and closed triad parameter scores are much higher than their standard errors, resulting in scores that are significant at the 0.05 level. The parameter values for 2-stars and 3-stars, although not significant, move in the direction one would expect: ties occur relatively rarely, indicating low-density, and the positive parameter for 2-stars suggests that actors have a tendency for wanting business partners, with this tendency capped by the negative 3-star parameter, indicating that local open structures do occur, yet for any one actor, it does not likely occur via many other partners.

Table 10.1   Results of p* analysis for marriage and business relations in Florentine families dataset

Network configuration	Marriage values (SE) and t-score	Business values (SE) and t-score
Edges (density)	−1.65 (0.98) t = −1.68	−4.24 (1.10) t = −3.85*
2-stars	−0.01 (0.34) t = 0.03	1.05 (0.64) t = 1.64
3-stars	−0.01 (0.13) t = 0.08	−0.64 (0.40) t = 1.6
Closed triads	0.24 (0.49) t = 0.49	1.32 (0.64) t = 2.06*

Note: findings indicated by * are significant at the 0.05 level.

ACTOR-BASED MODELS FOR LONGITUDINAL NETWORK DATA

As a foreword remark, I would like to say that I shall not spend too much time on this section pertaining to actor-based models, as many of the assumptions and considerations one needs to make with regards to the use of p* apply here.

What are actor-based models and how do they differ from p*?

Actor-based models were first discussed in Chapter 2. There, I noted that the stochastic, actor-based models developed by Tom Snijders and colleagues (Snijders, 2001; Snijders, 2010: 1001) are intended to model changes in network structure over time, and are thus to be used on longitudinal data. These changes are assumed to be the result of processes internal (i.e. endogenous) to the network itself, although external (i.e. exogenous) factors are also included in the model as attributes of actors. The Siena[1] application makes use of these models to investigate how a given network (or networks) change(s) over time.

If the network you are studying has some sort of behavioural variable, such as smoking, or attitudinal variable that can change, for example, political opinions, then one theoretical framework used in conjunction with Siena is that of social influence and social selection. These two theories were covered in Chapter 3, in the context of theoretical frameworks. Briefly, social influence considers how actors who share a social tie influence one another's behaviour, while social selection looks at how actors who share a similar sort of behaviour are attracted to form ties with one another. As social influence and social selection are seen as intertwined processes (Robins et al., 2001), making use of a set of models such as those found in Siena help the analyst unravel which process occurred first for a given set of actors.

The actor-based models found within Siena (there are three) make use of exponential functions with a given set of network 'effects' or statistics in much the same way as is done with p*. The theoretical assumptions behind the Siena models, however, are different. The actor-based models in Siena assume that each actor in a network is evaluating her position in the current network according to the specifications found in the model. More formally, when there is an opportunity for actor i to make a change, the probability of any given change is assumed to be proportional to the exponential transformation of the evaluation function, as shown in the textbox below (see Snijders, 2008). Thus the distribution of possibilities for an actor are provided by the actor-based models, and this distribution of

---

[1]Siena stands for Simulation investigation for empirical network analysis.

options happens via a stochastic simulation model, i.e. a computer simulation is used to generate a distribution of possible new network states for the given actor.

The three components of the actor-based model found in Siena include the evaluation function, the endowment function, and the rate function. In brief, the *evaluation function* models the likelihood of an actor changing her current state to a new state, given a range of specified options. In looking at the current state of the network, the evaluation function includes both network structural effects as well as behavioural (or attribute) effects. The *endowment function* can be seen as an extension to the evaluation function, and it models the value an actor places on ties that play a role when the tie is terminated, but not when it is created. Finally, the *rate function* models the speed by which a dependent variable (be that a network variable or behavioural variable) changes. For modelling network evolution, the evaluation function is considered the most important of the three models, followed by the endowment function and the rate function (Snijders et al., 2007).

The evaluation function

The probability of actor i going to some new state x is given by

$$\frac{\exp\big(fi(\beta,x)\big)}{\sum x' \epsilon C(x^0)\exp\big(fi(\beta,x')\big)}$$

Where

$$fi(\beta,x) = \sum_{k=1} \beta_k s_{ki}(x)$$

s_{ki} = network effects driving the network dynamics. Examples of such network effects include reciprocity, transitivity, behavioural similarity, and so forth.

β_κ = parameters that indicate the force of these effects and which are estimated from the data.

x = the potential new state of actor i's network. Example, the the potential that actor i drops a non-reciprocated tie to some actor j.

x' = other potential states for actor i's network.

x^0 = current state of actor i's network.

$x' \epsilon C(x^0)$ = the set of all permitted new states of actor i's network, which includes the current state (x^0). So, for example, if x refers to the possibility of i dropping a non-reciprocated tie to j, other new states (x')would include this option, as well as i's current state, and all other allowable options.

In words: the probability that actor i will make a specific change is a proportion based on the exponential function give above. This proportion is obtained as the *consequence* of making the specified change.

Given the fact that the evaluation function is the most important function driving the modelling process, and given the constraint in space for introducing this suite of models to the reader, I shall focus my attention on the evaluation function, explaining that in some detail, and then exemplify how to make use of this function in an example in Appendix 2.

The sorts of network effects that can be specified in the evaluation function include those identified earlier regarding Markov graphs and digraphs, as well as the higher order configurations such as alternating k-stars and triangles. There are additional effects not covered here, for example, interactional effects, and rate and endowment effects. Once you have worked through the material I present here, and if you have further interest, I suggest you visit the literature on these additional effects, e.g. the tutorial by Snijders et al. (2010). Estimation of the parameters happens in a similar fashion as p*, although different algorithms are used, and I encourage you to read Snijders (2001) if this is of interest to you.Finally, I strongly encourage the special issue in *Social Networks* on the topic of dynamic networks and actor-based models. Please see Snijders et al., 2010, which provides a good overview of the actor-based models, and then read all the articles within this volume for good examples of applications of these models.

Differences and similarities between ERGMs and actor-based models

As you can see from the discussion and representation of the evaluation model, the actor-based models found in Siena for analysing longitudinal data share a great deal of similarity with the ERG models discussed earlier. However, there are some distinctions between p* and actor-based models. Thus, in what follows, I summarize some of the key similarities and differences between the two sets of models:

- In general, ERG models are used for cross-sectional data, and the actor-based models found in Siena are used for longitudinal data.

- ERG models assume that the network being observed is already in an equilibrium state. The actor-based models do not make this assumption. Instead, they assume that networks can be modelled between different time periods, but that a network does not necessarily reach a stable structure. Having said this, the actor-based models do assume that networks exist in a 'state', meaning that there is some stability in the ties and that the network (or networks) does not change drastically from one time period to the next. Such state relationships are exemplified in relations such as close friendship, family and kinship.

- With longitudinal network data and the use of actor-based models, it is easier to distinguish the causal relationship between actor attributes and network structure and to disentangle whether attributes influence network structure or the other way around. This is reflected in the use of Siena for disentangling social influence from social selection processes (see for example, Agneessens and Wittek, 2008; Kleppera et al., in press; Mercken et al., 2009).

- Both the ERG and actor-based models assume that tendencies of actors are the same, e.g. the tendency to want to form ties with others, is the same across all actors, unless actor differences are explicitly modeled as depending on some observed nodal variable. This is known as the 'homogeneity constraint'.

- Both the ERG and actor-based models make use of computer simulations for generating a probability distribution of networks.

- The actor-based model is a Markov chain model; this roughly means that the current network provides all the information needed for understanding future dynamics. In Appendix 2, I introduce you to the Siena software package, created by Snijders and colleagues (2007) and offer an example for using Siena for conducting a p* analysis and longitudinal analysis.

Benefits of using p* and actor-based models

There are a number of key benefits of using these statistical models for network data over other forms of network analysis (although they do not necessarily replace the need to use other methods and approaches introduced in this book). These include the following: if you are interested in micro-macro linkages, then the p* and actor-based models can help you determine whether lower-level network configurations (such as reciprocity or transitivity) are more commonly observed in a given, observed network than might be expected by chance. Thus, an observed network with high density and centralization, two features that can be located on the macro-level, might contain a high number of transitive triads, and through use of these stochastic models, you can see whether or not such a tendency is statistically significant. Often, a global network structure can result from a combination of local, substructures in a network. The p* and Siena models help one assess these relative contributions. In addition, one can see the relative contribution of different substructures and actor attributes to the overall network structure. For example, is the level of clustering in the network a result of reciprocity between actors, or the similarity of actors' attributes, or both?

SUMMARY AND CONCLUSIONS

This chapter began with a discussion on statistical significance and the issues of testing network data, given the interdependencies found within the data. I began with an introduction into permutation tests, and then moved into a discussion of ERG models, such as the p* model, and actor-based models for longitudinal data analysis.

Some key differences between the different statistical techniques/options include the following: permutation testing controls for network structure, without attempting to explain it. Both ERG models and actor-based models attempt to explain network structure by looking at the local configurations for clues. ERG models are used on cross-sectional network data and actor-based models for longitudinal data.

Finally, a number of permutation tests exist within UCINET. For ERG models, you can make use of PNet, and actor-based models. I suggest making use of Siena, found within the StocNet application, and the R program.

REFERENCES

Agneessens, F. and Wittek, R. (2008) 'Social capital and employee well-being: Disentangling intrapersonal and interpersonal selection and influence mechanisms', *Revue Française de Sociologie*, 49: 613–37.

Frank, O. and Strauss, D. (1986) 'Markov graphs', *Journal of the American Statistical Association*, 81: 832–42.

Hubert, L. J. and Golledge, R. G. (1981) 'A heuristic method for the comparison of related structures', *Journal of Mathematical Psychology*, 23: 214–26.

Kleppera, M. D., Sleebosb, E., Bunta, G. V. D. and Agneessens, F. (in press) 'Similarity in friendship networks: Selection or influence? The effect of constraining contexts and non-visible individual attributes', *Social Networks*.

Krackhardt, D. (1987) 'QAP Partialling as a test of spuriousness,' *Social Networks*, 9: 171–86.

Mercken, L., Snijders, T. A. B., Steglich, C. and Vriesa, H. D. (2009) 'Dynamics of adolescent friendship networks and smoking behavior: Social network analyses in six European countries', *Social Science & Medicine*, 69: 1506–14.

Padgett, J. F. and Ansell, C. K. (1993) 'Robust action and the rise of the Medici', 1400–1434', *The American Journal of Sociology*, 98: 1259–319.

Pattison, P. E. and Robins, G. L. (2002) 'Neighbourhood based models for social networks', in R.S. Stolzenberg (ed.) *Sociological Methodology*. Boston, MA: Blackwell Publishing. pp. 301–37.

Robins, G., Elliott, P. and Pattison, P. (2001) 'Network models for social selection processes', *Social Networks*, 23: 1–30.

Robins, G., Pattison, P., Kalish, Y. and Lusher, D. (2007a) 'An introduction to exponential random graph (p*) models for social networks', *Social Networks*, 29: 173–91.

Robins, G., Snijders, T., Wang, P., Handcock, M. and Pattison, P. (2007b) 'Recent developments in exponential random graph (p*) models for social networks', *Social Networks*, 29: 192–215.

Skvoretz, J., and Agneessens, F. (2007) 'Reciprocity, multiplexity, and exchange: Measures', *Quality and Quantity*, 41: 341–57.

Snijders, T. (2001) 'The statistical evaluation of social network dynamics', in M. E. Sobel and M. P. Becker (eds), *Sociological Methodology*. Boston and London: Basil Blackwell.

Snijders, T. (2008) 'Longitudinal methods of network analysis', in B. Meyers and J. Scott (eds), *Encyclopedia of Complexity and System Science*. Berlin: Springer Verlag.

Snijders, T. A. B., Pattison, P. E., Robins, G. L. and Handcock, M. S. (2006) 'New specifications for exponential random graph models', *Sociological Methodology* 36: 99–153.

Snijders, T. A. B., Steglich, C. E. G., Schweinberger, M. and Huisman, M. (2007) *Manual for SIENA version 3.1*. University of Groningen: ICS/Department of Sociology; University of Oxford: Department of Statistics.

Snijders, T. A. B., Steglich, C. E. G. and van de Bunt, G. G. (2010) 'Introduction to actor-based models for network dynamics', *Social Networks*, 32: 44–60.

Wasserman, S. and Pattison, P. (1996) 'Logit models and logistic regressions for social networks: I. An introduction to Markov random graphs and p*', *Psychometrika* 61(3): 401–26.

Wilcox, R. R. (2005) *Introduction to Robust Estimation and Hypothesis Testing*. Amsterdam and Boston: Elsevier/Academic Press.

11

CONCLUSIONS AND FUTURE OF THE FIELD

This book started with the historical origins of SNA, proceeded with a discussion on how to study social networks, and then walked you through conceptual and analytical material pertaining to the different levels of networks, starting with the actor level and finishing with the network level. Then, you were introduced to advanced topics pertaining to the statistical modelling of social networks. In this concluding chapter, I would like to offer you some final remarks on the state of the SNA field, noting in particular what looks to be the big trends or hot topics for future social network analysts.

Social networks and network analysis has certainly grown in popularity over the years, and the number of articles published using this approach is steadily on the rise. As of December 2009, there were 3,180,000 articles listed in Google Scholar under the key terms 'social network analysis'. It does not seem that interest in the topic will die anytime soon.

So what can we expect to be the forthcoming trends in the field? Below is a small sampling and brief description of what a reader might expect.

POPULAR TOPICS

Small worlds

In the mid to late 1990s, the rise of the Internet and the renewed interested in small worlds, as discussed by the work of Watts and Strogatz (1998) in particular, drew wide attention from a variety of disciplines and fields to the topic of social networks and network analysis. This attention had an impact on the field of social network analysis. In particular, large-scale networks such as the Internet became a popular topic, and people began to look for 'underlying' network structural features to these networks, such as whether the network could be characterized as 'small world' or 'scale free' in nature (Barabási, 2000). A number of academics quickly became interested in looking at and studying large-sized networks via these two lens, i.e. 'small world' and 'scale free' (Newman et al., 2006). Examples include the Internet, food webs and transportation systems.

Social movements

The topic of social movements have steadily increased in popularity within the field of social network anlaysis (Bendell et al., 2009; Diani and McAdam, 2003; Ernstson et al., 2008; Smith, 2008; Stevenson and Greenberg, 2000). Social movements refer to group actions that are focused on specific political and/or social issues with the underlying goal of initiating or contributing to change. Network analysts tend to be interested in how individuals come together to form such movements, and in uncovering/describing the network structures of such groupings.

Social capital

Back in the 1990s, with the publication of Robert Putnam's (1993) book *Making Democracy Work,* social capital became a popular topic both within and outside academia, and with this rise in popularity came increased attention and interest in social networks and network analysis. Social capital refers to the ability to identify resources found within one's social networks, as well as the processes involved in accessing those resources (Lin, 2001). Perhaps social capital's popularity has decreased slightly (Borgatti, 2005), yet many continue publishing on social capital from a network perspective (Hsung et al., 2009; Lin and Erickson, 2008), and this trend is likely to continue for quite some time.

Social networking sites

The popularity of the Internet also brought with it, in recent years, a new set of technologies referred to as 'social networking sites'. Examples include spaces such as Facebook, MySpace and Bebo. These virtual spaces not only sensitized a new generation of people to the idea of social networks, but they also inspired academics into exploring ways to gather and analyse such social networking data.

Ecology and natural resources

Ecologists are starting to see the benefits of integrating a social networks' approach with ideas of systems ecology, as well as using SNA as a means to gain new insights into the ways natural resources can be managed and governed. This increase in interest in this topic is demonstrated by, for example, a recent special issue in *Ecology and Society* (see http://www.ecologyandsociety.org/issues/view. php?sf=48).

Of course, it is impossible to list all the different research areas and topics that are starting to benefit from social network analysis. In the most recent Sunbelt conference (the annual conference for the INSNA), a number of panels which were held focused on themes of social movements, political networks, geography and spatial concerns, online networks, natural resource management, cognitive networks and semantic networks. These themes stand alongside more 'classic' topics such as kinship and friendship networks, as well as organizational and inter-organizational networks.

MIXING WITH OTHER APPROACHES

Qualitative approaches

As awareness of social network analysis spreads to other disciplines, the methods and tools of SNA get applied to new kinds of data as well as mixed with other approaches. For example, in recent years ethnographers and qualitative researchers have started incorporating SNA into their tool-kits. In one respect, this new trend for 'mixed methods' can be seen as an extension of an earlier one, documented in Chapter 2, pertaining to social anthropologists such as Warner or Clyde Mitchell, both influenced by Radcliffe-Brown and both of whom incorporated SNA data and techniques into their wider anthropological studies. On another level, this trend to incorporate qualitative data into SNA studies or vice versa (include SNA data into qualitative studies) can be seen as offering some real advances in the way social network analysts currently conceptualize social relations.

Input–output analysis

Another mixed-approach gaining popularity in recent years is that of SNA and input–output analysis (Kagawa et al., 2009; Montresora and Marzetti, 2009; Studer et al., 1984). Input–output analysis, traditionally used within the fields of economics and policy analysis, is a quantitative technique developed by Leontief (1941) that models how certain sectors flow and interact with other sectors, and the data are structured in much the same way as the matrices used in SNA. As far back as the 1960s, scholars were noting the similarities between input–output analysis and social network analysis (Hubbell, 1965), and in a recent article, Borgatti and Li (2009) demonstrate how a number of techniques and analyses developed by Leontief (1941) are virtually the same as ones found in network analysis. As such, centrality and clique analyses, concepts and measures taken directly from the SNA field, are now starting to be applied to test all kinds of data.

Geographical and spatial approaches

Another blended approach gaining popularity is that of SNA with spatial measures and tools from geography (Bathelt and Gluckler, 2003; Johnson and Gilles, 2000; Martínez-López et al., 2009; Radil et al., 2010; Wong et al., 2006). Here, issues such as the role of geography and space on tie formation and network structure are explored, as well as how social network data can be combined, visually, with geographical information systems (GIS) maps.

Computer simulation/agent-based modelling

Agent-based modelling and computer simulation have become more popular in recent years within the social sciences (Gilbert, 2007), and combined with the improved computational tools available, this trend has inspired another pool of researchers to pursue themes of network formation and emergence. Here, earlier mathematical theorems such as those proposed by Jackson and Wolinksy (1996) on the efficiency of social networks, are challenged and explored within the context of simulation, thus revealing under which conditions 'efficient' networks arise and change over time (Doreian, 2002, 2006; Goyal et al., 2006; Hummon, 2000). More recently, simulations based on tie-based models such as p* (Robins et al., 2005) and actor-based models are being built to explore how certain network structures arise and under which conditions.

ADVANCES ON OLDER THEMES: TWO-MODE ANALYSIS AND THE VISUALIZATION OF NETWORKS

In addition to new topics and mixed methods, there are still a number of advances that are being made on 'older' social network themes. These include developing new measures for two-mode data. As this book has shown, the majority of analyses for social network analysis still take place on one-mode data. A recent conference in Amsterdam (October, 2009, see http://home.fsw.vu.nl/f.agneessens/2mode/overview.htm) focused on this topic, and a forthcoming special issue in the journal *Social Networks* attempts to address this gap in the literature.

In addition to increased attention on two-mode data, there is a growing group of computer scientists and network analysts re-thinking the ways in which networks are displayed visually (see, for example, the writings of Brandes et al., 1999, 2001, 2006). A number of software applications that specialize in the visualization of network data also exist, and these include KrackPlot, NetDraw (within UCINET), Sentinel Visualizer, Social Networks Visualizer (SocNetV), visone, and VisuaLyzer. Information on all of these can be found on the internet.

ADVANCES IN MODELLING NETWORKS

In the chapter on Advanced topics, I introduced both tie-based and actor-based models. Such models are used for the statistical analysis of networks, in particular, for explaining the kind of underlying network effects that give rise to network structures. Work and extension on these models continues; for example, Robins et al. (2010) are now extending the p* model to include a local configuration they term an 'edge-triangle'. This configuration, as the name implies, contains a closed triangle with a single edge attached to the triangle, and captures, on a micro level, the notion of 'brokerage' as described by Ron Burt (Burt, 2000, 2005). Other work looks at how p* can be used to model bipartite networks (Wang et al., 2009). Snijders and his colleagues continue to develop and apply their actor-based models to a wide range of behaviour in relation to network change (see Mercken et al., 2010; Snijders et al., 2010, for recent overviews).

A number of other advances in statistical modelling of networks exist, too many to include here. Work continues on looking at the effects of, and ways to handle missing social network data (Butts, 2003; Huisman and Steglich, 2008; Kossinets, 2006; Robins et al., 2004), as well as modelling networks from samples (Handcock and Gile, forthcoming). Still other work is looking at how to model and analyse fragmented networks (Snijders, in press).

SOFTWARE DEVELOPMENTS

The number of advancements in software development cannot be covered here, they are too numerous. However, I shall attempt to give a flavour of the range that currently exists; as mentioned above, the R application is increasingly being used for social network analysis, especially within the context of large networks and longitudinal network data. The Siena software package, for example, which was designed for analysing longitudinal networks through use of actor-based models, has recently been developed to run on R.

Although the more commonly known applications were originally developed for academic audiences (e.g. Pajek, for handling large datasets; EgoNet, for analysis of ego network data; and STRUCTURE), other applications have been more recently developed for more novice audiences. For example, the NodeXL application has been developed to run on Excel 2007. It is intended as a relatively easy software format that lets you perform some simple operations and visualizations, all within an Excel window.

Software has also been recently developed to run on open source applications. A sample of these include igraph, SocNetV and Tulip. In fact, it is very difficult to list and describe the number and variety of software applications that have been developed in recent years to support social network analysis (see for example Huisman and Van Duijn, 2005, for a review and comparison of a few different programs). The increase in software applications reflects the growing interest in the field, and the desire of software developers to explore different aspects of the field.

REFERENCES

Barabási, L. (2000) 'The large-scale organization of metabolic networks', *Nature*, 407: 651–4.

Bathelt, H. and Gluckler, J. (2003) 'Toward a relational economic geography', *Journal of Economic setgraphy*, 3: 117–44.

Bendell, J., Ellersiek, A. and United Nations Research Institute for Social Development (2009) *Noble Networks? Advocacy for Global Justice and the 'Network Effect'*. Geneva: United Nations Research Institute for Social Development.

Borgatti, S.P. (2005) 'Trends in social network analysis, keynote address', in *Oxford Conference on Social Networks*. Oxford University.

Borgatti, S.P. and Li, X. (2009) 'On network analysis in a supply chain context', *Supply Chain Management*, 45: 5–22.

Brandes, U., Kenis, P. Raab, J., Schneider, V. and Wagner, D. (1999) 'Explorations into the visualization of policy networks', *Journal of Theoretical Politics*, 11: 75–106.

Brandes, U., Raab, J. and Wagner, D. (2001) 'Exploratory network visualization: Simultaneous display of actor status and connections', *Journal of Social Structure*, 2.

Brandes, U. Kenis, P. and Raab, J. (2006) 'Explanation through network visualization', *Methodology*, 2: 16–23.

Burt, R.S. (2000) 'The network structure of social capital', in R.I. Sutton and B.M. Staw (eds), *Research in Organizational Behavior*. Greenwich, CT: JAI Press (pp. 31–56).

Burt, R. (2005) *Brokerage and Closure: An Introduction to Social Capital*. Oxford: Oxford University Press.

Butts, C. T. (2003) 'Network inference, error, and informant (in)accuracy: a Bayesian approach', *Social Networks*, 25: 103–40.

Diani, M. and McAdam, D. (2003) *Social Movements and Networks: Relational Approaches to Collective Action*. Oxford and New York: Oxford University Press.

Doreian, P. (2002) 'Event sequences as generators of social network evolution', *Social Networks*, 24: 93–119.

Doreian, P. (2006) 'Actor network utilities and network evolution', *Social Networks*, 28: 137–64.

Ernstson, H., Sörlin, S. and Elmqvist, T. (2008) 'Social movements and ecosystem services – the role of social network structure in protecting and managing urban green areas in Stockholm', *Ecology and Society*, 13 article 39 [Online]. Available at: http://www.ecologyandsociety.org/vol13/iss2/art39/.

Gilbert, N. (2007) *Agent-based Models*. London: Sage Publications.

Goyal, S., van der Leij, M. J. and Moraga-Gonzalez, J. L. (2006) 'Economics: An emerging small world', *Journal of Political Economy*, 114: 403–12.

Handcock, M. S. and Gile, K. J. (forthcoming) 'Modeling networks from sampled data', *Annals of Applied Statistics*.

Hsung, R. M. Lin, N. and Breiger, R. L. (2009) *Contexts of Social Capital: Social Networks in Markets, Communities, and Families*. New York: Routledge.

Hubbell, C. H. (1965) 'An input-output approach to clique identification', *Sociometry*, 28: 377–99.

Huisman, M. and Steglich, C. (2008) 'Treatment of non-response in longitudinal network studies', *Social Networks*, 30: 297–308.

Huisman, M. and Van Duijn, M. A. J. (2005) 'Software for social network analysis', in P. J. Carrington, J. Scott and S. Wasserman, *Models and Methods in Social Network Analysis*, Cambridge: Cambridge University Press, pp. 270–316.

Hummon, N. P. (2000) 'Utility and dynamic social networks', *Social Networks*, 22: 221–49.

Jackson, M. O. and Wolinsky, A. (1996) 'A strategic model of social and economic networks', *Journal of Economic Theory*, 71: 44–74.

Johnson, C. and Gilles, R. P. (2000) 'Spatial social networks', *Review of Economic Design*, 5: 273–99.

Kagawa, S., Oshita, Y., Nansai, K. and Suh, S. (2009) 'How has dematerialization contributed to reducing oil price pressure?: A qualitative input-output analysis for the japanese economy during 1990–2000', *Environmental Science & Technology*, 43: 245–52.

Kossinets, G. (2006) 'Effects of missing data in social networks', *Social Networks*, 28: 247–68.

Leontief, W. (1941) *The Structure of the American Economy 1919–1939*. New York: Oxford University Press.

Lin, N. (2001) *Social Capital: A Theory of Social Structure and Action*. Cambridge, UK and New York: Cambridge University Press.

Lin, N. and Erickson, B. H. (2008) *Social Capital: An International Research Program*. Oxford and New York: Oxford University Press.

Martínez-López, B., Perez, A. M. and Sánchez-Vizcaíno, J. M. (2009) 'Combined application of social network and cluster detection analyses for temporal-spatial characterization of animal movements in Salamanca, Spain', *Preventive Veterinary Medicine*, 91: 29–38.

Mercken, L., Snijders, T. A. B, Steglich, C., Vartiainen, E. and de Vries, H. (2010) 'Dynamics of adolescent friendship networks and smoking behavior', *Social Networks*, 32: 72–81.

Montresora, S. and Marzetti, G. V. (2009) 'Applying social network analysis to input-output based innovation matrices: An illustrative application to six OECD technological systems for the middle 1990s', *Economic Systems Research*, 21: 129–49.

Newman, M. E. J., Barabási, A.-L. and Watts, D. J. (2006) *The Structure and Dynamics of Networks*. Princeton: Princeton University Press.

Putnam, R.D. (1993) *Making Democracy Work: Civic Traditions in Modern Italy*. Princeton, NJ: Princeton University Press.

Radil, S. M., Flint, C. and Tita, G. E. (2010) 'Spatializing social networks: Using social network analysis to investigate geographies of gang rivalry, territoriality, and violence in Los Angeles', *Annals of the Association of American Geographers*, 100: 307–26.

Robins, G., Pattison, P. and Woolcock, J. (2004) 'Missing data in networks: Exponential random graph (p*) models for networks with non-respondents', *Social Networks*, 26: 257–83.

Robins, G., Pattison, P. and Woolcock, J. (2005) 'Small and other worlds: Global network structures from local processes', *American Journal of Sociology*, 110: 894–936.

Robins, G., Pattison, P. Snijders, T. and Wang, P. (2010) 'The statistical modelling of network processes: Activity, closure and brokerage', in *6th UK Social Networks Conference*. Manchester, UK.

Smith, J. (2008) *Social Movements for Global Democracy*. Baltimore: Johns Hopkins University Press.

Snijders, T.A.B. (in press) 'Conditional marginalization for exponential random graph models', *Journal of Mathematical Sociology*.

Snijders, T. A. B., van de Bunt, G. G. and Steglich, C. E. G. (2010) 'Introduction to stochastic actor-based models for network dynamics', *Social Networks*, 32: 44–60.

Stevenson, W. B. and Greenberg, D. (2000) 'Agency and social networks: Strategies of action in a social structure of position, opposition, and opportunity', *Administrative Science Quarterly*, 45: 651–78.

Studer, K. E., Barboni, E. J. and Numan, K. B. (1984) 'Structural analysis using the input-output model: With special reference to networks of science', *Scientometrics*, 6: 401–23.

Wang, P. Sharpe, K. Robins, G. L. and Pattison, P. E. (2009) 'Exponential random graph (p*) models for affiliation networks', *Social Networks*, 31: 12–25.

Watts, Duncan J. and Strogatz, S. H. (1998) 'Collective dynamics of small world networks', *Nature*, 393: 440–2.

Wong, L. H. Pattison, P. and Robins, G. (2006) 'A spatial model for social networks', *Physica A: Statistical Mechanics and its Applications*, 360: 99–120.

APPENDIX 1

GETTING STARTED WITH UCINET

Throughout this book, I have offered you instructions on how to use UCINET to analyse for different social network concepts. Here, I offer a brief introduction on getting started with UCINET, and I also demonstrate how to unpack, transform, analyse and export data files using UCINET. The dataset I will be demonstrating is the Freeman Electronic Exchange System data (Freeman and Freeman, 1979), which is found as one of your UCINET datafiles. I have chosen this dataset and the analyses for this example for a particular reason: the resulting data transformations you do here, in Appendix 1, will be used in Appendix 2. That is, if you are interested in learning about Siena, and how to conduct a p* and longitudinal analyses, then the datafiles you generate here, in Appendix 1 will be used in the examples provided in Appendix 2.

Please launch UCINET and start having a look around. For example, please go to the Help menu found in UCINET. You will notice a Help Topics option and also an option called Hanneman tutorial. The Help Topics is the help file that Borgatti and Everett have developed for this software. The Hanneman tutorial is an online tutorial developed as a teaching tool for using UCINET. Both the UCINET Help Topics and the Hanneman Tutorial will make for useful additional resources for you as you attempt to learn this software and the concepts introduced in this book.

GETTING STARTED

You will first need to set up the various directories in UCINET. In general, you need all folders to point towards the same directory. By default, UCINET points the directories to the 'Datafiles' directory.

If you have installed UCINET onto a PC, and onto the C: drive, then the pathname for the Datafiles directory will probably look similar to the following:

C:\Program Files\Analytic Technologies\Ucinet 6\DataFiles

The important part, however, is that the end directory, 'Datafiles', has the same pathname across all relevant directories/folders. To make sure this is the case, in UCINET:

1 Press the 'file cabinet' button on the far right, bottom-hand side of the window. Navigate to the 'Datafiles' folder. Double click on it to open the folder. Click OK.

2 Go to Options/Scratch Folder. Make sure 'Datafiles' is selected, with the same pathname as above.

3 Go to Options/Output Folder. Make sure 'Datafiles' is selected, with the same pathname as above.

Please note that this is a procedure you should check at the beginning of each session. You need to make sure that your various directories (input, scratch and output folders) are all pointing towards your 'datafiles' directory. Otherwise, this will cause problems with UCINET functioning.

DISPLAYING DATA

Select *Data – Display*. At the 'dataset:' prompt, press the ellipses ('..') button to access the file menu. Select Freeman's_EIES. Then press 'ok'. You should see something Figure. A1.1

There are three datafiles in Freeman's_EIES. To become familiar with each of these, read briefly what UCINET has to say about them. Go to Help/Help Topics/Standard Data Sets. Click on the link called ' FREEMAN'S EIES DATA'. Read the description offered to learn about the three networks.

For our purposes, we will be using the first two networks (Time 1 and Time 2). Essentially, these data are acquaintanceship data that range in strength from 1 = 'have heard, but never met this person' to 4 = 'close personal friend'.

UNPACKING DATA

To gain access to these two network files, we need to unpack the data. To do this go to *Data – Unpack*. In the window entitled 'input data set:' select the button with '...' This will enable you to browse for the Freeman's_EIES file. Once you have selected the Freeman's_EIES file, press the OK button, and your files should be unpacked into two data sets: TIME_1 and TIME_2.

```
Matrix #1:  TIME_1

                              1 1 1 1 1 1 1 1 1 1 1 1 2 2 2 2 2 2 2 2 2 3 3 3 3 3 3 3 4 4 4 4 4
                  1 2 3 4 5 6 7 8 9 0 1 2 3 4 5 6 7 8 9 0 1 2 3 4 5 6 7 8 9 0 1 2 3
                  1 2 3 6 8 0 1 3 4 6 7 8 9 0 1 2 3 4 5 6 7 8 9 0 1 2 3 4 5 6 7 8 9 0 1 2 3 4 5
                  - - - - - - - - - - - - - - - - - - - - - - - - - - - - - - - - - - - - - - -
  1   1   0 4 2 2 2 2 2 1 1 1 1 1 2 2 2 2 2 2 2 2 2 2 2 2 2 2 2 2 2 2 3 3 3
  2   2   4 0 2 2 2 2 2 2 2 2 2 2 2 2 2 2 2 2 2 2 2 2 2 2 2 2 2 2 3 3 3 1 2
  3   3   2 2 0 1 3 0 1 2 2 2 2 2 2 2 2 2 2 2 2 2 2 2 2 2 2 2 2 3 4 4 4 2 4
  4   6   2 0 1 0 4 1 2 2 2 2 2 2 2 2 2 2 2 2 2 2 2 2 2 2 2 4 4 4 4 4 4 1 1
  5   8   3 0 0 2 0 1 2 2 2 2 2 2 2 2 2 2 2 2 2 2 2 2 2 3 2 2 2 2 2 2 2 3 4
  6  10   0 2 0 3 2 0 2 2 2 2 2 2 2 2 2 2 2 2 2 2 2 2 2 2 0 2 0 2 0 0 0 0 0
  7  11   3 2 1 2 2 2 0 3 2 2 2 2 2 2 2 2 2 2 2 2 2 2 2 2 2 2 2 2 2 2 2 2 2
  8  13   3 2 2 3 0 2 2 0 2 2 2 2 2 2 2 2 2 2 2 2 2 2 2 2 2 2 2 2 2 2 2 2 0
  9  14   4 0 2 2 2 2 2 2 0 2 2 2 2 2 2 2 2 2 2 2 2 2 2 2 2 2 2 2 2 2 2 0 4
 10  18   2 2 2 2 2 2 2 2 2 0 3 2 2 2 2 2 2 2 2 2 2 2 2 2 2 2 2 2 2 2 2 2 0
 11  19   1 3 3 1 2 1 1 0 1 2 0 2 2 2 2 2 2 2 2 2 2 2 2 2 2 2 2 2 2 2 2 1 1
 12  20   3 1 2 1 0 1 0 3 0 3 2 0 2 2 2 2 2 2 2 2 2 2 2 2 2 2 2 2 2 2 2 2 0
 13  21   1 2 0 1 2 0 0 3 0 2 2 2 0 4 2 2 2 2 2 2 2 2 2 2 2 2 2 2 2 2 2 2 0
 14  22   3 1 3 1 0 2 1 2 1 3 1 3 4 0 3 2 2 2 2 2 2 2 2 2 2 2 2 2 2 2 2 1 1
 15  23   3 2 2 3 3 2 3 1 0 3 0 3 0 3 0 2 2 2 2 2 2 2 2 2 2 2 2 2 2 2 2 1 1
 16  24   2 2 2 0 2 0 3 0 3 0 3 0 2 2 2 0 2 2 2 2 2 2 2 2 2 2 2 2 2 2 2 2 2
 17  25   3 2 2 2 2 0 0 0 2 2 0 0 2 2 2 2 0 2 2 2 2 2 2 2 2 2 2 2 2 2 2 2 0
 18  26   4 1 1 4 2 4 1 2 1 1 3 3 1 2 2 0 2 0 2 2 2 2 2 2 2 2 2 2 2 2 2 1 0
 19  27   2 0 3 4 2 0 4 3 2 0 0 2 2 1 1 3 0 3 0 2 2 2 2 2 2 2 2 2 2 2 2 0 4
 20  32   2 2 2 4 3 0 3 0 2 2 1 3 0 3 3 1 0 2 2 0 2 2 2 2 2 2 2 2 2 2 2 0 2
 21  33   2 2 0 4 2 0 3 2 2 0 2 0 0 3 0 3 0 3 0 2 0 2 2 2 2 2 2 2 2 2 2 2 0
 22  35   3 3 2 3 2 2 3 2 3 0 3 3 3 2 3 3 3 2 3 3 2 0 2 2 2 2 2 2 2 2 2 3 4
 23  36   2 2 2 2 0 0 2 0 0 0 0 0 0 0 1 0 0 0 0 0 0 0 0 2 2 2 2 2 2 2 2 2 3
 24  37   2 2 0 3 2 0 0 1 2 0 1 0 0 1 0 0 0 0 0 0 0 0 0 0 2 2 2 2 2 2 2 2 0
 25  38   2 1 4 4 2 2 2 0 2 0 0 1 3 4 3 2 3 1 4 1 2 3 4 3 0 2 2 2 2 2 2 4 0
 26  39   1 1 1 2 1 1 0 3 0 0 1 0 1 1 1 0 1 3 3 0 1 3 1 1 2 0 2 2 2 2 2 1 2
 27  40   4 2 0 0 0 0 0 0 2 0 0 0 0 0 0 0 0 0 0 0 0 0 0 0 0 1 0 2 2 2 2 4 0
 28  41   3 2 2 0 0 0 2 0 0 0 2 0 2 0 0 0 2 0 3 0 0 3 0 0 2 1 0 0 2 2 2 3 0
 29  42   3 2 3 2 2 0 2 2 0 0 2 2 0 3 0 0 2 3 0 2 0 3 0 0 3 2 0 0 0 2 2 4 0
 30  43   3 4 4 4 2 0 2 2 4 0 2 2 2 2 2 2 3 2 3 2 2 2 2 4 0 2 4 4 0 0 2 4 4
 31  44   4 4 4 4 0 0 1 2 2 0 2 2 2 1 1 2 0 2 2 2 2 2 2 1 1 2 0 0 0 2 0 0 4
 32  45   3 0 1 2 0 3 2 2 2 2 2 2 0 1 1 0 2 0 2 0 2 0 0 0 2 2 2 2 2 2 2 4 0
```

```
Matrix #2:  TIME_2

                              1 1 1 1 1 1 1 1 1 1 1 1 2 2 2 2 2 2 2 2 2 3 3 3 3 3 3 3 4 4 4 4 4
                  1 2 3 4 5 6 7 8 9 0 1 2 3 4 5 6 7 8 9 0 1 2 3 4 5 6 7 8 9 0 1 2 3
                  1 2 3 6 8 0 1 3 4 6 7 8 9 0 1 2 3 4 5 6 7 8 9 0 1 2 3 4 5 6 7 8 9 0 1 2 3 4 5
                  - - - - - - - - - - - - - - - - - - - - - - - - - - - - - - - - - - - - - - -
  1   1   0 4 2 2 3 0 3 3 4 2 1 3 1 3 3 2 3 4 3 2 2 2 2 2 2 2 2 2 2 2 3 1 4
  2   2   4 0 2 0 0 2 2 2 2 2 3 1 2 1 2 2 2 2 2 2 2 2 2 2 2 2 2 2 2 2 2 1 4
  3   3   3 1 0 4 0 0 1 2 2 2 2 2 2 3 2 2 2 2 2 2 2 2 2 2 2 2 2 3 4 4 4 2 4
  4   6   2 2 3 0 2 2 2 2 2 2 2 2 2 2 2 2 2 2 2 2 2 2 2 2 2 4 3 4 4 4 4 1 0
  5   8   3 2 0 2 0 2 2 2 2 2 2 2 2 2 2 2 2 2 2 2 2 2 2 3 2 2 2 2 2 2 2 3 2
  6  10   4 2 0 3 0 0 3 2 2 0 2 2 2 3 2 2 2 2 2 2 2 2 2 2 0 2 0 2 0 0 0 0 0
  7  11   3 2 1 2 2 3 0 3 2 2 2 2 2 2 2 2 2 2 2 2 2 2 2 2 2 2 2 2 2 2 2 2 2
  8  13   2 2 2 4 2 2 2 0 2 2 2 2 2 2 2 2 2 2 2 2 2 2 2 2 2 2 2 2 2 2 2 2 0
  9  14   3 2 2 2 2 2 2 2 0 2 2 2 2 2 2 2 2 2 2 2 2 2 2 2 2 2 2 2 2 2 2 0 4
 10  18   4 2 2 2 2 2 2 0 2 0 3 2 2 2 2 2 2 2 2 2 2 2 2 2 2 2 2 2 2 2 2 2 0
 11  19   3 3 3 0 0 1 1 0 1 4 0 2 2 2 2 2 2 2 2 2 2 2 2 2 2 2 2 2 2 2 2 1 2
 12  20   3 1 1 2 2 0 0 3 0 3 2 0 2 3 2 2 2 2 2 2 2 2 2 2 2 2 2 2 2 2 2 2 0
 13  21   1 1 0 1 2 2 0 3 0 2 2 2 0 4 2 2 2 2 2 2 2 2 2 2 2 2 2 2 2 2 2 2 0
 14  22   3 2 3 3 1 3 1 3 1 3 3 3 4 0 3 3 2 2 2 2 2 2 2 2 2 2 2 2 2 2 2 1 1
 15  23   4 0 2 3 3 2 3 2 0 3 0 3 0 3 0 2 2 2 2 2 2 2 2 2 2 2 2 2 2 2 2 1 1
 16  24   2 2 2 2 2 0 3 0 3 1 3 0 2 3 2 0 2 2 2 2 2 2 2 2 2 2 2 2 2 2 2 2 2
 17  25   3 2 3 2 2 0 0 0 2 1 0 0 2 2 2 2 0 2 2 2 2 2 2 2 2 2 2 2 2 2 2 2 0
 18  26   4 2 4 4 2 4 1 2 1 4 3 4 1 4 2 3 3 0 3 2 2 2 2 2 2 2 2 2 2 2 2 1 0
 19  27   3 2 3 4 3 0 4 3 2 2 3 2 2 2 2 3 2 4 0 2 2 2 2 2 2 2 2 2 2 2 2 0 4
 20  32   2 2 2 4 3 2 3 3 2 2 3 3 0 3 3 2 2 2 2 0 2 2 2 2 2 2 2 2 2 2 2 0 2
 21  33   3 2 2 4 2 2 3 2 2 2 2 2 0 3 0 3 2 3 2 2 0 2 2 2 2 2 2 2 2 2 2 2 0
 22  35   3 3 3 3 2 3 3 2 3 3 3 3 3 2 3 3 3 4 3 3 2 0 2 2 2 2 2 2 2 2 2 3 4
 23  36   3 3 2 2 3 0 2 0 0 0 0 0 0 2 2 0 0 2 0 0 0 0 0 2 2 2 2 2 2 2 2 2 3
 24  37   3 2 2 3 2 0 0 1 2 3 1 0 0 1 0 0 0 2 0 0 2 0 0 0 2 2 2 2 2 2 2 2 0
 25  38   2 2 4 4 2 2 2 0 2 0 2 1 3 4 3 2 3 2 4 3 2 3 4 3 0 2 2 2 2 2 2 4 0
 26  39   3 3 1 2 1 1 0 3 0 2 1 0 1 1 1 0 1 3 3 2 1 3 1 1 2 0 2 2 2 2 2 1 2
 27  40   4 2 2 3 0 0 0 0 2 0 0 0 0 0 0 0 2 0 0 0 0 0 0 0 0 1 0 2 2 2 2 4 0
 28  41   3 2 3 3 2 2 2 0 0 3 2 2 2 2 2 2 2 2 3 3 0 3 2 2 2 1 0 0 2 2 2 3 0
 29  42   3 2 3 2 2 0 2 3 2 0 3 3 0 3 3 0 3 3 0 3 2 3 0 0 3 2 0 0 0 2 2 4 0
 30  43   3 4 4 3 3 0 2 2 4 0 2 2 2 2 2 2 3 2 3 2 2 2 2 4 0 2 4 4 0 0 2 4 4
 31  44   4 4 4 4 2 2 2 2 2 0 2 2 2 2 2 2 0 3 2 2 2 2 2 1 2 2 0 0 0 2 0 0 4
 32  45   4 2 4 0 0 3 2 2 2 2 2 2 0 1 1 0 2 0 2 0 2 0 0 0 2 2 2 2 2 2 2 4 0
```

Figure A1.1   Matrices of Freeman datafile

Matrix #3: NUMBER_OF_MESSAGES

	1	2	3	4	5	6	7	8	9	10	11	12	13	14	15	16	17	18	19	20	21	22	23	24	25	26	27	28	29	30	31	32
	1	2	3	6	8	10	11	13	14	18	19	20	21	22	23	24	25	26	27	32	33	35	36	37	38	39	40	41	42	43	44	45
1 1	24	488	28	65	20	65	45	346	82	52	177	28	24	49	81	77	77	73	33	31	22	46	31	128	38	89	95	25	388	71	212	185
2 2	364	6	17	17	15	0	30	20	35	20	22	15	15	15	15	50	25	8	0	15	15	15	15	0	15	15	10	24	89	23	163	39
3 3	4	5	0	0	0	0	0	5	0	0	0	0	0	0	0	0	0	0	0	0	0	0	0	0	0	0	0	0	0	0	0	0
4 6	52	30	0	4	0	2	0	32	21	34	9	0	0	0	0	5	4	2	35	0	0	0	0	12	0	0	12	5	20	4	19	33
5 8	26	4	0	4	0	4	8	4	4	4	4	4	0	0	4	4	6	4	4	0	4	8	4	14	4	0	4	3	4	7	4	4
6 10	72	23	0	2	0	34	0	16	0	7	15	0	0	0	8	7	0	0	0	0	0	0	0	14	0	0	7	3	34	3	22	0
7 11	14	0	0	0	0	0	0	0	0	0	15	0	0	0	0	0	0	0	0	0	0	0	0	0	0	0	0	0	4	3	6	0
8 13	239	82	5	37	3	34	5	10	12	18	164	18	0	0	0	30	53	27	20	4	0	5	4	55	0	9	34	0	146	216	88	288
9 14	24	25	0	2	0	0	0	8	16	0	15	2	10	0	0	0	5	0	0	0	0	0	0	29	0	0	15	0	10	6	30	44
10 18	43	15	0	32	0	12	10	8	0	5	25	0	4	0	0	10	10	0	20	0	0	5	0	29	0	4	10	0	47	0	22	19
11 19	178	36	0	11	0	19	172	14	39	28	29	3	0	0	0	23	15	24	0	15	8	0	0	29	10	11	22	0	46	0	119	34
12 20	0	5	0	0	0	0	0	0	0	0	0	0	0	0	0	0	0	0	5	0	0	0	0	0	0	0	0	0	53	0	5	9
13 21	5	0	0	0	0	0	0	0	0	0	0	0	0	0	0	0	0	0	0	0	0	0	0	0	0	0	0	0	0	0	5	0
14 22	12	0	9	0	0	0	0	0	0	0	0	0	0	2	0	12	0	0	0	0	0	0	0	0	0	0	0	0	35	0	8	0
15 23	120	0	0	0	0	4	0	0	0	0	0	5	0	0	78	0	0	0	5	5	0	0	0	0	0	0	8	0	35	0	32	0
16 24	58	25	0	10	0	0	20	20	0	5	10	5	0	5	0	15	10	0	0	5	5	0	5	5	0	0	0	0	58	0	10	0
17 25	63	18	9	7	0	0	0	36	0	5	9	0	0	5	0	5	0	4	0	2	0	0	0	0	0	0	15	0	35	9	15	9
18 26	58	5	5	4	0	6	0	4	0	5	18	0	0	5	8	0	0	0	5	0	0	0	0	0	0	0	20	0	10	10	48	0
19 27	5	5	0	25	0	0	0	10	0	5	0	0	0	5	0	0	0	4	0	0	4	0	5	0	0	0	0	0	8	0	10	0
20 32	0	0	0	0	0	0	0	0	0	0	3	0	0	0	0	0	0	0	0	0	0	0	0	40	0	0	0	0	4	0	0	0
21 33	9	0	0	0	0	0	0	0	0	0	0	0	0	0	0	5	0	0	5	4	0	0	0	0	0	0	0	0	5	0	0	5
22 35	10	5	0	0	0	0	0	0	0	0	0	0	0	0	0	0	0	0	0	0	0	0	0	0	0	0	0	0	15	0	5	0
23 36	5	0	0	0	0	0	0	0	0	0	3	0	0	0	0	0	0	0	5	0	4	58	0	0	0	0	0	0	14	0	0	5
24 37	89	17	5	14	14	18	8	41	4	19	31	4	4	9	4	14	4	9	4	4	4	0	4	5	18	14	9	4	156	4	56	10
25 38	32	5	0	0	0	0	0	0	0	0	0	0	0	15	0	0	0	0	0	4	0	10	0	23	10	0	0	0	0	9	15	0
26 39	35	5	0	0	0	0	0	0	0	5	0	0	0	0	4	0	0	15	0	0	0	0	0	0	0	0	0	3	10	0	13	0
27 40	50	28	0	13	0	0	19	0	29	5	8	0	33	0	0	0	10	0	0	0	0	0	0	10	0	0	0	3	32	0	13	33
28 41	9	6	0	0	0	3	0	19	0	0	0	0	0	0	4	0	10	0	0	5	0	0	0	0	0	0	0	3	0	0	0	6
29 42	559	132	5	24	21	29	0	155	15	98	69	89	37	76	80	63	15	4	9	18	43	108	29	218	0	15	66	0	6	14	91	126
30 43	39	21	0	6	3	3	0	140	0	7	0	2	0	0	0	0	9	5	0	5	5	0	8	0	0	8	2	8	18	2	20	8
31 44	82	125	10	22	10	15	15	70	35	23	114	20	16	15	24	30	28	49	30	5	0	15	0	53	25	8	21	8	65	28	0	67
32 45	239	99	0	27	3	0	0	268	101	18	35	4	0	0	0	0	7	0	0	0	0	14	0	5	0	0	50	6	71	7	107	219

TRANSFORMING YOUR DATA EXAMPLE: DICHOTOMIZING

The TIME_1 and TIME_2 datafiles are valued data, as can be seen by looking at the matrices shown in Figure 1. We shall dichotomize the data, so that we only look at the stronger ties. By this I mean, we will convert the two digraphs to two binary matrices, i.e. matrices only containing 0s and 1s, where a 1 will mean the presence of a strong tie, i.e. one where the respondent says the alter is either a friend or close friend, and a 0 represents no tie. I have chosen to only focus on the strong ties in the dataset, as such strong ties in this context represent friendship ties, and friendship ties are something we shall be looking at more carefully in Appendix 2.

To transform the data so that we only focus on friendship ties, we must dichotomize the data. I have chosen the cut-off value for dichotomizing to be 3 or above, as 3 = a friendship tie and 4 = a friendship tie, for these data.

1 To dichotomize TIME_1 and TIME_2 files, go to *Transform – Dichotomize*.

2 In the window that appears, select the TIME_1 data file:

   a. Choose 3 as the cut-off value.

   b. Make sure the cut-off operator is greater than or equal, as we wish to contain tie data at the value of 3 and above.

   c. Make sure that the output dataset is called Time_1GE3 (this is done auto-

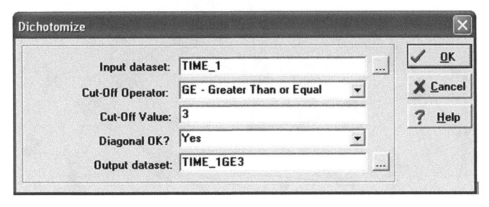

   matically for you).

3 Select OK. You should receive an output file that shows you a new matrix, one that contains 0s and 1s, displaying only those ties of value 3 or more in the original network datafile.

4   Repeat steps 1–3, but this time for the TIME_2 data file (be sure to call the output file TIME_2GE3).

VISUALIZE YOUR DATA THROUGH NETDRAW

1   In UCINET, Press the 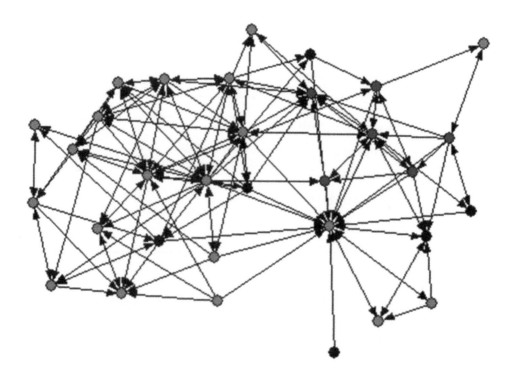 button to start NetDraw. The NetDraw application will launch.

2   In NetDraw, press the Open File button and load the TIME_1GE3 dataset. This loads the network data, and a digraph should appear in the screen.

3   In NetDraw, go to *File – Open – Ucinet datafile – Attribute file*. Select the Freeman's_EIES_Attribute file. The attribute file is now loaded onto NetDraw. There are two attributes saved: the number of citations/academic and each actor's academic discipline. We will visualize the digraph incorporating the Disicipline attribute:

(a)   To include the Disipline Attribute as part of the digraph, go to *Properties – Nodes – Symbols –Color – Attribute based*.

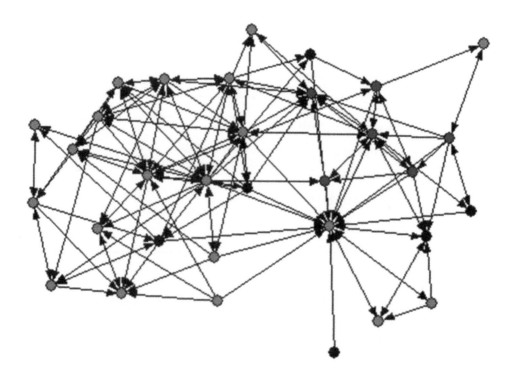

(b) In the window that appears, choose from the menu of attributes 'Discipline'. You will see a digraph with the nodes coloured according to Discipline:

ANALYSIS EXAMPLE: IN AND OUTDEGREE CENTRALITY

I shall now walk you through a simple example of using UCINET for analysis purposes. We shall measure for indegree and outdegree centrality for the TIME_1GE3 dataset. To do this:

1 In UCINET, go to *Network – Centrality – Degree*.

2 In the window that appears, select TIME_1GE3 as the Input dataset.

3 Select the option 'No' for 'treat data as symmetric'. These network data are directional (i.e. asymmetric) and so we shall be distinguishing between incoming and outgoing ties.

4 Click OK. The output that appears should look like Figure A1.2.

Here, the indegree and outdegree raw scores and normalized scores are given. You can see that actor 14 is the most active, while actor 1 is the most popular, both by a large margin. The Descriptive Statistics reinforces the idea that these data are skewed; both indegree and outdegree have mean scores of 4.8 (rounded) and standard deviations scores of 3.5 (again, rounded).

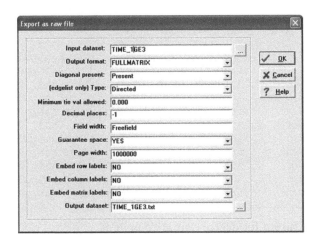

	1 OutDegree	2 InDegree	3 NrmOutDeg	4 NrmInDeg
14 22	17.000	9.000	54.839	29.032
2 2	10.000	8.000	32.258	25.806
21 33	9.000	8.000	29.032	25.806
24 37	9.000	6.000	29.032	19.355
22 35	9.000	11.000	29.032	35.484
25 38	8.000	4.000	25.806	12.903
17 25	7.000	3.000	22.581	9.677
13 21	7.000	2.000	22.581	6.452
20 32	7.000	6.000	22.581	19.355
16 24	7.000	6.000	22.581	19.355
3 3	6.000	4.000	19.355	12.903
32 45	6.000	3.000	19.355	9.677
9 14	5.000	4.000	16.129	12.903
10 18	5.000	4.000	16.129	12.903
15 23	4.000	2.000	12.903	6.452
1 1	4.000	17.000	12.903	54.839
28 41	4.000	0.000	12.903	0.000
23 36	3.000	4.000	9.677	12.903
31 44	3.000	6.000	9.677	19.355
26 39	3.000	1.000	9.677	3.226
29 42	3.000	5.000	9.677	16.129
30 43	3.000	3.000	9.677	9.677
11 19	2.000	3.000	6.452	9.677
18 26	2.000	3.000	6.452	9.677
19 27	2.000	5.000	6.452	16.129
7 11	2.000	2.000	6.452	6.452
5 8	2.000	2.000	6.452	6.452
4 6	1.000	7.000	3.226	22.581
12 20	1.000	3.000	3.226	9.677
6 10	1.000	0.000	3.226	0.000
27 40	1.000	2.000	3.226	6.452
8 13	0.000	10.000	0.000	32.258

DESCRIPTIVE STATISTICS

		1 OutDegree	2 InDegree	3 NrmOutDeg	4 NrmInDeg
1	Mean	4.781	4.781	15.423	15.423
2	Std Dev	3.533	3.471	11.397	11.196
3	Sum	153.000	153.000	493.548	493.548
4	Variance	12.483	12.046	129.900	125.348
5	SSQ	1131.000	1117.000	11768.991	11623.310
6	MCSSQ	399.469	385.469	4156.803	4011.121
7	Euc Norm	33.630	33.422	108.485	107.811
8	Minimum	0.000	0.000	0.000	0.000
9	Maximum	17.000	17.000	54.839	54.839

Figure A1.2   Output for degree centrality analysis

EXPORT DATAFILE

For our next exercise, found in Appendix 2, we will be making use of these Time_1GE3 and Time_2GE3 files. The format of these files, however, needs to change, as StocNet (see Appendix 2) does not accept UCINET datafiles. Thus, we need to export the files into a suitable format.

One format that Siena does accept is text, ASCII files. To convert and export UCINET datafiles into this format:

1   In UCINET, go to *Data – Export – Raw.*

2   In the window that appears, select Time_1GE3 as the input file.

   (a) make sure that the output format selected is 'Fullmatrix'

   (b) Select that the diagonal is 'Present'

   (c) Select that the edge type is 'Directed'

3   Press OK, and the .txt file is created. You will see that no labels are included, only the contents of the cells. This is exactly the kind of format we need for our next set of exercises in Appendix 2.

4   Repeat steps 1–3 for Time_2GE3.

SUMMARY AND CONCLUSION

You have created two datafiles in this exercise Time_1GE3 and Time_2GE3. Both these files will be used in the next Appendix in exploring the use of the Siena application for p* and actor-based models.

REFERENCE

Freeman, S. C. and Freeman, L. C. (1979) 'The networkers network: A study of the impact of a new communications medium on sociometric structure', *Social Science Research Reports*, No 46. Irvine, CA: University of California.

APPENDIX 2

EXPONENTIAL RANDOM GRAPH MODELLING AND LONGITUDINAL MODELLING THROUGH SIENA

In this Appendix, we will be using the Siena application, which is located within StocNet. In the time period in which this book was written, Siena has moved from the StocNet environment to the R environment. You can still make use of StocNet and Siena, yet the developers have decided to make all future changes and developments within R. Thus, one can still download and make use of StocNet, yet in future years, if a reader decides to continue making use of the statistical models presented here, then s/he would be advised to start exploring R and RSiena.

Thus, it may feel slightly unsettling to be taught via StocNet, only to find out that StocNet is no longer being supported! However, the main reason I have decided to keep this working example of Siena for the present book is that the StocNet environment is a bit more user friendly. To make use of more recent Siena versions (which are called RSiena) requires knowledge of R and some R programming. For many scientists learning SNA, especially those just trying to get to know some basic SNA concepts, learning R is not a top priority. Thus, even though RSiena does provide a Gui interface, one still needs to learn a bit of code to get RSiena up and running, whereas the Gui interface found within StocNet is still a bit more user friendly.

Thus, in this Appendix, you will first conduct a p* analysis (ERGM analysis) in Siena using the older StocNet environment. This will be followed by a longitudinal analysis using actor-based models, again in Siena. In both cases, we shall be using a dataset from UCINET, the Freeman Electronic Exchange System data (Freeman and Freeman, 1979). These data include relational data on 32 academics (actors). The data we will be analysing are the relational data at two time periods (Time_1 and Time_2), as well as the data on each actor's academic discipline (found in the Freeman's_EIES_Attribute file).

In Appendix 1, you learnt how to unpack the Freeman datafile, how to convert the network data from valued data to binary data. As a result, you created two text files entitled Time1_GE3 and Time2_GE3. You shall be using those files here. In addition, you will be using one of the attribute vectors found in the Freeman's_EIES_Attribute file, this being the Discipline variable. In the below instructions, I shall show you how to convert those data into a format suitable for Siena.

Before getting started however, please go and download StocNet, and place StocNet in your C://drive. You can download this program for free from the following website: http://stat.gamma.rug.nl/stocnet/. Please follow the instructions on the website for installation.

ERGM ANALYSIS IN SIENA

Step one: Download and install StocNet

If you have not done so already, you need to download and install StocNet onto your computer. This application is for free and can be downloaded at the following URL: http://stat.gamma.rug.nl/stocnet/. Helpful manuals are also found on this site. The website for Siena is http://stat.gamma.rug.nl/siena.html

Step two: Assemble your data

You need to make use of an adjacency network file in ASCII (or 'text') file format. In Appendix 1, you were shown how to export the UCINET datafile to a raw text file by going *Data – Export – Raw*. Through that procedure you should have created two text files for Time_1GE3 data and Time_2GE3 data. For the p* analysis we shall only use Time_1GE3 data, but later on, we shall import the second network datafile for conducting a longitudinal analysis.

In addition, you need to create text files for your attribute data. For Siena, each text file represents one attribute. The number of columns in that text file represents the number of time periods for which that particular attribute was measured. Thus, for the present example, we have attribute data on each actor's academic discipline, and these data are for one time period only (i.e. they are a constant variable for this dataset). Thus, the attribute data found in UCINET needs to be adjusted slightly. Please follow these steps:

1 In UCINET, select the spreadsheet icon found at the top of the menu bar. A spreadsheet should open.

2 Go *File – Open* and select the Freeman_EIES_Attribute file. The attribute data, consisting of two columns (Citations and Disciplines) should appear.

3 Copy the column of numbers (do not copy the label) from the Disciplines column.

4 In the Notepad (or comparable) application, copy these data. You should now have one column of numbers only, with no other numbers or text present.

5 Save these data as 'Disciplines' under your StocNet/Actfiles directory. Make sure the format of the file is a text/ASCII file.

In Figure A2.1, I have drawn the digraph of the Time1_GE3 data, and the nodes shading reflect the four different disciplines represented by these actors. The corresponding matrix data and attribute data are also found in the Figure A2.1.

Step three: Copy datafile(s) into StocNet

In step two, you saved your Disciplines folder to the StocNet/Actfiles. You need to make sure your network data are in the correct directory as well. Within the StocNet directory, you will see a folder (directory) entitled 'Networks'. Drop your Time1_GE3 datafile in here.

Step three: Importing data in Siena

1 Launch StocNet and you will see a window entitled 'Data Definition' and places to import your 'Networks' and 'Actor attributes' files.

2 Select the Add button under the 'Networks' window. Here, a window appears, allowing you to browse and select your datafile.

3 Select your Time1_GE3 text file from the datafiles listed. You may need to switch the 'file type' to text files in order to view your datafile.

4 Select the Add button under the 'Actor attributes' window. Here, a window appears, allowing you to browse and select your attribute datafile.

5 Select your Disciplines text file from the datafiles listed. You may need to switch the 'file type' to text files in order to view your datafile.

6 Once you have selected and opened your datafile, you should see these data names appear alongside the label 'Network 1' and the label 'Attribute 1'. You have now successfully imported your data into Siena.

Diagraph of Time1_GE3 network data

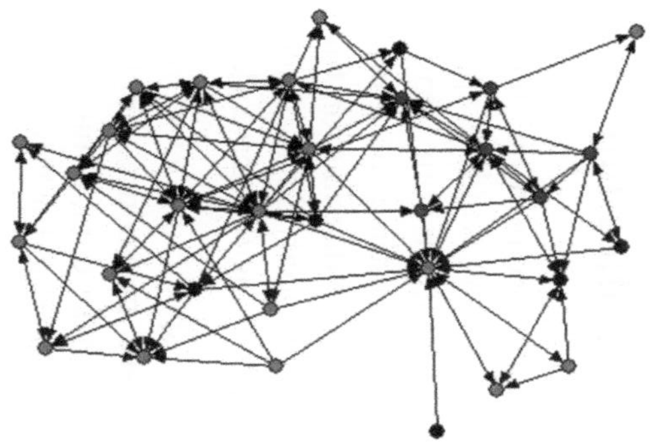

Matrix of Time1_GE3 network data	Disciplines attribute file
0 1 0 0 0 0 0 0 0 0 0 0 0 0 0 0 0 1 0 0 0 0 0 0 0 1 0 0 0 0 1 0	1
1 0 0 0 0 0 1 1 1 0 1 0 0 0 0 1 0 0 0 0 1 0 0 0 0 0 0 0 0 1 1 1	2
1 0 0 1 0 0 0 0 0 0 1 1 0 1 0 0 0 0 0 0 0 0 1 0 0 0 0 0 0 0 0 0	4
0 0 0 0 0 0 0 0 0 0 0 0 0 0 0 0 0 0 1 0 0 0 0 0 0 0 0 0 0 0 0 0	1
1 0 0 0 0 0 0 0 1 0 0 0 0 0 0 0 0 0 0 0 0 0 0 0 0 0 0 0 0 0 0 0	4
1 0 0 0 0 0 0 0 0 0 0 0 0 0 0 0 0 0 0 0 0 0 0 0 0 0 0 0 0 0 0 0	4
1 0 0 0 0 0 0 0 0 0 0 0 1 0 0 0 0 0 0 0 0 0 0 0 0 0 0 0 0 0 0 0	4
0 0 0 0 0 0 0 0 0 0 0 0 0 0 0 0 0 0 0 0 0 0 0 0 0 0 0 0 0 0 0 0	2
1 1 0 0 0 0 0 0 0 0 0 0 0 0 0 0 0 0 0 0 0 1 0 0 0 0 1 0 0 0 0 1	2
0 0 1 1 0 0 0 0 0 0 0 1 0 0 0 0 0 0 0 1 0 0 1 0 0 0 0 0 0 0 0 0	1
0 1 0 0 0 0 0 1 0 0 0 0 0 0 0 0 0 0 0 0 0 0 0 0 0 0 0 0 0 0 0 0	1
0 0 0 0 0 0 0 0 0 1 0 0 0 0 0 0 0 0 0 0 0 0 0 0 0 0 0 0 0 0 0 0	1
1 1 0 0 0 0 1 1 0 0 0 0 0 0 0 0 0 0 0 0 0 0 0 0 0 0 1 0 0 0 1 1	2
1 0 1 0 1 0 0 1 0 0 0 1 0 0 1 1 1 0 1 1 1 1 1 1 1 0 0 0 1 1 0 0	1
1 0 0 1 0 0 0 0 0 0 0 0 0 1 0 0 0 0 0 0 0 0 0 0 0 0 0 0 1 0 0 0	1
0 0 0 0 1 0 0 1 0 0 0 0 0 1 0 0 1 0 0 0 1 1 0 1 0 0 0 0 0 0 0 0	3
1 0 1 0 0 0 0 1 0 0 0 0 0 1 0 0 0 0 0 1 1 1 0 0 0 0 0 0 0 0 0 0	4
1 0 0 0 0 0 0 0 0 0 0 0 0 0 0 0 0 0 0 0 0 0 0 0 0 0 0 0 0 0 1 0	1
0 0 0 1 0 0 0 0 0 0 0 0 0 0 0 0 0 0 0 0 0 1 0 0 0 0 0 0 0 0 0 0	1
0 0 0 0 0 0 0 0 0 1 0 0 0 1 0 0 0 0 0 0 1 1 0 1 1 0 0 0 1 0 0 0	1
1 1 0 0 0 0 0 1 0 0 1 0 0 0 1 1 1 0 0 0 0 1 0 0 1 0 0 0 0 0 0 0	3
0 0 0 1 0 0 0 0 1 0 0 0 0 1 0 1 0 0 1 1 1 0 0 1 0 0 0 0 1 0 0 0	1
0 0 1 1 0 0 0 0 0 1 0 0 0 0 0 0 0 0 0 0 0 0 0 0 0 0 0 0 0 0 0 0	1
0 0 0 0 0 0 0 1 0 0 0 0 0 1 0 1 0 0 1 1 1 1 0 0 1 0 0 0 1 0 0 0	1
0 0 0 0 0 0 0 0 0 1 0 0 0 1 0 1 0 0 0 1 1 1 1 1 0 0 0 0 0 0 0 0	1
1 0 0 0 0 0 0 0 0 0 0 0 0 0 0 0 0 1 0 0 0 0 0 0 0 0 0 0 0 0 1 0	1
0 0 0 0 0 0 0 0 0 0 0 0 1 0 0 0 0 0 0 0 0 0 0 0 0 0 0 0 0 0 0 0	3
1 0 0 1 0 0 0 0 0 0 0 0 0 0 0 0 0 0 1 0 0 1 0 0 0 0 0 0 0 0 0 0	1
0 0 0 0 0 0 0 0 0 0 0 0 0 1 0 0 0 0 0 0 0 1 0 1 0 0 0 0 0 0 0 0	1
1 1 0 0 0 0 0 1 0 0 0 0 0 0 0 0 0 0 0 0 0 0 0 0 0 0 0 0 0 0 0 0	2
1 1 0 0 0 0 0 0 0 0 0 0 0 0 0 0 0 1 0 0 0 0 0 0 0 0 0 0 0 0 0 0	4

Figure A2.1 Network and attribute data for Time 1

Step four: Saving your session

Now save your session. In the lower right-hand corner, you will see an Apply button. Select this button, and you will be asked to save your session. Save your session with a name you will easily remember or recognize. I tend to give a name for the data and a date (e.g. Freeman 1Dec09).

Step four: Data specification

1 At the top of the menu bar, you will see an icon with the label 'Model'. Select this 'Model' icon. This takes you to the data and model specification window.

2 Here, you will see an option for 'Model Choice'. Siena should be automatically selected for you.

3 Select 'Data Specification'. This takes you to a new window entitled 'Siena data specification', where you will see your Network 1 data (your Time1_ GE3 file) listed under 'Available networks' and you will see File 1 data (your Disciplines file) listed under 'Specify actor attributes'.

4 Select Network 1 and move it to the window entitled 'Dependent networks in seq. (sequential) order'. Select File 1 and move it to the 'Constant covariates' window. Your attribute file has only one time period, and thus it shall be treated as a constant variable.

5 Select the OK button, and you return to the Siena window.

Step five: Model specification

1 Now select the 'Model specification' button, which is next to the 'Data Specification' button. A new window appears, entitled 'Siena model specification'. Here you can specify your network effects and also specify some options for model type and estimation. Recall from your centrality analysis in Appendix 1, that the degree distribution for these network data are skewed. As such, we shall need to specify Siena to accommodate for this skewness. We shall do this before specifying the network effects.

2 Model options: before specifying network effects, we shall tell Siena how the steps in the MCMC procedure should be specified to account for the degree distribution in these data. Thus, select the 'Options' tab, and under the drop-down menu selection for 'Model code', select option '20. MH fixed out degrees'. In fixing the outdegrees, you are essentially controlling for the

skewness in the data (please note, if your data are not skewed, you can simply work with the default option provided by Siena).

Now select the network variable tab to take you back to the network effects page.

3 Specifying network effects: here, we shall choose network effects that reflect Markov dependence assumptions. Thus, select the following effects:

(a) reciprocity

(b) transitive triplets

(c) in-2-stars

(d) in-3-stars.

Please note that you do not need to select the out-star effects, as you are keeping outdegree measures constant.

Once you have selected the above effects, click on the 'OK' button.

Step six: Running the model

Now click the button 'Run' to start the simulation/estimation process, and a new window appears, showing the simulation process running. After a few minutes, some output should appear in the Results window.

Step seven: Looking at initial results

The Siena output gives you a great deal of information, and I encourage you to download and read the Siena manual for details on all data output. I shall focus here on some initial, interesting results that are important to note:

1 *Number of observations* Scroll down the window until you find the heading, 'Observed values of target statistics'. Here you will find the observed frequency counts for each of your specified network effects:

```
Number of mutuals (reciprocal ties)        43.00
Number of transitive triplets             326.00
in-2-stars                                482.00
in-3-stars                                132.00
```

At this point, there are no parameter values associated with these observed counts.

2 *Look for convergence* For your results in Siena to be meaningful, your model needs to 'converge'. Essentially, this means that the model results Siena offers are a good 'fit' to the data. To look whether these data have converged well, go to the heading 'Information for convergence diagnosis'. Here, you are offered averages, standard deviations, and t-ratios for each of the four network statistics. What you are looking for here is whether the t-ratios are close to 0 (zero) in actual value. If these t-ratio values are too large, Siena will alert you with an error message:

```
Good convergence is indicated by the t-ratios being close
to zero. One or more of the t-statistics are rather large.
Convergence of the algorithm is doubtful.
```

In present case, this is the result we attain, and so we have a few options:

(a) Re-run the model, using the parameter values attained from the previous analysis as the starting parameter values;

(b) Re-specify the model (e.g. use higher order configurations that go beyond Markov assumptions).

It is recommended that you first try to run the model a subsequent time, to see if new starting parameter values will yield better convergence. Thus, this is the option we shall try here.

Step eight: Re-run the model

Go back and select the 'Run' button. You do not need to re-specify or alter your Model Specifications in any way. Simply click on the 'Run' button, and re-examine your results.

1 Look at the initial parameter values. In the Results page, you should notice, under the heading, 'Initial parameter values', that none of the values are 0. All have adopted the last run's values as starting values.

2 Look at the t-ratios under the convergence diagnosis. Here, the t-ratios should be much closer to 0, and Siena offers a comment telling you that good convergence has been reached: 'Good convergence is indicated by the t-ratios being close to zero'.

3 Autocorrelations. Ideally, for the results under the heading 'autocorrelations', we want values less than or equal to 0.4. All of the values are above this amount, and thus, one is advised to re-run the Model, but in doing so, to increase the value of the Multiplication Factor. I have gone ahead and done this, increasing the value to 5, and the values for the autocorrelations have drastically improved. For now, however, let's just proceed with interpreting

our findings (you can read-up more on fine-tuning your model according to these issues in the Siena manual).

Now we can continue looking at our results.

Step nine: Interpreting the results

Assuming that the model has converged well, we now move onto interpreting the results of the network effects specified in the model. Here, what we are looking for, essentially, is to see the extent to which our network statistics are significant. If they are, we can feel reasonably confident that these statistics are helping to explain the overall structure of the network.

Recall what network statistics we are testing: reciprocity, transitive triplets, the presence of in-2-stars and in-3-stars. We have opted to fix our outdegrees, and so we are not testing for the out-stars.

Also recall, from an earlier discussion, what we hope to expect, given what previous research on social networks suggests, and the nature of our data. Previous research on friendship studies (Kadushin, 1966; Martin and Yeung, 2006; Skvoretz, 1991; Wellman et al., 1991) although see Carley and Krackhardt, 1996 for exceptions) notes a strong tendency for actors to reciprocate their ties (so if I call you a friend, you are likely to do the same for me), and also a strong tendency of friends of friends to become friends (i.e. the transitivity effect, as discussed in Chapter 5). Thus, given that these data consist of actors who nominate others as either friends or close friends, we would expect to see strong tendencies toward reciprocity and transitivity.

The findings are shown below, where the estimates and standard errors are give. Please note that your values will be slightly different, as this is a stochastic process, and as such, there is an element of randomness in the model. Your results, however, should approximate those found below. I have gone ahead and calculated the t-ratios, to help in interpretation:

```
reciprocity                  2.15 (0.32) t-ratio = 6.72
transitive triplets          0.19 (0.05) t-ratio = 3.80
in-2-stars                  -0.10 (0.09) t-ratio = 1.11
in-3-stars                   0.02 (0.01) t-ratio = 2.00
```

The above findings indicate that reciprocity and transitivity are statistically significant, and the low presence of 2-stars, although not significant, show a patterning that one would expect in friendships, i.e. that one is not too eager to have too many friendship partners. The high presence of 3-stars, however, while not significant, suggests that a few actors might be having many friends, and looking at the digraph presented earlier, as well as the degree distributions conducted in Appendix 1, it seems like the presence of a few highly popular actors are indeed present.

Step ten: Including actor attribute effects

Now, let's re-run the Model one final time. This time, we will include the 'same Attribute 1' effect, which tests the extent to which actors form ties with others who share exactly the same attribute. In our example, this translates into seeing the extent to which people in the same discipline are friends with each other.

1 In Model specification, leave all Markov network statistics originally selected. In addition, scroll down and select 'same Attribute 1'.

2 Go back and press the 'Run' button.

3 Interpret the results. Your latest run should have converged, and the Autocorrelation values should be better. The attained values for your test statistics results should be similar to the ones below:

```
reciprocity              2.06 (0.33) t-ratio = 6.24
transitive triplets      0.21 (0.05) t-ratio = 4.20
in-2-stars              -0.08 (0.10) t-ratio = 0.80
in-3-stars               0.01 (0.01) t-ratio = 1.00
same Attribute1          0.84 (0.17) t-ratio = 4.94
```

Once again, reciprocity and transitivity exhibit positive, significant results. The same Attribute 1 effect also attained a positive, significant value, implying that, in addition to exhibiting strong tendencies for reciprocity and transitivity, this network also is prone to actors befriending others within their same discipline.

BEYOND p*: ANALYSING LONGITUDINAL DATA IN SIENA

In Siena, you can easily extend the above analysis to now consider longitudinal data. As I have gone slowly through the process of using Siena for conducting a p* analysis, I shall move more quickly through analysing for longitudinal data.

1 Import text file. Import the text file 'Time2_GE3' into Siena through Adding a network file under the Data Definition window.

2 Data specification. Under the Data Specification window, select your Network 2 data, and bring these data underneath your Network 1 data, in the 'Dep.

Networks in sequential order' window. Leave your attribute datafile in the Constant Covariate window. Select OK.

3 Model specification. Under the Model Specification window, you will see a slightly different listing of possible network effects to choose from. Again, for this example, let's continue working with Markov assumptions. Thus, we shall select the following network effects:

(a) Density

(b) Reciprocity

(c) Transitive triplets

In addition, we shall again select effects to test whether, across the two time periods, actors befriend others in the same discipline as themselves. In addition, however, we shall also see if attributes play a role in the indegrees and outdegrees of actors (e.g. if being in a particular discipline coincides with having more ties). Thus we will include the attribute alter and attribute ego effects as well:

(d) Same attribute effect

(e) Attribute alter

(f) Attribute ego

Positive parameter values associated with e and f above imply that higher attribute values coincide with higher indegrees or outdegrees for actors, respectively. As value 1 = Sociology; 2 = Anthropology; 3 = Mathematics/Statistics; and 4 = other, we will have to take these values into account in interpreting our results.

   Leave all other model options in their default mode.

4 Run the model. After selecting the above network effects, run the model again by clicking on the 'Run' button. After a few moments, your results should appear.

5 Interpret results. Look to see that the t-ratios under your convergence diagnosis are close to zero, indicating that good convergence has occurred. Proceed onto the parameters output. Your output/results should be similar to those below (again, I have gone ahead and calculated the t-scores for you):

```
outdegree (density)        -1.65  (0.44) t-score = 0.04
reciprocity                 1.21  (0.32) t-score = 3.78
transitive triplets         0.21  (0.05) t-score = 4.20
Attribute 1 alter          -0.31  (0.14) t-score = 2.21
Attribute 1 ego             0.14  (0.22) t-score = 0.64
same Attribute 1            0.50  (0.50) t-score = 1.00
```

The results are similar to the p* findings: reciprocity and transitivity receive positive significant values, indicating that the network exhibits strong tendencies towards these two effects. Different from the p* analysis, there is no significant finding for the same attribute effect, although a negative, significant result is found for the attribute alter effect. Thus, although in this case actors do not appear to be choosing friends according to the same attribute, there is a tendency for sociologists and anthropologists to have higher indegree scores. Keep in mind, though, that there are simply more sociologists and anthropologists in this dataset than other disciplines.

This was an example of how to use Siena for both p* and actor-based models. In Appendix 3, you will see an example of the maths for the actor-based model, the evaluation function.

REFERENCES

Carley, K. and Krackhardt, D. (1996) 'Cognitive inconsistencies and non-symmetric friendships', *Social Networks*, 18: 1–29.

Freeman, S. C. and Freeman, L. C. (1979) 'The networkers network: A study of the impact of a new communications medium on sociometric structure', *Social Science Research Reports*, *No 46*. Irvine, CA: University of California.

Kadushin, C. (1966) 'The friends and supporters of psychotherapy: On social circles and urban life', *American Sociological Review,* 31: 786–802.

Martin, J. L. and Yeung, K.-T. (2006) 'Persistence of close personal ties over a 12-year period', *Social Networks,* 28: 331–62.

Skvoretz, J. (1991) 'Theoretical and methodological models of networks and relations', *Social Networks,* 13: 275–300.

Wellman, B., Frank, O., Espinoza, V., Lundquist, S. and Wilson, C. (1991) 'Integrating individual, relational and structural analysis', *Social Networks,* 13: 223–49.

APPENDIX 3

CALCULATING PROBABILITY FOR TRANSITIVITY USING ACTOR-BASED MODELS

In this Appendix, I am offering you an example of calculating the probability distribution for a single actor (actor i), through use of Tom Snijders' evaluation function (Snijders, 2005). Please keep in mind that this example I provide here is not intended to replace more rigorous, detailed texts on the topic of multinomial functions, and similarly, if readers are interested in delving deeper into the mechanics and applications of this actor-based model, then I would advise you to read Snijders' own writings on the topic (e.g. Snijders 2001, 2005; Snijders et al., 2010). However, this example provided here can help you get started in 'unpacking' the evaluation function, and seeing how it works to create a probability distribution.

As a general overview, please keep in mind that (as with all multinomial functions), one needs to have all possible options (in this case, all new situations that could result from this change; i.e., all alters toward whom ego could change his tie variable) in the denominator of the formula, and then the one option of interest (a specific other actor towards whom a tie variable could be changed) in the numerator.

The visual graph below shows you the network for actor i at Time 1. Please note, actor i refers to the actor for whom the probability is being calculated, i.e. the probability that actor i will take some kind of action (or no action) with regards to his/her network state. In the example below, j refers to those actors to whom actor i is tied. This is an adaptation from the example provided by (Snijders et al., 2010).

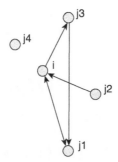

Figure A3.1 Evaluation function and digraph for actor *i*

STEP 1: CALCULATE THE CURRENT STATE OF THE NETWORK (CALCULATING X⁰)

Before you can calculate the probability of ego (actor *i*) making a change to her network, you first need to understand what is ego's current value for the evaluation function. Thus, the first step is to calculate the current state of the network for actor *i*, and this in turn involves (i) calculating the current state of each network 'effect', e.g. how many outgoing ties does ego have (outdegree effect), and (ii) insert the parameter value for each network effect.

A note before we begin: in Chapter 10 on network statistics, I offered a description on parameter estimation, and I suggest readers return to that section if they are curious about that topic. In continuing with the rest of this example, I shall make use of the parameter values that were estimated in Appendix 2 for the Freeman dataset.

Calculating current value of each network effect

Your parameter values are used with your network effects to calculate the evaluation function for ego. This is illustrated below for each of the network effects. For example, the network effect for outgoing ties (called the 'outdegree effect', and expressed below as s_{1i}) has the below formula:

$$s_{1i} = \sum_j x_{ij}$$

and when combined with its associated parameter (β_1), the formula used in the evaluation function becomes

$$\beta_1 \sum_j x_{ij}$$

This translates into counting the instances of a particular effect, and then multiplying that number with the associated parameter value. In what follows, I briefly discuss how these two pieces of information, the parameter and the network effect, are brought together in the evaluation function.

Network effects

Outdegree effect for actor i

The formula for the outdegree effect is:

$$s_{1i} = \sum_j x_{ij} \text{ with } \beta 1 = -1.65$$

This effect has an associated parameter estimate of -1.65. This means that there is a fairly strong tendency for an actor to *not* form outgoing ties. Thus, for this example, because actor i has 2 outgoing ties,

$$s_{1i} = 2(-1.65) = -3.30$$

Thus, the overall contribution of the outdegree effect to the evaluation function for ego is -3.30.

Reciprocity effect

The formula for the reciprocity effect is:

$$s_{2i} = \sum_j x_{ij} x_{ji} \text{ with } \beta_2 = 1.21$$

So there is a fairly strong tendency for a tie to become reciprocated in this current example. Thus, we count how many reciprocated ties there are, and multiply this by the parameter of 1.21.

$$s_{2i} = 1(1.21) = 1.21$$

Thus, the overall contribution of the reciprocity effect to the evaluation function for actor i for this example is 1.21.

Transitivity effect

$$s_{3i}(x) = \sum_{j,h} x_{ij} x_{ih} x_{jh} \text{ with } \beta_3 = 0.21$$

So there is a fairly strong tendency for a tie to become embedded in a transitive triad. For this example, there is one such transitive triple (i connects to *j*3, and i connects to *j*1, and *j*3 connects to *j*1). So:

$s_{3i} = 1(0.21) = 0.21$

Thus, the overall contribution of the transitivity triples effect to the evaluation function for actor *i* for this example is 0.21.

STEP 2: CALCULATING THE VALUE OF A TIE BASED ON THE EFFECTS ABOVE

The effects presented above, and their associated parameter values, inform the value of a tie for ego. Taken together, we can state:

- the value of adding a non-reciprocated, outgoing tie is −3.30

- the value of adding a reciprocated tie is −2.09 (as this is 1.21 −3.30)

- The value of adding a reciprocated tie to make a transitive triple is $0.21 - 2.09 = -1.88$

- The value of adding a non-reciprocated, outgoing tie to make a transitive triple is $0.21 - 3.30 = -3.09$

These above values thus inform actor *i* of the level of *attractiveness* in deciding an option for changing or not changing her network.

STEP 3: DECIDING ON THE OPTIONS FOR ACTOR I

Thus, when actor *i* has the opportunity to make a change (or doing nothing) with her network, these are the options for her:

1 Drop the reciprocated tie to *j*1. Keep in mind that this is not only a reciprocated tie, but it is also a tie that is part of a transitive triple. If ego drops the tie to *j*1, then ego also decides to drop the transitive triple (ego would still be part of something called a cycle, but not a transitive triple).

So for this particular tie to *j*1, given the fact that it is (i) reciprocal and (ii) transitive, one must bring these two values together:

$$-2.09 + 0.21 = -1.88$$

Thus, this option has a value of -1.88, and in the evaluation function, this becomes $e^{-1.88}$.

2   Reciprocate the tie from $j2$. Again, a reciprocated tie would be worth -2.09. The transitivity effect does not contribute, because no additional transitive triplets are formed. So in the evaluation function, this option is translated as $e^{-2.09}$.

3   Drop the non-reciprocated tie to $j3$. A non-reciprocated, outgoing tie has the value of -3.30, and this particular outgoing tie is part of one transitive triple, thus making the total value of this particular tie -3.09. Thus, in the evaluation function, this translates as $e^{-3.09}$.

4   Initiate a new tie to $j4$. Initiating a new outgoing tie is worth -3.30, and this translates as $e^{-3.30}$.

5   Do nothing. So, $e^{0.00} = 1.0$.

So there are five options for ego, and we shall now look at the probabilities of these options being chosen by ego.

STEP 4: CALCULATING THE PROBABILITY DISTRIBUTION FOR EGO

As discussed in Chapter 10, the probability distribution is captured in the formula of the evaluation function. In calculating the probability distribution for ego, we can make use of this evaluation function: all options become part of the denomination and the numerator contains the option in question. This is illustrated below:

Option 1:

$$\frac{e^{-1.88}}{e^{-1.88} + e^{-2.09} + e^{-3.09} + e^{-3.30} + e^{0.00}} = 0.11$$

Option 2:

$$\frac{e^{[-2.09]}}{e^{-1.88} + e^{-2.09} + e^{-3.09} + e^{-3.30} + e^{0.00}} = 0.09$$

Option 3:

$$\frac{e^{[-3.09]}}{e^{-1.88}+e^{-2.09}+e^{-3.09}+e^{-3.30}+e^{0.00}}=0.04$$

Option 4:

$$\frac{e^{[-3.30]}}{e^{-1.88}+e^{-2.09}+e^{-3.09}+e^{-3.30}+e^{0.00}}=0.03$$

Option 5:

$$\frac{e^{[0.0]}}{e^{-1.88}+e^{-2.09}+e^{-3.09}+e^{-3.30}+e^{0.00}}=0.73$$

So here, you can see that each option is calculated, and when one totals the results from all five options, the sum total is 1. Thus, each option can be seen as a probability, where higher probabilities are the more attractive options for ego. In this distribution, the option with the highest probability of occurring is Option 5, to do nothing. That is, doing nothing is the most attractive option for ego for Time 2.

The above example illustrates how a probability distribution gets created for a single ego. This process is repeated for all egos in the network, thus creating an overall probability distribution for the entire network.

REFERENCES

Snijders, T. (2001) 'The statistical evaluation of social network dynamics', in M. E. Sobel and M. P. Becker (eds), *Sociological Methodology*. Boston and London: Blackwell.

Snijders, T. A. B. (2005) 'Models for longitudinal network data', in P. Carrington, J. Scott and S. Wasserman (eds), *Models and Methods in Social Network Analysis*. New York: Cambridge University Press. pp. 215–47.

Snijders, T. A. B., Steglich, C. E. G. and van de Bunt, G. G. (2010) 'Introduction to stochastic actor-based models for network dynamics', *Social Networks*, 32: 44–60.

INDEX

978-1-84787-907-3

978-1-4129-2226-5

978-1-84920-417-0

978-1-84860-034-8

978-1-4129-7517-9

978-1-4129-7457-8

978-1-4129-7044-0

978-1-84920-595-5

978-1-4129-7959-7

Find out more about these titles and our wide range of books for students and researchers at **www.sagepub.co.uk**

EXCITING RESEARCH METHODS TEXTS FROM SAGE